Mary Russell has an MA in Peace Studies from the University of Bradford and took her first solo journey in her mid-forties,

_____

___ advices her ___

___ a regular contributor to _The Irish Times._

has broadcast one of her plays and her short stories have been published in Ireland, the UK and Australia. She has previously been published in _Amazonian_, a collection of travel writing by women.

JOURNEYS
OF A
LIFETIME

Mary Russell

POCKET BOOKS

TOWNHOUSE

A VIACOM COMPANY

First published in Great Britain and Ireland by Pocket/TownHouse, 2002
An imprint of Simon & Schuster UK Ltd and TownHouse and
CountryHouse Ltd, Dublin
Simon & Schuster UK is a Viacom Company

1   3   5   7   9   10   8   6   4   2

Simon & Schuster UK Ltd
Africa House
64–78 Kingsway
London WC2B 6AH
www.simonsays.co.uk

Simon & Schuster Australia
Sydney

TownHouse and CountryHouse Ltd
Trinity House
Charleston Road
Ranelagh
Dublin 6
Ireland

A CIP catalogue record for this book is available from the British Library

ISBN 1-903650-08-9

Typeset by Palimpsest Book Production Limited,
Polmont, Stirlingshire
Printed and bound in Great Britain by Cox & Wyman Ltd

Permission granted by Faber & Faber Ltd to quote from W. H. Auden's poem
'Atlantis' and from Canongate Books for permission to quote from *The Complete
Poems of Anna Akhmatova*, published in 2000 by Canongate Books, Edinburgh.

Author's Note
When it comes to Arabic spelling there are many variations and therefore
I have always tried to remain faithful to the actual pronunciation, as the
Arabic language itself is phonetic.

For Eta, Isabella and Charlie

In memory of their grandfather, Ian Graham Rodger

Acknowledgments

I would like to thank the following people: Patsey Murphy, who said do it; Mercer Simpson for permission to quote from his collection of poetry, *Rain from a Clear Blue Sky*; Professor Paul Rogers for his lecture on the 1975 oil crisis; and Carol Fox for the politics and the music.

Thanks also to Robert Paine, Frankie and Rafique Mottiar, Abdel Nabi and Rima es Staif, Barbara Harrell-Bond, Jane Val Baker, Conor O'Clery, Jan and Trevor Johnson, Marie Meehan, Aideen Ryan, Peter Emerson, Hillbourne Frank, Bill Heine, Toby, Yanto and William Wain, Eamonn Slater, Rune and Sirpe Leskinen, Germaine Dalton, al-Abbas Shiblak, the League of Arab States, UNIPAL, POLISARIO and APSO; Tom Burke and the Royal Dublin Fusiliers Association; family members in South Africa and friends in Burgersdorp.

Thanks, too, to Russell, Deirdre and Freya for reading part of the MSS.

I would also like to say thanks to the many people who welcomed me into their homes, during my travels, especially those who probably wished they hadn't.

I would particularly like to acknowledge my debt to the Saami in Enontekiö, the Caribs of Dominica and St Vincent and the Anangu of Uluru. Thanks also to the Saharawi people of Western Sahara for their generous hospitality.

Mary Russell
Corkerbeg, 2001

Contents

All the little household gods
Have started crying, but say
Good-bye now, and put to sea.
Farewell, my dear, farewell: may
Hermes, master of the roads,
And the four dwarf Kabiri,
Protect and serve you always;
And may the Ancient of Days
Provide for all you must do
His invisible guidance,
Lifting up, dear, upon you
The light of His countenance.

W. H. Auden, 'Atlantis'

Introduction

On a whim, I take McGeehan's bus from Dublin, leaving behind the fumes of cars tailgating through the evening rush hour. This is a recurring dream journey made while I'm walking the dusty roads of some distant country. In my mind's eye, I see the rhododendrons scattering across the bog as the bus rocking-horses its way over Pettigo Mountain. Far off to the west, is the outline of Ben Bulben, Yeats's flat-topped mountain.

The main, tarred road ribbons on, linking Donegal town and the smaller town of Ardara before running all the way up to the tip of Donegal – Ireland's most northerly county.

Just after ten, the bus climbs a forested hill and we stop at a crossroads invisible to everyone but myself. Altcore, my drop-off point, marks the spot where the intersecting road curves off secretly into time – grass growing up the middle of it, its bordering ditches gleaming with wild flowers. If I shut my eyes, I can see them now – pale yellow primroses, electric-blue bluebells, tiny orchids, purple and perfect.

Each road round here, travelled or not, has its own name: the Spink, the Dark Road, the Brae, the Line. Mine – the one I always take – is the Spink.

I strap on to my bike the saddlebags packed with laptop, books, a bottle of whiskey, food for a week and ride off into another world. No sound here but the occasional clink of pedals, the chesty breathing of a shadowy cow in a nearby field, the song of meadow larks bringing their day to a close. Reluctant to intrude on the intermittent stillness, I keep silent although my heart is sparking with the excitement of being here again. I breathe deeply, taking in the fresh, grass-sweetened air, which inexplicably smells of toffee.

There are no houses to be seen along this stretch of road, nothing in sight but fields lumpy with reeds and flags of bog-cotton flickering against the shade of early night. You couldn't call it dusk, this luminosity, for dusk is an urban word belonging to drawn curtains, pavements and street lamps. Up here, pale streaks of light – yellow, blue, green and orange – still flood across the western sky where the moon, crescented and calm, patrols the growing darkness, accompanied by two bright, minder-stars.

The bike bumps down another hill, skids round the corner and there it is – the house – standing patiently, silently, in the last light of the day, exactly where I left it. Where I knew I would find it.

But *do* I know this? Has it been here all the time – while I was in the Sahara, the Arctic, the South African bush? While I rode camels and skidoos? While I slept in some far-off, cockroached hotel room or in a flapping tent?

While I lowered my forehead in a Buddhist temple, took off my shoes to enter a mosque, lit soft wax candles in an eastern church? Was it here . . . or did I only imagine it? Does it fill an empty space in my traveller's heart, conjured up by loneliness, longing and exhaustion? Will I return one day and find it gone? Find that the Bishop Berkeley magic has ceased to work? George Berkeley said that things existed only as long as we were there to look at them. Look away, and, like the leprechaun, they disappear. His philosophical ideas were later gently ridiculed by Ronald Knox:

> There was a young man who said 'God
> Must think it exceedingly odd
> If he finds that this tree
> Continues to be
> When there's no one around in the quad.'

I often think about Berkeley's thesis. Does it apply to everything? If a coconut crashes to the ground in the bush and there's no one there to hear it, does it make a sound?

The key is in the tin kettle by the door and, letting myself into the house, I begin replaying the old, comforting ritual: I am here, I tell myself, as I unscrew the top of the whiskey bottle, because I need time for reflection after two months travelling in Australia. Last time, it was a long hot autumn in a dusty township on the edge of the Karoo. Before that, the white reaches of the tundra. Before *that*, the glittering blue of the Caribbean.

The next destination lies in some future not yet travelled but wherever I find myself, the needle on my spiritual compass will point me to the townland of Corkerbeg, in the county of Donegal, for the journey ends here.

I celebrate my arrival with a hot whiskey, pouring boiling water over the half spoonful of crunchy brown sugar before adding the Jameson. Then, carefully, I insert a row of cloves into a half moon of lemon before floating it in the steaming, golden liquid. Preparation adds to the anticipation and the aroma spices my nostrils, making my eyes water. After the first glass, I have another and then another. Two too many probably, but I've arrived safe and sound, relieved to find my little three-roomed, whitewashed house still here with its roof on, though battered by winter gales. Waiting.

Although it's now eleven o'clock, dispersed light from the vanished sun hangs light as a veil across house, grass and trees, giving a gleam to the last of the day. I take a walk up the lane to the raised mound where, on summer evenings, the old people used to gather to chat as they watched the sun go down. From here, I can pick out the lights of one or two houses lying along the road to Dunkineely and, down in the dip by the bridge, the place where the Corker and the Tullintain rivers join up to become the Oily.

Inexplicably, I think of Tom who, for one glorious year, was my sweet, illicit lover. But that was all before I stumbled through the door that opened on to a world whose borders ran far beyond school runs, the weekly shopping and secret love trysts. On the other side of it, I found that affairs of the heart shrank when set against the enormity of the Sahara, the surge of the Blue Nile, the sand-red mystery of Khartoum. And that was only Africa.

I walk back along the lane and, not for the first time, think I see Ian's figure come towards me out of the night

4

shadows. Eric Newby explained this phenomenon to me once, after I had challenged his assertion that he had seen the statue of the Virgin at Ballinspittle moving.

'No, it's true,' he protested. 'Honestly. If you just keep staring at something, it happens. Like a sentry on duty, staring out into the darkness. Your eyes conjure up an imaginary shape that you *know* is there.'

It was an insane metaphysical theory that appealed to me. The certainty at the heart of the unknown. Bishop Berkeley again: if I stare long enough at the dark patch at the end of the lane that leads to eternity, Ian will emerge from it, materialized. But I look away and hurry back into the house. In my childhood, ghosts lurked in the yawning darkness at the top of the stairs, waited for me by the banging door of the outside lavatory, sprang into action in that long second between opening the bedroom door and managing to switch on the light. I am still nervous about them.

In a sense, of course, Ian *is* here for, one starlit, frosty New Year's Eve, I scattered the last of his ashes among the rocky ruins of the nearby cottage known as the Poet's House – where yellow flag irises now grow. And the night raven sings.

I have a last look up at the inky sky, step inside, shoot the bolt on the door, make another whiskey, get into the bed which has a concrete block propping it up at one corner and fall asleep to the intermittent creaking of the tin roof as a north-westerly blows in off the Atlantic. I am home and have no further need to dream.

CHAPTER ONE

One Second Class Lady: Lesotho 1981

Makobe and I had been down to look at the cave paintings at Ha Khotso. 'You see here,' he said, pointing at a red ochre drawing on the rock, 'this is a Bushman and here, this is a Bushman woman.' Something caught my eye. 'Wait a minute,' I said. 'Why's your nail *that* long?' It was a generous inch, at least. By way of answer, Makobe stuck it first into his ear and then up his nostril. 'For cleaning,' he said and then returned to the business of tapping the rock to show me the chiselled picture of a San man and woman – descendants of the Stone Age hunter-gatherers who once inhabited Lesotho. Beside them were carved representations of their familiars: snakes, buffalo and vultures.

Climbing back up the red, dusty track, the tall grasses on both sides obscuring my view, the afternoon sun beating down on my unprotected head, I stood aside to let a party-goer pass. The urgent drumming on the other side of the gorge made her quicken her own reply, which she was beating out on an old biscuit tin. She and the two other teenage girls, following in single file, had rouged their black cheeks with white powdered tree bark. Bright bits of shredded plastic bag fluttered from their short stubby plaits like ragged ribbons. They were three cool cats, on their way to party over on the other side. Plastic bags are used a lot in Lesotho. A yellow one tied to a stick outside a rondavel denotes maize for sale, a red one for meat and a green one for vegetables. White is for an off-licence selling *joala*, the local beer made from sorghum.

I'd already been to a party myself that day – a wedding between a Canadian aid worker and a local woman, also an agriculturist. Development aid was a sacred subject with the Canadians who somehow took on the devout air of pioneering missionaries whenever the subject came up, with some justification. A group of them, members of a religious order, had built a hospital up here way back in the 1930s, using donkeys to drag the planks of wood up from Maseru. The pieces of timber were always one foot longer than was needed in order to compensate for the wear and tear of getting them up the 7000 foot high mountain.

At the wedding feast, we stuck our bottoms out behind us and, singing the same two musical phrases over and over again, shunted in a crocodile round and round the community hall, an activity which I knew could go on till all hours and which I was glad to be eventually released from when Makobe called to take me to see the cave paintings.

The Kingdom of Lesotho is the 'Roof of Africa'. Its ancient mountains – wrinkled brown claws of eroded rock curling into themselves like an arthritic hand – lie close to the sky, for even the lowest point of this tiny kingdom is 1000 feet above sea level. Without roads – and there are still whole mountain communities without any – the only way to get around was, traditionally, by pony. Silhouetted against the wide expanse of blue sky, the Basotho horseman, wrapped in a bright-coloured blanket, his coned straw hat topped with an intricately woven knob of straw, is the icon of Lesotho, the image freeze-framed on to a million postcards and tea towels but fast becoming anachronistic as cars and buses take over.

This shift away from the traditional means of transport had its origins in the Boer Wars when the British, challenged by the Afrikaners, dug in, determined to hang on to southern Africa. To a seagoing nation, the region's position, overlooking two oceans, was a prime strategic prize and its mineral wealth an even greater one. Noting that the Boer farmers got about everywhere on horseback, an order for horses to be shipped out from England was dispatched. 'Send only the best,' it said. The order duly arrived: frisky, nervous Arab stallions which were fleet of foot and elegant to look at but totally useless in the bush or for getting across mountains. Perplexed, the British looked around and, seeing how good the tough little ponies ridden by the Basotho were, commandeered as many of them as they could. They killed off the mares destroying – for generations to come – the country's public transport system.

Then, in 1975, the Irish Taoiseach, Garrett Fitzgerald, engaged in initiating the Irish Bilateral Aid Programme, found himself on a plane returning from a UN conference. Halfway through the flight back to New York, he was accosted by a couple of other delegates. 'Do you know you're undone,' one of them told him. This was not a reference to a *coup d'état* back home but merely an indication that he should do up another button or two. The delegates turned out to be Basotho, from Lesotho, and he was able to tell them he had just set in train one of Ireland's most imaginative projects: two Connemara ponies, both champion of champions, would be donated to the Kingdom of Lesotho where they would be used to replenish the National Stud.

The two breeds of ponies – from Ireland and Lesotho – are broadly similar. Both are strong and heavy, with good conformation and accustomed to rough, rocky terrain. The two champion of champions were to form part of the new Third World development programme. Ireland, at that time, was emerging as a busy, prosperous little country, ready to play a modern role both in Europe and within the United Nations. As a public affirmation of this, the Government set up its Bilateral Aid Programme which, since Ireland was not a wealthy country, came in the form not of cash but of agricultural expertise, which was second nature to a people who could dig a good sod of turf, knew a spade from a shovel and were expert at making silage.

There was nothing new, really, in the idea of the Irish going abroad to do good. Nuns and priests had been doing it for centuries but in the 1970s this did not fit well with Ireland's new self-image of modernity. From now on, its involvement with the developing world would be secular. Its programmes would be budgeted by civil servants, administered by bureaucrats and executed by development aid workers. Consultancies were set up and feasibility studies undertaken. Mission statements were made, reports sent back, targets aimed at – and often achieved. There were seminars and workshops and, of course, expense account lunches all financed from the budget still known as 'aid', for these undertakings were not yet acknowledged openly as being commercial investments.

In place of nuns and priests, project officers were recruited to work in Lesotho. Courses for Basotho financial planners and hospital administrators were offered. A major training scheme for pilots was established. Lesotho, surrounded by apartheid South Africa, was dependent on it for air transport. An airline of its own, however small, would increase its growing independence. Aer Lingus was sent in to help and advise, with the hope that it would eventually get the contract for running the whole operation. All aid comes with a price.

I came upon the Basotho Pony Project while researching a Masters degree at the School of Peace Studies at Bradford University. Intending originally to present my thesis on the subject of fasting and hunger striking (it was the year when ten young Irishmen, led by Bobby Sands, went on hunger strike in protest at being treated as criminals rather than as the political prisoners they perceived themselves to be), I attended a lecture given by Paul Rogers, now Professor of Peace Studies at Bradford, in which he examined the political and economic consequences of the 1973 oil crisis. The lecture made me realize how small and interdependent the world was. It also raised the question of the economic development of the emerging democracies. The 1960s had seen the former colonies of Africa break the bonds of servitude, some of them simply to fashion a new set of restrictions for their hapless citizens. ('Why go for change if it means more chains?' a Caribbean woman had said to me when I doorstepped her during a British Labour Party canvas.)

Lesotho was especially interesting since it had many things in common with Ireland: both were small countries with an agricultural-based economy, their populations were depleted by immigration and each was struggling to emerge from under the shadow of a large, powerful neighbour. And so, even as the hunger strikers in Belfast's Long Kesh prison were dying one by one, I turned away from the subject of fasting. From now on, my research would be into the economics of Third World aid and, in particular, Ireland's involvement in Lesotho. This meant I would have to travel to Lesotho, meet up with the Basotho as well as with some of the aid workers and persuade them to explain to me what their projects were all about.

I borrowed £350 from the campus bank manager – having first flattered him by writing a witty feature in the *Guardian* about loans in which he appeared as a benignly generous figure – and set off for Lesotho. Up till then, the longest journey I had made had been a camping holiday to Yugoslavia with Ian and our three children. This time the journey was different, I was going to Africa and I was going alone.

There are two ways of getting up to Thaba Tseka: you either do the nine-hour car drive or you take your chances with the plane. The Thaba Tseka Tango, it was called. I chose to tango. At the check-in, I put my rucksack down beside me on the enormous scales, because baggage and bodies were treated as one. The rucksack was modest and had the extra virtue of staying put, whereas the woman behind me had to deal with a basket of restless hens, while in front a man wrestled with an undisciplined ironing board. Crossing the cracked tarmac to the little eight-seater plane, I asked the man walking beside me what the routine was. 'There isn't any,' he said a little grimly as he climbed into the pilot's seat. Seated beside him, I spent the short journey reaching for the handbrake as we hurtled straight for jagged mountain faces only to slip through a cleft which appeared, miraculously, at the last minute.

As we came in to land at Thaba Tseka, I noticed a cloud of dust speeding along the dirt road to the landing strip. The Irish manager of the National Stud, with whom I was to stay, was engaging in one of his pastimes, attempting to get from his house to the plane before the propellers stopped turning. Another trick they indulged in on a windy day, I later discovered, was to load the windsock with stones. When the pilot saw this, he assumed there was no wind and descended to land, flying smack into a force ten gale. You had to make your own entertainment in Thaba Tseka.

The ponies at the National Stud terrified me. Unused to horses of any sort, I had been expecting something if not as small as a Shetland then certainly nothing as big as the Connemaras. They were huge creatures, heavy as shires with heads that reared up like dragons. Helped up on to one, my legs splayed out around its grossly bulging stomach. There were no brakes, no reverse gear, I couldn't see over the top and I was immediately crushed against a fence as my stallion noticed a mare in the next field and tried to cosy up to her. The size and sex of the whole thing put me off. This was research that would have to be done at one remove.

*   *   *

Two evenings later, sex again raised its awkward member. An agriculturist, working on an Irish farming project, invited me to come and see his work. One of the few people in Ireland not raised on a farm, the fields full of something green (lucerne, I learned later) looked as interesting as a concrete footpath. I pretended to listen while he droned on about fodder production and how it would revolutionize the farming practices of the average Basotho. Fodder, silage and slurry were not words that occurred regularly in my vocabulary but I made assiduous notes while performing my favourite displacement activity: working out, in my mind, whether I had enough money left to see me to my next destination.

That night, I joined up with a group of people and the drink flowed. Some time after midnight, I crawled into bed with a head that clanged with every movement, only to be wakened after a few minutes of sleep by the agriculturist groping under the sheets. As I was his guest, I felt it incumbent upon me to remain polite. 'Go away,' I mumbled. 'I have a *terrible* headache.' He did, but ten minutes later my door crashed open and he hurled himself across the room, this time on top of me. Had he been standing outside the door all that time trying to control himself? My head now felt as if it were a square of lead and my tongue smelled like a dodgy drain. In fact, I thought that I was probably going to vomit. But, convent educated, I failed to smack the intruder in the face and chose polite- ness instead. '*Please* stop,' I said. 'I'm here to work.' Somehow I imagined this would convey to him that far from being Diamond Lil on the loose in Lesotho, I was a mature, MA student engaged in serious research. And that

I needed my sleep. He withdrew and next morning, as I emerged from my room, he looked at me anxiously, fearful no doubt that I was going to make something of his behaviour. But I was too hung over to care about anything except my painful head. In his relief, he invited me to spend the following Sunday with himself and his family. My non-committal groan obviously freed him from all fear of exposure and he spent the rest of the morning whistling cheerfully as we made our way up and down yet more rows of lucerne.

It's a story I often recount when questioned about the perceived dangers of women travelling on their own, relishing the discomfiture of the questioner when I reveal that the sexual harassment I endured while in Lesotho was perpetrated not by a fearsome black man with the proverbial large, threatening dick, but by a fellow Irishman. I might just as well have stayed at home.

Julia was the stud manager's maid. When we were alone, she and I chatted about children and husbands but at other times it was different. 'Julia,' the manager called out over his shoulder, 'breakfast for two, please.' And Julia, eyes downcast, served us silently, speaking only when she was spoken to. We were sisters no longer.

I was due to fly back down to Maseru after a few days, but when high winds prevented the frail little plane from landing I had to spend an extra night up in the mountains. Next day, with the wind still blowing, they sent a Belfast Hercules troop carrier to collect us. Through the gaps in the metal plates of the floor, I could see the spiky, snow-capped mountain peaks not very far below and shivered as the cold air coming off them hit us as we sat on our metal benches, glum as troops being carried to war. Down in Maseru again, I found it full of admonitory statements: 'Enter to learn, depart to serve,' it said at the entrance to the Agricultural Training Centre. 'Bring down high prices,' someone had written on a shop front. And if I needed evidence of the grandiose aspirations of the average shop-keeper it was there in the small general store with the decrepit, one-armed bandit proudly stationed in the middle of the floor and a sign hammered on the outside wall which read: The Chicago Disco.

The Basotho have a creative handle on language, but when it came to officialdom there were sometimes prob-lems. Some things are better not talked about and in Mosotho, the language spoken in Lesotho, there are no words for the sex organs. At the Lesotho Distance Learning Centre, therefore, they'd been trying to work out how to write a biology handbook without mentioning what the tutor – a former Catholic priest from the Netherlands – called 'the interconnecting bits'. It was indeed a problem and when the Centre finally published their handbook, with a chapter on contraception in which the word vagina appeared, it was banned within a month. There were semantic problems also with marketing local goods for sale abroad, which was a term that often meant simply South Africa. Mohair goats thrive in the mountains of Lesotho and their wool makes up into excellent suits. Promoting them in South Africa, however, required a degree of com-mercial subterfuge. The apartheiders were suspicious of anything made by black people, believing them to be of inferior quality. Therefore, fine mohair suits made in Lesotho found their way on to the South African market with only the trade name Berea on them. Berea is an area in Lesotho but is also a suburb of Johannesburg.

I took the plane to Gaborone and sat at the bar of the Holiday Inn there, wondering where I was going to stay and if I should phone Ian and tell him I missed him. But I was here and he was in England, dealing with family meals, disco runs and the dustbin collection. I sighed and decided to have another drink instead. The distance was too great and in any case, though it took me a while to admit it, I didn't want home intruding into my new-found world. I had become a stranger to myself. I was not a wife, not a mother but a woman on her own, without a history. It was an image I felt I could develop. A black woman seated herself beside me at the bar, wearing a peaked Union Jack cap.

'You live here?' I asked.

She shook her head: 'Zimbabwe.'

'*Zimbabwe?*' I was still a novice traveller, excited by unknown destinations. 'I'm going there after this.'

There was no reaction. Going to Zimbabwe was clearly no big deal. We lapsed into silence and I engaged in some mental arithmetic, trying to work out if I had enough for another Castles beer.

The woman in the cap drank on, steadily and morosely. Over the PA came a call for someone called Mrs Hailstones. I put down my glass: it was time to call home.

The President Hotel where I ended up staying was down-market from the Gaborone Holiday Inn but still expensive: a room with a bath and breakfast cost £18. 'In the unluckly event you have difficulties, please call the management,' said the notice on my door.

From the bar stereo came the sound of the Nolan Sisters, telling us they were in the mood for dancing. Pasted on the wall of the bar was a notice advertising the impending Miss Ebony Competition, with music by Sheik Mania. I ordered a Castles and thought about Tom. Ian had told me on the phone that he had suffered a massive heart attack and had been unconscious now for a week.

My love affair with Tom had ended two years previously when he told me, unexpectedly, that he no longer felt emotionally involved. In a way, I could understand why. We had slipped into a routine of clandestine meetings and lovemaking that bore little resemblance to the earlier fire that erupted, taking us both by surprise.

'Shall we meet?' I'd said after we had slow-danced at a party and he'd dipped his body so that the soft roundness of his sex tucked itself neatly into mine. It was an act of boldness that took my breath away.

'Yes, but when?' he asked.

'Early January.'

'Not before?'

'No.' Christmas was for families. His and mine.

He phoned just after Christmas. 'When?'

'I wish it could be now, tonight.'

'Me too.'

'First week in January some time?'

'I'm away that week.'

More waiting.

'It'll be all the sweeter,' he promised.

I nodded into the phone. Then hearing a door open downstairs, I whispered: 'Got to go', and hung up.

We met and it was indeed sweet.

'Don't worry,' Tom said, after an afternoon's lovemaking when my violent desire for him had erupted and taken me by surprise. He touched my face and smiled: 'It's only passion.'

Our friendship developed on different fronts. I relished the extra companionship, the chance to talk to someone who was at once close and new. Like all lovers, we celebrated the things we had in common and glossed lightly over our differences. We listened to each other recounting the joys, the minor irritations, the anxieties of our marriages, taking care never to be judgmental of our respective partners since we were both happily married and had no intention of taking this relationship any further. Our marriages, we both agreed, were not at stake. 'What we have is external to all that,' said Tom, touching the tip of his finger to his tongue before slowly drawing a circle round my aureole. The fire consumed us for a year, fuelled by the stomach-tightening nature of its illicitness. Houses had to be borrowed, alibis found or invented. Like a criminal falling into a life of crime, I slipped into one of subterfuge, amazed at how easy the half-lies came. But it was a man's world, this. Tom had lots of male friends and colleagues all only too ready, it seemed, to help each other out. I, on the other hand, had no one. Told no one. We made love wherever we could – in borrowed houses, in summer meadows, in dark parks locked for the night. We watched out for field gates that could easily be climbed over, risking discovery by passing tractors. Rent-a-field, Tom called it. Sometimes, with our partners, we went out together as a foursome, our fingers sparking as they touched when pouring a glass of wine or lighting a cigarette. Once, in a restaurant, I dined deliciously with Tom's foot between my legs while above the table cloth we all discussed Labour Party policies.

Eventually, we settled into a routine of weekly meetings and it was this very routine, I guessed, that led to Tom's disenchantment. He was in love with his wife, he said, had always been, whereas now, with me, he no longer felt emotionally involved. His announcement sent me spiralling into a dark hole of hopelessness around which the everyday cycle continued as usual. I moved into automatic mode cooking family meals, washing up, doing the shopping, the car run, the late-night teenage party collection, sharing my bed and body with Ian. But it was all an illusion. Surrounded by noise, music and voices I heard only silence. Foolishly, I'd thought I could continue for ever with a husband and a lover, two complementary relationships. They knew each other and got on well, especially when it came to politics. 'Ian is my brother,' Tom had said. I was twice blessed having two men and hoped, rather than knew for certain, that some of the excitement from my lovemaking with Tom commuted to both our marriage beds. Life was as near perfect as it could be, I'd thought.

There's nothing more lonely than the ending of a secret love affair. I had confided in no one and now had no one to talk to about my sorrow and loss. The very person I would normally turn to for comfort was the one person to whom I couldn't speak. Life carried on around me as usual while I marked the empty days in a shell of silence. We still, occasionally, went out together as a foursome and once, at a night-time, open air concert, I overheard Tom murmur to his wife: 'We should go away somewhere and rent a field.' I stopped eating and grew thin. Then one day, as I sat disconsolately on the side of my bed, trying to find the energy to get dressed, I looked at my thinning body. What was the use in feeding it now that it was no longer tended by my lover's passionate hands? And hearing these thoughts articulated so clearly in my head, I realized the folly of wasting away like this, mourning for a love affair that was now dead. In that second, some survival instinct I didn't know I had kicked in and, energized, I got dressed, went downstairs, made a large pot of coffee for myself and Ian and spent the morning clearing weeds from the garden path, my burden of sadness lifted. There was life beyond a broken love affair. I *would* survive. My life would change. I would do new things, though what exactly I didn't yet know. But I would read more books, tend to my family, look after my body – and be a good wife. I didn't add fidelity to this list of strictures for what Tom and I had had was quite distinct from the rock upon which my marriage was built. Our relationship had been a thing apart and because of this, I had not, I knew, been unfaithful to Ian.

Two months later, while washing, I glanced down and saw a splash of blood bloom brightly on the white ceramic of the washbasin. I stared at it, mesmerized by the vividness of its colour and the strange beauty of its shape. Had I inadvertently cut my finger? Bitten my lip? Then, as I looked, a second drop splashed down beside it and moving my gaze from the washbasin to my breast, I saw a tiny balloon of blood already oozing from my right nipple.

There was something blocking one of the milk ducts, the consultant said. They would try to see what it was. But I already knew: my mourning for Tom had eaten away from the inside. I had made myself ill.

'We need another one or two of these,' said the radiographer, reaching for a couple more *Reader's Digests* to prop up my meagre breast on the cold metal. Then she clamped it tightly between the X-ray plates. Looking at the mottled flesh turn grey as it was pressed flat under the glass, I felt myself engulfed by a wave of nausea. Nothing showed up on the X-rays and when, later, I had a heat photograph taken that too proved inconclusive. The consultant shook his head: 'We'll have to do a biopsy.' The houseman who came to examine me the evening before the operation was young, good-looking and new to the job. He sat on the side of my bed: 'Do you mind if I look at your breast – as they say,' and he smiled apologetically. My eyes filled with tears. After the machinery that had exposed, photographed and squashed me, the businesslike nurses who handled, shoved and poked me, his words and his embarrassed smile made me mourn what it seemed was about to be taken from me. With Ian, my breasts had been a rich source of nourishment for our children, pillows of comfort for him. With Tom, they had become sensuous again, newly discovered highly charged triggers of erotica that gave pleasure to both of us. That night, in the hospital ward, wondering what else might happen to my womanhood, I turned on my side and closed my eyes tight against my lost love. Next morning, the nurse came with a thick felt-tip pen and marked a black X on my right breast. 'They sometimes do the wrong one in the theatre,' she explained. 'Have to be extra careful.'

The wait for the results of the biopsy was interminable. I wept at unexpected moments but Ian was resolute. 'Do you *feel* ill?' he asked and I didn't. 'Then you're not', and

I knew his words made sense. But how could I tell him that the illness had taken hold months before, when I *did* feel ill. When I was indifferent to life itself.

'No, you are not ill,' he said firmly, knowing but not knowing. Years later, when his time came, I grieved that I was never able to give him the same reassurance.

The results arrived: the tumour within the duct had been tiny, located right under the nipple and therefore hard to see. And it was benign. I had been given a second run at life. I slept, made love, laughed and sang. Hugged my new-found Ian. By way of thanksgiving – and for future insurance – I made a donation to cancer research. I celebrated the sun and the rain, smiled at my beautiful children, whistled while I scraped garden mud off my shoes, dried the dishes with vigour and swore never again to feel sorry for myself. I had come through a dark, silent tunnel and felt no desire to look back. I saw Tom occasionally, looked at him from a distance, as someone I had once known a long time ago. And when, clumsily, he tried to rekindle our affair I felt embarrassed for him that he had failed to realize that this time it was I who was no longer emotionally involved. Now he lay in hospital, covered with a white sheet, wired up to a monitor, his wife weeping by his bedside. I felt sorry for her and glad I was in Africa. It was all happening too far away, in a place I could not connect with.

I moved even more downmarket, to the Gaborone Hotel, which was cheaper and located more or less on the railway station. The railings of the station were hung with drying nappies, the platform crowded with people waiting overnight for the uptrain train from Johannesburg to Bulawayo.

With many of the waiting passengers lying side by side in neat rows, wrapped up in their blankets, the place looked more like a hospital ward than a railway station. I'd been told the Gaborone was a brothel but that struck me simply as white-speak for a predominantly black hotel. There wasn't much to it, just a series of rooms with their doors opening on to a long veranda patrolled by a security guard with a stick and a dog. My room, with its single bed and one chair, was small and clean and I felt safe.

Early next morning, a crowd formed around the ticket window. 'Mister Ticket Conductor, I think you should attend to my request,' called out one polite but impatient traveller. Mr Ticket Conductor, however, was an imperturbable Scot used to, and therefore unmoved by, large crowds. He checked my destination. 'One second class lady for Bulawayo,' he called out to his assistant.

Leaning out of the window of my carriage, I watched as a man (white) sauntered along to the first-class car, dropping disused bits of paper behind him as he went. Following him was one of the station cleaners (black) whose job it was to pick up all the discarded rubbish on the platform – by hand. I constantly saw images like this, clicking a mental shutter to store them away for later. I'd learned early on not to comment on such things for it was often explained to me, by white South Africans, that I must not confuse apartheid with economic reality. Workers, it seemed, were exploited not because they were black but simply because they were poor and of the working class. It happened in every country, I was told.

The night was freezing and I encased my feet in a plastic bag against the chill dawn air. Next day, we crossed the

Botswana border and rattled on northwards over into Zimbabwe. One year previously, the head teacher at the ghetto comprehensive in Oxford, where I was then working as a school counsellor, announced at assembly that today was a great day. 'Zimbabwe has become independent,' he told a mystified group of teenagers. They so rarely crossed the ring road that separated their large working-class housing estate from the privileged square mile which enclosed the university that Zimbabwe might have been France for all they knew. 'He was doing a mental in there, Miss, wasn't he?' said Andy taking a packet of cigarettes from the pocket of his denim bomber jacket as I came through the door of the classroom for the first lesson of the day. I let both the comment and the provocation pass. Timing was Andy's thing. He liked to call my bluff in front of his classmates by slowly taking out a cigarette, putting it to his lips and then idly flicking his lighter on and off. 'Like one, Miss?' he'd say, watching for signs that I was about to break. I never broke and he never lit up but we worked through our ritual on a daily basis, each knowing exactly what was expected of the other. I was fond of Andy. I thought of him when, at the Zimbabwean border, a customs man got on to the train and checked my passport. 'Congratulations on becoming independent,' I said. He looked up in surprise and then shook my hand. But it was what I had come for, after all.

I walked in the neighbourhood close to the hotel in Bulawayo, afraid to stray too far in case I got lost for there was no one around to ask the way in this English area of neat flower-beds and well-kept lawns. Gates and doors were shut, curtains drawn, gardens empty. The air was silent as a hot Sunday afternoon. A wave of indescribable misery spread over me. I felt lonely and confused. Expecting noble Africa I had wandered, instead, into suburbia, marooned in an arid desert of bright flowers and trimmed, controlled greenery. Further afield, beyond my reach, lay black Zimbabwe, still divided by internal strife. 'We're not Shona here in Bulawayo,' the taxi driver had told me, 'we're Nkomo's people – Ndebele.' On the TV, Comrade Mugabe – the victor in the power struggle with Nkomo – talked to us in Shona. He had won not just the civil war but also the war of words.

Because Zimbabwe had received help from many different quarters, there were news programmes from Chile, Yugoslavia, China and the West Bank. Then in the evening the TV announcer digressed to tell us Bobby Sands had died after sixty-five days on hunger strike.

I lay on the large double bed reading the Song of Solomon from the hotel's Gideon Bible: 'I am black but comely, Oh ye daughters of Jerusalem. As the tents of Kador, as the curtains of Solomon.' And heard Ian's voice take up the next verse: 'His right hand is under my head and his left caresses me', as he laid his hand between my legs.

Ian, Ian Graham Rodger. I had first fallen in love with him when, one wet Saturday afternoon in a friend's flat in Notting Hill Gate, we had sat on the floor together and he had read to me Dylan Thomas's 'Do Not Go Gentle', his ex-public school voice sounding strange but intriguing to my Irish ears. *His* travelling had all been done many years before, hitching round France just after the war, when the bridges were still being rebuilt and when people came to him, a young, blond Englishman, and shook him by the hand. Later, being sent by his newspaper editor to doorstep a woman whose son had just been hanged, he had walked away from the Scottish *Daily Mail* and taken a boat to Sweden, going from there on an icebreaker up into the Arctic before returning to live in Stockholm where he had set two of his novels. Later, he moved to the Netherlands where the first of his many radio plays was broadcast on the Hilversum station. That was all before, at the age of thirty-three, his travelling days over, he had settled down to write and have children with me.

I put the Bible to one side and turned back to the TV. An American circus programme was showing which included an act involving tame, toothless lions. The local news followed: a woman and her three children had just been attacked and eaten by a lion. Africa – dark and swarming with dangerous animals – was out there some-where beyond the flower-beds. Waiting. But I was new to travelling, still clinging to safe areas like hotel bars. Besides, both my time and my money were running out. I had to catch the train back to Botswana.

Passing through Gaborone again, I returned to the President Hotel to get a room. 'Sorry,' said the receptionist, 'we're completely booked.'

This was bad news. I knew that the Gaborone Hotel too was totally booked and I certainly couldn't afford the Holiday Inn.

'But I made a booking before I left last week.'

The receptionist looked surprised. 'You did? Well, there's no record of it here.'

'I made a booking. Definitely,' I lied firmly. 'Perhaps you failed to write it in.'

My persistence was rewarded and I was given a pleasant double room. Later that evening, however, the receptionist accosted me angrily: 'You've taken someone else's room. He's just arrived and he *had* booked. We have the reservation here. Now we've had to put a bed for him in one of the squash courts.' I had been caught out.

The train stood motionless. Heat shimmered on the chrome of the door handles. A lizard scurried across the sleepers. We had stopped at a trading post called Pitsane. A small shanty town had grown up round the halt – one-roomed shacks with tin roofs, lean-tos, cars with their wheels removed. Beyond the wire fence, a woman was washing clothes in a big tin bath and a little girl, no more than six, had the job of ferrying water from a nearby standpipe. Back and forth she walked, cradling the empty can in her arms, placing it under the standpipe until it was filled, then carefully putting a leaf on top of the water to stop it spilling before lifting the can on to her head and walking back along the track to her mother.

As the youngest in the family, it had been my job, too, to bring the water back from the well when, each year, we went to our cottage in Ballycorus for the summer months. Although it was only twelve miles from Dublin there was no running water, no electricity, no phone. The lavatory was an earth closet, unless I needed just to pee, in which case a quick dash behind the fuschia bush was enough.

I hated going to the well. The long wet grass on either side of the path clawed at my bare, eight-year-old legs like a hungry, multi-tongued creature. And despite stretching out one arm for balance, I could never prevent some of the water spilling over from the pail into my wellingtons. But if going to the well was bad, going for the milk was far worse. We got our milk from Suzanne whose lined old face was brown as turf and who lived, with her farmhand Jemmy, in a near-derelict farmhouse three fields away.

'You'll watch, won't you,' I'd beg my mother as I set out on this perilous journey and when I got to the first stile I would turn and look back, knowing she'd be standing at the cottage door, ready to give me an encouraging wave, her presence going with me all the way to the next stile.

Sometimes, if she was milking the cows, Suzanne would turn the udder in my direction, aiming a jet of warm milk straight into my face. Then, bringing me into the house, she'd swipe from the shit-covered kitchen table the hens which had come in through the window from the orchard, sending them flapping and squawking on to the floor. When I got to the farm gate, I'd shout out for Suzanne and she would come to shoo away the flock of geese which always congregated there, cackling herself at my fear. One blow from an outstretched wing could break a man's arm, I knew, and thinking about it made my own eight-year-old arms feel brittle as match sticks.

Now, leaning out of the train window and watching the small black girl working so industriously for her mother, I wondered what childhood dangers lay in store for her, but my mind was blank. I had, I realized, no concept of what life was like for a small African child.

In my own childhood, danger lay just beyond the farm gate. If Suzanne wasn't there, I'd have to brave the geese and go into the house alone where I knew Jemmy would be waiting for me and where my mother's protective, watchful eyes could not follow. 'Will I pull it offa yeh?' Jemmy would say, sliding his hand up the leg of my knickers and tweaking that small part of me that had no name and I would laugh politely and let him do it because he was a grown-up and I'd been taught to be polite to grown-ups. Then, skipping back across the fields, relieved to be free of his farm-dirty, prying fingers, I'd swing the lidless milk can round in an arc without losing a drop, knowing nothing about centrifugal force, equating it simply with all the other mysteries of life such as the Virgin Birth and the Change of Life which made women get embarrassed about perspiring. When I reached the cottage my mother would ask: 'What on earth kept you?' 'Nothing,' I would reply, the memory of those possessive fingers already carefully buried. Some days, going for the milk, it was Paddy, the horse, I had to watch out for. Bitten by a gadfly, he would often rear up in pain and gallop around the field in demented circles. Threatened by malevolent nature, therefore, I always made sure to locate a hole in the hedge through which I could escape should a gadfly get Paddy or the geese become overly angry and block my way. Locating my escape route is a habit that persists to this day so that no matter what situation I find myself in – whether emotional or physical – I still make a mental note of the emergency exits. I like my panic buttons to be within easy reach.

But despite the geese and the gadflies, the Ballycorus summers were idyllic. I went up into the woods with a sack to collect fir cones for the evening fire, played cards with my mother on wet days, climbed trees, pulled myself across the weed-strewn pond by a rope slung from one side to the other and, on warm summer evenings, sat outside on the granite steps, tucked in between the grown-ups, listening to them talking and singing ('Now you can't get to heaven, in a wee Ford car . . .') until the light faded and the night clouds started to move across the sky from the Three-Rock Mountain opposite, drawing down a dark blind upon the day. And so, in the heat of the African day, I looked at the little girl carrying her pail of water and saw myself.

Next morning, the risen sun was bright, so bright its memory imprinted itself on my retina so that when I looked away from it, the blue sky was covered with a thousand glowing discs. Below them, a mist hung over the valley.

The train continued to trundle southwards all day through the dry, yellow countryside of Botswana. Behind us lay Zimbabwe, twenty-four hours ahead lay Johannesburg and in a few hours we would arrive in Mafikeng, which was a surprise to me as, so hazy was my colonial geography, I had always thought Mafikeng was a border town somewhere in India. But it turned out to be a small town just over the South African border where passengers had to change trains. Faced with an eight-hour wait there, I roamed around the town and discovering the dull, dusty museum signed my name in the visitors' book: 'May 9th, 1981, the day on which Bobby Sands, British MP, was buried.' Then I legged it out of the building and down the street, fearful someone would think I was connected with the IRA.

I hated being in South Africa. Hated the armed police with their thick necks, the whites-only benches on the railway platform. Felt uncomfortable when a white friend, who had lived in South Africa for many years, dismissed Steve Biko as a nonentity who had only come to prominence because of his brutal death at the hands of the agents of the apartheid regime. In the white neighbourhoods, guard dogs barked and razor wire climbed like clematis over garden walls. At the Rand Show, I held in my hand a 25 kilogram bar of gold still warm from the furnace – and shivered. Apartheid South Africa, it seemed, was with us for ever. I couldn't wait to leave.

When I got back to Brill (the village in Buckinghamshire where Ian and I lived) I turned up as usual to the Friday night poker school, full of tales of my journeying: the brutish customs men at Johannesburg airport with their shaved heads, fat stomachs and holstered guns; the beauty of the smart Basotho women against whose dark skin their silver jewellery glowed; the brown-uniformed hit squad of the Lesotho Government, menacing as they rode on horseback around Maseru; the clusters of rondavels, seen from an aeroplane, clinging to the side of a mountain, no link visible between them and the outside world. I wanted to talk about the foul-tasting home-brewed raisin beer and how I ate sticky mealie with my fingers. There was the performance of Dario Fo's *Accidental Death of an Anarchist*, put on at Barney White's Market Theatre in Johannesburg, only spitting distance from Smith Square, headquarters of the South African Police, from which building many political activists had been hurled, just as happened in Fo's play. I had travelled, seen it all and couldn't wait to tell everyone. 'Hi,' said the dealer, 'how's the rest of the world?' But before I could answer, he'd shuffled the cards and placed them in front of me. 'Your turn to cut,' he said, 'and we're shy in the middle.'

Over the next few years, my work took me to other parts of Africa, to other parts of the world and it wasn't until

1994 (thirteen years later) that I was able to return to Lesotho, this time to write something about pony trekking in the mountains. I stayed the night at the Maseru flat of a friend, which turned out to be a night of crises. One of her colleagues had drunk one drink too many and had been carted off to hospital, leaving someone – anyone – to look after his child. The flat below had flooded and water was pouring across the living room and down through the ceiling into the flat of a tight-lipped Taiwanese couple engaged on some aid project or other. Within minutes of arriving, I found myself barefooted and with my trousers rolled up, sweeping wave after wave of water out the front door and on to the balcony from where it fell in cascades on to the cars in the car park below.

Next morning, I left Maseru for the trading station where I was to hire a pony. The old clapboard building smelled of rubber gloves and paraffin, reminding me of Conroy's, the little red-painted shop at the bottom of the Ballycorus hill. My guide was Robert who, I later learned, was called Sebeli Senone, the Robert bit a sop to Europeans unable to get their tongue round an African name. Our destination was a village 7000 feet up in the Thaba Putsoa mountain range. With us was another horseman leading a packhorse, with our water, food and bedding, and a flabby, sandalled woman connected to the British Council, who kept falling from her pony. Riding behind her on a pony called Rosie, I could chart each steady and inevitable decline as the pony, clambering up and over rocks, dislodged her rump until, with a deep groan of despair and in a tangle of desperately waving arms and legs, she would slither to the ground yet again. Eventually, in tears – and to my relief – she begged to return to base accompanied by the other horseman, leaving Robert and myself to continue on. Trekking up a mountain on a pony in Lesotho is not unlike climbing an unending flight of steep stairs, but on horseback. Ascending, the pony's head rises up in front of you at an alarming angle. Descending, your whole body pitches forwards and the only thing that keeps you on top and in place is faith in your mount and a pair of knees strong enough to grip tight when the scrambling stage is met. Climbing upwards all morning in the hot sun, we paused on the plateau to take in the enormity of Lesotho's mountain peaks and to eat a piece of bread and brew up some tea. Then we pressed on, descending to the river bed so that this time I was in danger of sliding down the banister that was Rosie's neck, continuing over her head and landing on the rocky path. The only way to avoid this happening was to lie back and rock in the saddle with each step.

We had three mountain peaks to negotiate as well as the River Makhaleng and when we clambered down to the river bed the ponies had a long cool drink before splashing across to start the climb up the side of the next mountain, stepping carefully across a rushing stream covered, at one point, by a treacherously uneven layer of ice. At the sight of the ice, Rosie hesitated and I urged her on with my boots but Robert held up a warning hand: 'No, no. Wait. She's working out which is the best way to go. Give her time.' Carefully, Rosie lowered her head to the sheet of ice and stared hard at the water running fast below it, assessing its depth. Then, when she was ready, we started our perilous navigation of the slippery ice, each step deliberate and chosen with care. Once, losing her footing, she stumbled then backed up, unable to edge her way round the tight corner of an over-hanging rock. Water foamed through a crack in the ice, creating a froth of icy whiteness that left me shivering. Robert, having got to the other side of the rock, called across to me: 'Just do as I say. First, pull her round a little. Now a little bit more. Careful. Now this way, over towards me. That's it. Wait! Give her a chance to see where she's going. Now, let her come across.' Once on the other side of the ice, the tension flowed away from my body and I patted Rosie: her wisdom and experience in these matters far exceeded mine.

We rode into the mountain village of Rabetsane in the late afternoon and found it deserted but for some small children and a few old women. Everyone, including the chief and his family, had walked to another village further up the mountain to attend a party for a man just returned from South Africa. The majority of Basotho men still worked as migrant labourers in the mines of South Africa, leaving the women behind to farm the land. The men's other source of income was as journeymen sheep shearers. In South Africa's Eastern Cape, just over the Lesotho border, I had often seen lorry loads of Basotho shearers being taken round the Boer farms during the shearing season. Khotso, the chief (his name meant peace), had not become a migrant, however, but had stayed at home to look after his village and his stock. That night, on his return from the neighbouring village party, he carried a huge brazier to the door of our rondavel and his wife, Majala, handed round pieces of dried dung for us to break up and throw on it, the dung sending bright golden flames sparking upwards into the night. All the creatures – oxen, mohair goats and sheep

– were safely corralled and on the stone wall the white-feathered fowl were roosting, crooning quietly to themselves. Across the valley we could see other braziers flaring up in the darkness but soon, they, like our own, died away.

Khotso brought us into his mother's rondavel where she and the children were sitting round a dung fire in the middle of the floor, popping corn. The blackened husks sizzled and spat, hopping around the mud floor sprightly as fleas which the children tried to catch. On the wall hung a framed copy of Khotso's and Majala's wedding certificate. It was a warm place to be, full of firelight and happiness, and I pulled out the few Mosotho words I knew: '*Ke thabile hoba mona,*' I said, expressing, I hoped, my pleasure at being a guest in the chief's house. Next morning, a Sunday, the village would have to stir early as it was a two-hour walk to the nearest church, which meant a five o'clock start. Before that, the animals had to be milked, fed and watered. Khotso and Majala, wrapped in their blankets, walked me back to my rondavel. The night was still, with only the occasional ring of a bell as the oxen shifted in their pen. Above, the sky glimmered with stars and the air was bitterly cold. I went into the rondavel warmed now by the glowing brazier. Down in Maseru, they would all be gathered round the TV in the Italian restaurant there: Ireland was playing in the quarter-finals of the World Cup in Italy. Bedding down on the floor, I held my watch up to the light of the fire and smiled to discover I was going to sleep on a Saturday night and it wasn't yet eight o'clock.

Next morning, after a bowl of strong, sour tasting motoho mealie, we saddled up again. Ahead lay the cone-shaped mountain of Ntsupe with, beneath it, the giant Ribaneng waterfall.

Apart from the advent of Christianity, the village of Rabetsane had remained relatively untouched by the outside world. No international aid had found its way up there. There was no road, no electricity, no newspapers, no television. Water came from a spring.

Down in Maseru, thirteen years on, things hadn't gone quite as expected. KLM and not Aer Lingus had got the airport contract. The Connemara Pony Project, conceived twenty years previously with such enthusiasm and hope, turned out to be a flop: the Irish ponies failed to thrive in the hot climate of Lesotho. Interbreeding did nothing to improve the native stock and now the crossbreeds are used mainly for giving rides to tourists.

CHAPTER TWO

Is it OK to Eat the Tray Cloth?
Sudan 1982

Abdel Gadir took me by the arm and drew me aside: 'Before we go into my house for breakfast, I want to tell you,' he said in a low voice, 'I have two wives.'

'Lucky you.' It was a silly, flirtatious reply but I couldn't think of what else to say and it seemed to be an acceptable one for Abdel Gadir's top row of gold teeth semaphored delight. '*El hamdhu lilah*,' he agreed. Thanks be to Allah. We walked up the steps to the shady veranda of his house and washed our hands at the tap, before joining his male staff for breakfast.

There was a slow feel to the plantation. The cotton picking season was nearly over and the seasonal workers – nomads, mostly – would soon leave. The water level in the channels was low, delaying the onset of the sowing season. There was nothing to do but wait for more water to be released into the Gezira from one of the dams further up the Nile. Sudan's Gezira is a miracle of water engineering.

A broad piece of land shaped like a saucer, it lies south of Khartoum. Flowing alongside to the west of it, is the Nile. Tip the waters of the Nile over the rim of the saucer and you have a major, gravity-flow irrigation system that floods the rich, cotton-producing soil. Egyptian cotton (Sudan was once part of Egypt) is among the best in the world, due to the density of the weave and the length of the thread which gives it its distinctive softness.

The Gezira had presented itself to me as a gift. Before I'd even left southern Africa, that first time, I knew that I would be back. Not necessarily to Lesotho but to somewhere in Africa. Anywhere. Something of the hot stillness, the wide open skies, the dusty roads had lodged like a longing in my heart. In any case, I wanted to be away. I was growing out of cooking family meals, of weekly trips to the supermarket, of the sameness of my days. I was growing out of village politics, growing out of Brill, even, where we had lived for nearly twenty years.

The cost of the journey to Lesotho had been partly covered by some newspaper features I'd subsequently written and these had come to the notice of the Irish Department of Foreign Affairs. Would I write an information booklet for them, they asked, on all the good things Ireland was doing for Africa? The request fitted neatly with the ending of my year at Bradford University where, in the course of my researches, I'd discovered that Sudan was another of Ireland's partners in the development aid programme, chosen because it was an Arab country. Arab, that is, provided you ignored the south which the Islamic colonists had so far not managed to pacify. Sudan would have to be included in the booklet.

The money offered by the Department was small but I had become cunning, starting to learn the survival strategies of the traveller, the techniques of the beggar, now more politely known as networking. I wrote lots of letters in advance of a journey taking up contacts from the most tenuous connections. Distant acquaintances had only to mention that they had a relative or friend in some far off place for me to write their name and address in my notebook. I found I could borrow from the bank, travel, write about the journey when I came home and then pay off the bank loan. On paper, the theory was perfect, its execution less so. The sale of features to newspapers or radio rarely covered either the cost of the air ticket or the expenses incurred while travelling. Having a free bed came with a price. It meant always having to be interesting and vivacious. Never being dull or feeling tired. Occasionally, I managed to make myself useful by reading *Thomas the Tank Engine* to the children of the house, cooking a meal or helping with the shopping and these tasks I relished as they gave me a feel for living in a place rather than passing through it. Although each journey left me in greater debt, on reflection, I knew I'd have been in debt anyway. And besides, travelling was quite a pleasant way of getting in the red.

The day before going to see the cotton plantation, I'd gone looking for some fabric in the market in Khartoum. The one I liked was pale blue cotton with a silvery sheen to its thread which felt silky when I rubbed it between my fingers. I bought a length and took it to one of the tailors whose sewing machines tick-tacked on the pavements. 'Could you make a djellabiya,' I asked and he nodded.

'What size?' 'It's for my husband,' I lied. 'He's the same size as me.' Women don't wear djellabiyas in Sudan. The tailor measured me – height and then width across the shoulders – holding the tape measure close to my shoulders but being careful not to touch them. Islam discourages men from touching women other than their wives. 'It will be ready in a few days,' he said, and bowed, putting his hand on his heart.

'I bought some cotton in Khartoum yesterday,' I told Abdel Gadir during breakfast.

'Ah,' he said proudly, selecting a choice piece of pigeon breast from his own plate and placing it, with delicate fingers, on mine. 'Sudanese cotton. It is the best.' Abdel Gadir was a kindly man whose round stomach, silhouetted beneath his djellabiya, gave him an avuncular look. He had studied agriculture at Alexandria and had fond memories of Egypt. One of his tasks, as Block Inspector, was to police the flow of water in this part of the Gezira. The flow is first pumped through from the heart of the Nile. It divides into arteries, fanning out to take the water across the Gezira to various plantations. Then it divides again, narrowing down to veins which feed the individual projects on the plantation. Finally, it flows through capillaries or channels no more than a foot wide, bearing its precious gift to each farmer. And it's here that the trouble starts for whenever there was a shortage of water, farmers – desperate to get their cotton plants growing – could, by judicious damming, divert into their own channels more water than they were entitled to. All that was needed were a few twigs. It was one of Abdel Gadir's jobs to see that those rogue twigs were removed.

Like cotton, breakfast in Sudan was also the best and the table was laid with fermented milk, salad, *ful* (Egyptian beans), pigeon, omelette and cool yoghurt. After their ablutions, the men seated themselves round the table with Abdel Gadir placing me on his right. The talk was of water, the weather and of cotton planting. Another project had recently been introduced and there was much discussion about its hoped-for success. This project involved the donkeymen whose job it was to ride round collecting milk from the farmers and then sell it on to customers. Up till now, milk had been transported in cans which meant it often arrived at its destination sour. The new idea was the construction of a dairy where the milk would be sterilized before being put into individual, pint-sized plastic pillows for the donkeymen to deliver. (When I later came to write about this for an Irish paper a sub-editor edited out the word donkeymen as he feared it sounded offensive, which is an interesting reflection on attitudes in a country where, until some fifty years ago, many rural families not only had a donkey and cart but depended on them.)

As always, we talked in whatever language came to hand, in this case a mongrel mix of English and Arabic. Our exchanges were not elegant but together with smiles, nods, hand signals and a general projection of goodwill they were tools that served us well. When the coffee was brought in and the cups and saucers distributed, I found the men had been given plain cups while I was given a tiny one rimmed with gold. 'I feel like a queen,' I said. 'Then you must meet my prince,' said Abdel Gadir and called out to someone in house. A baby boy was carried through and handed to ming father. Amir (the name means prince) was

Abdel Gadir's pride and joy. A tiny tuft of dark hair stuck up on the top of his head, insurance in the event of an early death. Should he die while still a baby, he could be plucked straight up into heaven by this tuft of hair. For further safekeeping, a leather pouch containing a verse from the Koran was tied to his fat little wrist.

Although Amir was the prince of the family, he was not the only child. All through breakfast, two small girls, in their best dresses, had stood staring at me but whenever I tried to speak to them had slipped behind their father, fingers in mouth. When the meal was over and the men gone, Abdel Gadir brought me into the house to meet the womenfolk. Here, his marriage arrangements became clearer. His first wife had had three miscarriages and had subsequently failed to conceive. However, instead of divorcing her, as was his right under Islamic law, he had introduced into his household a second wife who had promptly borne him three children. The family room was busy with women working, talking and cuddling children. Abdel Gadir's mother, a shrivelled nut of a woman, sat at a table chopping green leaves, patiently pushing her veil away from her face across which it constantly fell. Opposite her sat Abdel Gadir's mother-in-law – which one I wasn't told – gathering up the chopped leaves and putting them into a bowl. At the stove stood his first wife, dressed in a long brown gown, her head shrouded in a brown veil. She kept her face averted, eyes downcast and it was only when Abdel Gadir spoke her name and introduced her to me that she looked up. In the instant our eyes met, I saw in her sad ones the shame of the barren woman. I looked away quickly but not before some of the sadness detached itself from her, to stay with me for ever. Beside Abdel Gadir stood his second wife – young and vivacious, wearing a brightly coloured European dress, her head uncovered, her dark, perfumed skin adorned with gold. In her arms, she held Amir, her passport to happiness and security.

At the entrance to the plantation, where I waited for the bus to Gedaref, a new nightwatchman arrived bringing with him his straw house which he carried like a large umbrella over his head. It cost £500 to build a permanent watchman's house, Abdel Gadir told me, but a straw one was only £2, took two days to build and had the added advantage of portability.

Excitement pinched the pit of my stomach as the bus drew into Gedaref: I had arrived in an unknown place, no one knew where I was and I had made no advance sleeping arrangements. In fact, I didn't know if there was even such a thing as a hotel in Gedaref.

'You want a taxi?' asked a driver.

'Well, I want to get to the police station.' As a foreigner, I had to register my arrival with the police.

'Just where I'm going,' said the driver, deftly swinging his car round in the other direction. Along the way, we overtook a herd of swaying camels loaded with bundles of straw, making for the straw market.

'You know, a camel never forgets,' the taxi driver shouted back to me.

'I thought that was elephants.'

'Elephant? No, camel.'

He'd once known a man, he said, who had a fractious camel. The man dealt with it sharply, beating it to try to make it behave. Eventually, losing patience, he sold it but years later, bought it back again. The very first time he went to saddle it up, ducking underneath it with the straps, the camel swung its stomach at its former owner, hitting him on the head with its belly bone and killing him. 'They never forget,' said the taxi driver, shaking his head. 'Never.'

A couple of soldiers lounged at the door of the police station, one of them in boots far too big for him, the laces undone. Boots were not things he was used to. I sat on an upturned bucket and waited, though for whom I wasn't certain. After half an hour, one of the soldiers handed me his rifle to look after while he went off to find me a glass of tea. Eventually, tired of waiting, I set off through the town for the refugee office and found Elsir who worked for the United Nations High Commission for Refugees. 'You must stay with me,' he said, 'I'll show you my town.' And that evening, he did. In the smart white UNHCR Land Rover, we cruised up one sandy street and down another. Lanterns hanging outside shops and market stalls gave off an orange glow, which, filtering through the dust of the night, threw an eerie underworld pall over everything. After an hour, I grew restless and, conscious we were wasting precious fuel, asked pointedly how much petrol cost. Elsir laughed: petrol was not a problem. 'No one pays the official rate,' he said. 'Everyone buys whatever they want on the black market.'

Back at the house, we pored over my English–Arabic phrase book. This entailed Elsir slapping me on the back a lot and laying a hand nonchalantly on my knee as he leaned over to draw my attention to a word or phrase that interested him. Sleeping arrangements were discussed. Would I like to sleep inside or outside? But I refused to say, until I found out where he thought *he* was sleeping.

He pressed me and eventually I made a definite decision: I would, I told him, either take my bed outside or leave it inside. Finally, Elsir brought me through to his room which was, it seemed, to be my room. The table was strewn with combs, oils and creams – all the things needed to make him beautiful. In truth, Elsir *was* beautiful, tall, slim and slender as an ash plant. I guessed he was a Dinka from the south. My surreptitious examination of Elsir's toiletries was interrupted by Mohammed, a moustached sixteen-year-old neighbour who wanted to try out his English on me. Mohammed roared out the names of authors he'd studied at school, as proud as if he had actually written their books for them. Also proud, I told him I came from the same place as some of the writers. 'Yes,' he shouted, 'Oscaw Wile, vair good writah. Eenglish. Yorgia Bernaard Chaw – vair good writah. Americaan.' He was so pleased with this information that it seemed churlish to argue. Mohammed's proud possession was his bike which he wheeled into the bedroom to show to me. It was Chinese-made, called the Flying Pigeon and came with something I'd never seen before: a built-in lock.

My day had begun at 4.30 a.m. when I had set out for the cotton plantation and I was now tired and sticky and accepted with relief Elsir's offer of a wash. The shower, which was out in the yard, was a concrete telephone box of a thing with a hole in the floor through which the water drained. To activate it, you dipped a jug into a bucket of water and poured it over yourself. I unwrapped the bar of perfumed soap that had been left for me and filled the jug with cold water. It was the best shower I have ever had.

It took a couple of days in Gedaref to fix a visit to the

nearby Tawawa refugee camp which, as well as gathering material for the Irish Aid information booklet was another reason for coming to Sudan. Tawawa had been set up as a place of safety for people fleeing the war between Eritrea and Ethiopia. The Canadian Government was in the process of creaming off educated refugees and many of the people in Tawawa, being nurses, engineers and teachers, stood a good chance of getting to Canada. They were cheerful people, demanding, ebullient, sure of their hopes. But there were some – the ones who clearly wouldn't get to Canada – who were too tired and depressed to care about anything beyond their day-to-day survival.

I squatted over the hole in the latrine in Tawawa, thinking about Sudan. Bordered by eight countries, most of which seem to have had wars at some time or other, it had become home to the thousands who streamed in from Uganda, Ethiopia, Eritrea and Kenya. The Sudanese, in fact, had taken in more refugees than any country in fortress Europe, something rarely acknowledged by those who finger the purse strings in Brussels. I reached for the broad leaf and bottle of water left for latrine users, wondering if the latrine was one of Ed Schroeder's. Ed was an American environmentalist who had once lived on Skid Row making fishing nets and was now living in Gedaref. He had cracked Tawawa's latrine problem. A new road-building scheme had been initiated by the Chinese and Ed had struck up a deal with the foreman: in return for English lessons the foreman would supply Tawawa with empty tar barrels which, when sunk in the ground, made excellent latrines. 'And you know what the foreman was called?' Ed asked me. 'Mr Liu.'

At lunchtime, Hassan invited me to join the Eritrean

health orderlies who were sitting on the ground round a huge bowl of food. 'Why do you eat with your left hand?' he asked me. I faltered. It was true, I'd forgotten my manners and had been using it to dip into the communal bowl of *ful*. 'I'm left-handed,' I said, trying to cover up. But this information was no excuse: the left hand is reserved for nose picking and arse cleaning. The others scolded Hassan, however, for his apparent unmannerliness. I was an ill-bred foreigner who could not be expected to know any better. He should have made allowances for me, they told him.

There were lots of babies at the camp, poor miserable crying infants being nursed by listless mothers. Everyone, in fact, was tired, including the doctors and nurses, who, labouring under difficult conditions, occasionally lost their bedside manner. 'For God's sake, woman,' I heard someone shout as I ducked my head to go into the medical tent, 'hold her bloody hips still.' It was Jed, an Australian doctor, in boots and bushwhacker hat, trying to deal with the dreadful injuries of a child who had fallen into a pot of lentils cooking on an open fire. The distressed child was given a shot of valium and then put on a drip because she had become dehydrated.

Jed took off his hat, scratched his head and sat back on his heels to take a breather in his makeshift clinic. 'Always the same – bloody *tukul* fires.' *Tukuls* are made of bamboo stakes with mud plastered in between them, the whole construction covered outside with rush matting, the roof thatched with reeds. They have a pleasing, graceful look to them, are cheap and easy to make but a death trap if they catch fire. Lying on a mat to one side of Jed's tent was another small boy who had been badly burned when the roof had caught fire and flaming straw had fallen in on him. His mother had been cooking *ful* inside the *tukul* at the time.

I felt dispirited after visiting Tawawa. Although this was the first refugee camp I had ever visited, I felt as if I'd seen it all before: the resignation, the unquestioning acceptance, the anxious, helpless trust put in authority. In a way I *had* seen it all before when I had worked in a ghetto school on a council estate in Oxford where those at the bottom of the economic and social pile accepted their powerlessness with the same tiredness I saw on the faces of the refugee mothers. The more valiant of the council tenants railed against it in a way I knew would be simply misunderstood if not actually derided by those set above them. Which is why I worked for a time in educational counselling, trying to bridge this communication gap. One of my tasks had been to deal with a small boy called Billy, whose mother had left home. 'She just fecked off,' said Jack, Billy's father. Jack had solved some of his household problems – the electricity had been cut off for non-payment of bills – by reconnecting directly to the electricity pole outside his council house. His living room had several television sets: one he used for sound, another for vision while the third was on standby.

In his own way, Jack was a good father. He encouraged Billy to go to school though was rarely up early enough in the mornings to ensure that the seven-year-old got there on time.

But teachers are teachers and they were censorious of Jack. He was not a good father. He drank. He didn't come to parents' evenings, didn't reply to notes, didn't send Billy to school in clean clothes. As a result, the staff were of the opinion that the boy should be taken into care.

Social workers were called in, meetings held and reports written. These reports, I soon learned, were handled more secretively than newspaper D-Notices. Few people were allowed to read them, certainly not the people about whom they were written. And having read one or two of them and seen how judgmental and offensive they were, I could understand why they were always marked confidential. However, this was the 1970s, the dawn of openness, of discussion, of exploring relationships – relationships even between teachers and recalcitrant parents – and I was part of it. In any case, I had recently completed a postgraduate teaching course at Oxford where, during one lecture, we had discussed the damaging nature of some school and social services reports. The only way to avoid falling into the same trap, we decided, was never to write anything in a report that we would not be prepared to discuss with the subject. Thus, one afternoon, after a meeting at which Jack's many failings had been dicussed, I called to see him.

'What did those feckers have to say?' he asked, reclining in an armchair with his beer.

'The usual – Billy's a bright boy and it's a shame he misses school so often. They think he should be sent away.'

'Hmm. Let's have a look.' I handed him the notes of the meeting to read which, for once, were inoffensive.

'You mustn't tell anyone I showed you that folder. It's confidential, you know.'

'What folder?' he asked, handing it back to me. He was a subversive after my own heart.

We had a talk about the proposals in the report but Jack

was adamant: 'Billy's going nowhere,' he said. 'And if he *does* go somewhere, it'll be back to Northern Ireland where my sisters live. They'd have Billy any time. They'd be *honoured* to have him but I'm not letting him go. He stays here with me.'

If Billy knew one thing, it was that his father loved him but this was so clearly not a view shared by the school that eventually the time came for a bit of constructive intervention.

'You must come to the school on parents' evening,' I told Jack. 'Then they'll see you really care about Billy's schooling.'

'In the name of God, what are you talking about? I *do* care about Billy's schooling. It's just that I don't like schools. I never did. I had an auld bitch of a teacher once and that was enough for me. They're all the same . . . But don't be saying I don't care about Billy because I do.'

'I know, but they have to see it. You have to humour them. Teachers aren't always the brightest of God's creatures,' I said, enjoying my treachery.

'OK, don't worry. Name the day and the time and I'll be there. I'll take them all on, one by one. When is it?'

'You should have already had a note about parents' evening. Billy should have brought it home.'

'A note? Sure I never read any of that rubbish.'

On parents' evening, I primed Billy's teacher: 'Jack is coming in to see you especially. He wants to talk about Billy's progress. I think you'll find he really is interested in what you're doing.'

Later, towards the end of the evening, I heard shouting coming from one of the classrooms. 'Take that man out of here,' Billy's teacher was saying. 'Get him *out*. He has no right to come in here in that condition.' Jack emerged from the classroom wearing a tie – something I'd never seen him in before – and carrying an exercise book and pencil, presumably to make notes on his historic visit to the school. But something was drastically wrong. As he came along the corridor, shepherded by Billy, who was running from side to side like a sheepdog, I could see that Jack was swaying and knew, without asking, what had happened. On the way to parents' evening, he had called in to the pub to fire himself up for the ordeal. It was the end of the road. Social Services drew up yet another report, the home was visited, the number of televisions noted and Billy's educational profile investigated. But before anything could be finalized, Jack and Billy slipped away to Ireland and were never heard of again. Secretly, I wished them *bon voyage*.

The poorer of the refugees in Sudan – those who would *not* be creamed off – had no energy left to rail against the circumstances that had forced them to flee their homes and seek refuge in a strange land. They had walked for days to reach safety on this side of the Sudanese border and were both exhausted and dispirited. In any case, who was there to rail against? The people they might have complained about were the same people they had to turn to for help. There were now so many displaced people in the world, so many refugees, both economic and political, that they had come to be known not as the Third but as the Fourth World. When I returned home, I decided, I would try to find out more about these issues. I had no idea where and what that decision would lead to.

The bus back to Khartoum was due to leave Gedaref at seven in the morning and, to be on the safe side, I got there at six, which was lucky as it left half an hour early. When I arrived, activity at the bus station was already peaking. A small boy was selling sunglasses from a tray hung round his neck and not doing too badly considering some of the frames had only one lens in them. As a sideline, he sold single cigarettes. The cold drinks man was disinterring blocks of ice which had been buried overnight in sawdust. These were lowered into metal containers which acted as a cooler. A coffee seller walked up and down, a copper coffee machine strapped to his back, the metal cups which hung from it clinking in time to his step. Beside the bus stop, the bread stall was serving rounds of freshly baked bread. I bought a cup of strong, steaming coffee and some hot bread and while I was enjoying my breakfast a young Kenyan came up to me for a chat. 'What tribe do you belong to?' he asked. 'The Irish tribe,' I replied and he nodded. He'd heard of us.

The Khartoum bus belonged to Abu Arabi Travel and was a dangerous looking number. The windows were unglazed and the interior lined with chipboard. The ceiling and sides, however, were papered in a bright mosaic of Arabic patterns. I couldn't wait to get on it. I managed to get one of the last tickets (£4 all the way) and pushed my way through to the last vacant seat in the back row which I shared with seven men. By eight o'clock, the desert heat was clogging my throat and whenever we overtook a bus or lorry, the rush of stinging grains of sand hit my face and arms like a violent attack of sharp needles. Everyone on the back seat had wound their turbans round their faces to protect them from the sand and rooting about in my bag I pulled out my towel and did the same.

As we got up speed going through the desert, the slip-stream increased and my eyelids felt as if they were being blown back behind my eyeballs. Leaning my elbow on the window frame, I found that every so often I got a welcome rush of cool moisture on my arm. Perhaps it was some freak of nature in the desert. I knew that droplets occasionally materialized then evaporated as soon as they were felt. Whatever the cause, it was God-given and I thanked Allah for it. The bus trundled along the road, sometimes heaving outwards to overtake on the inside when an overturned lorry or a broken-down truck blocked its way. Once, to see what was happening, I leaned my head out of the window. At the front of the bus, an old man, the tail of his turban loose and blowing in the wind, leaned far out of his window, hawked and then spat. I quickly withdrew my head just as the spray of cooling spittle hit my arm.

At half past nine, we stopped at a roadside stall for break-fast. Everyone made for the tap to wash their hands which was how I, the unclean foreigner, inadvertently found myself at the top of the food queue. The meal was delicious, or *lazees*, as I was learning to say. *Ful*, cooked in oil and garlic and crushed with a lemonade bottle. This tasty, nutritious mush was scooped up with a piece of warm, fresh bread. I bought a glass of coffee, preening when the man serving it understood my request: *suukar qaleel* – only a little sugar. Most Sudani take four or five spoonfuls of sugar in their coffee and become anxious for your mortal wellbeing if you take anything less.

I left the bus when we were halfway to Khartoum. A

near collision with a lorry piled high with durum flour had sent us shooting to the other side of the road where the bus wavered for a few seconds, undecided whether or not to capsize. Returning finally to its own side of the road, the sudden swerve brought all the luggage from the overhead racks tumbling down on top of us. A few miles further along the road, we caught up with the lorry and our driver stopped, waved it down and then pulled the lorry driver out of his cab in order to pummel him, a bare-knuckle fight that was only stopped by a soldier who happened to be travelling on our bus. By the time we got to Wad Medani, I had had enough. In any case, it was the Easter weekend and I had friends there with whom I could stay. I met up with Mike Green, an engineer from Scotland, on Good Friday, while sitting beside him in the shallow waters of the Nile. Most of the ex-pats had brought books and were sitting in the shallows reading paperbacks, which is why the weekly gathering was called the Nile Book Club.

Mike and I talked. Trouble lay ahead for Sudan, he felt. While the Sudani were away making megabucks in the Gulf, the land was being worked by Nigerian blow-ins, the Felladi. When the Sudani returned, he said, they could well find their country being run by Nigerians. There was also the trouble down south. Sudan is divided between the Arab north, which is mainly Islamic, and the African south, which is animist. Sporadic fighting had been taking place between the southerners and the government forces for some years. 'Take last week,' said Mike, pushing away his dog Fable (because he had a long tail) who was shaking himself dry in his face. 'Last week, a young lad here was suspected of having a molotov cocktail and was shot dead. At his funeral, his body was being carried through the streets when some of the soldiers from the south thought his spirit was coming back from the dead to haunt them and so they shot him dead again, but this time they also killed the four pallbearers.'

Therese, with whom I was staying, had asked me to go to the market to get some tomatoes, but I'd had to return empty-handed. '*Mafish*,' I told her. All gone. This morning, however, as I was walking through the market again, someone called out: 'Hey, you!' I didn't look round but when the call became more insistent: 'You! Hey, *you*!' I did turn and found the tomato seller beckoning me with a delighted smile. Used to being addressed by his white bosses in such a way, he assumed, I suppose, that it was the correct form of address for everyone. 'Look,' he cried, 'today plenty', and selecting two of the brightest, reddest tomatoes from the huge pile on his trestle table held them up for inspection. When I nodded, he spat on them before polishing them enthusiastically with the sleeve of his djellabiya. I had no option but to buy them. It would have been unmannerly to have done otherwise. On the way home, I stopped off at a little craft stall and bought a dagger. I somehow had the romantic idea that every male Sudani should own both a camel and a dagger. Having my own dagger was as close to the romantic ideal as I was going to get. Waiting to pay, I found myself standing beside Margaret whose husband managed an agricultural project. She was full of advice for the novice traveller and, since she was a nurse, I listened with interest.

'You don't drink the iced water here, do you?' she asked.

'God, no,' I lied.

'Good. Because it will give you diarrhoea. We've both had it very badly. Got it from the water. And of course, ice cream is totally out.'

'Oh, of course. I'd *never* touch that.' I was getting into the swing of lying.

'And as for sex . . .'

'Sex?'

'Yes, sex. Have you noticed all the phallic symbols everywhere?'

I hadn't.

'The minarets,' she continued, 'sticking up like that. And the daggers. Look at *your* dagger, for instance.' I looked at it and saw what she was talking about. The tip of the tooled leather sheath was a perfect, mushroom shape. I ran my fingers over it thoughtfully.

'You see,' said Margaret breathlessly, 'It's everywhere.'

I quickly withdrew my hand. Doing it in private was one thing but in the souk, where everyone could see?

Easter Saturday evening, Therese and I picked our way along the broken pavement to go to Mass. There had been a power failure and through the luminous red haze, figures materialized and faded again like wraiths at the gates of hell. I hadn't been in a church for a long time but curiosity about what a Mass in Africa might be like made me overcome my reservations. It turned out to be pretty much the same as a Mass in Dublin, with the addition of drumming and keening.

'I'm going up to Communion,' whispered Therese, 'are you?' I shook my head. I'd long since cut loose from the practices of the Catholic Church, regarding most of them as repressive both in regard to men and women. Having had my teenage bra strap twanged by a randy priest as he chatted with apparent innocence to his flock of schoolgirls, been misled over the question of the Immaculate Conception, and harassed by Rome when it became evident that I was going to marry Ian in a registry office rather than in a Catholic church, there seemed no good reason to remain a member of it. It wasn't, after all, like a political party that you stuck with out of loyalty when its leaders seemed to have, temporarily you hoped, gone off course. I had therefore freed myself long ago of the invasive influence of the Church. Now, faced with the opportunity of participating again in one of its rituals, I recoiled. '*No*,' I whispered to Therese, 'I'm not going up there.' But as I thought about it, I realized that if I had such strong feelings of repugnance about going to Communion, I clearly hadn't freed myself. I tapped Therese on the shoulder: 'Move up. I'm coming too.' I took the white disc in my mouth. The priest had dipped it in wine which gave it a pleasant, effervescent taste. I thought about what it represented, this eating of the flesh of a man put to death 2000 years ago because his politics were unacceptable to the colonial powers. Ritualistic cannibalism was a strange thing to be participating in particularly in a country where, if legend was anything to go by, missionaries were put in the stewpot by the dozen.

Warsama was waiting for me when I came down the stairs of the El Sharak hotel in Khartoum. I didn't recognise him at first – he looked like any other Arab in his long white flowing djellabiya and his turban with the tail, Sudan-style, hanging down his back, like the hair of a wanton woman. I'd first noticed him in a lecture theatre at an Oxford conference on famine in Africa. He had looked cool and smart in his pale blue safari suit and I learned he was a Sudani, working in President Nimeri's office in Khartoum. 'Where are you staying?' he'd asked when I arrived in Khartoum but shook his head when I told him. It was the cheapest hotel in town and, as usual with such places, was considered unsuitable for a single, European woman. 'You can't stay there. I'll find you a better one,' he said. 'It's got to be cheap,' I said nervously. My budget was strictly worked out. 'Don't worry,' he soothed me, 'it'll be all right.' In fact, El Sharak was more than all right: it was perfect. It was used mainly by local people and had a small dining room where, served by a kindly old man in a grubby djellabiya, I had breakfast each morning: coffee and fried eggs swimming in oil with lots of fresh bread to soak it up. My room was a small cell with a single bed, a chair and a curtained window giving on to the communal balcony. A fan spun slowly and unsteadily on the ceiling and my worst fear was that it would detach itself from its fitting and slice into my neck. Outside on the balcony sat a team of boys always on call to bring me a glass of tea, a jug of iced water, stamps or whatever else I might need. Sometimes, they brought me these things before I even knew I needed them.

In the heat of the day, I occasionally lay on my bed at El Sharak and fantasized about Warsama. He would come to my room, his dark eyes soft with longing, his turban in delicious disarray. He would apologize for being so much younger than me and undoubtedly being far less experienced and then, despite my better judgment, we would make love. He had told me once that he wished he was married and for one giddy moment I imagined myself living in Khartoum, belonging to this lovely, dusty city, pottering about the market in the early mornings, dining under the stars at the old colonial Sudan Club, taking trips out into the desert. His wish to be married, however, had a practical objective. 'If I had a wife, I could bring you to my house and she would cook you a meal,' he explained. I had to rethink my fantasy. The cooking duties of a Khartoum wife hadn't figured in it.

Today, Warsama was wearing his djellabiya because it was Friday, his day off work. It was also my last day in Khartoum. Tomorrow, early, I flew home.

We drove across the Nile to see the old city of Omdurman and to visit the Mahdi's tomb close to the defence works his followers had thrown up against the British attack on their city. I'd first came across the Mahdi when I read a remark made in the House of Commons in 1913. The subject under discussion was the militant action being taken by the suffragists. 'They are,' thundered an MP, 'as mad as the Mahdists.' The Mahdi, I discovered, were a group of political activists dedicated to resisting British domination whose leader, a devout Muslim, came from the prominent Mahdi family of Omdurman. Things had come to a head when, in 1885, the British were making their way down the Nile, fighting to keep control of Egypt and to regain Khartoum, which was being besieged by the Mahdi from their position in Omdurman on the opposite bank of the river. The British made their push southwards and were within two days of relieving the city when a troop of Mahdi burst into the residence of the Governor General, Charles Gordon, and ambushed him as he walked down the great curving staircase. It was a brutal assassination and the anger of Westminster was total: the Mahdi must be subdued. It would be another fourteen years, however, before the city was finally retaken, and when it was, a new street plan was drawn up in the shape of the Union Jack. Britain had made an indelible mark on at least one of her colonies.

History, of course, wrote it otherwise. With Warsama, I peered through the red clay gun emplacements directed across the river on Khartoum, and imagined their thunder and the answering roar from the guns of General Horatio Kitchener, later to be Britain's Secretary of War, who had finally come to avenge Gordon's death. Among his troops was a twenty-three-year-old, freckled-faced, red-haired lancer, Winston Churchill, a future Prime Minister. Now, however, there were no guns. The bright dome of the Mahdi's tomb gleamed in the sun, brilliant against the blue sky. Down by the banks of the Nile, women were washing their clothes and men cleaning their lorries. A boat builder worked on the bony skeleton of a dhow. The imperialists had long since gone and the problems Sudan now had to contend with were of its own making.

On our way back, we stopped at a market so that Warsama could buy me a gift. It was an earthenware coffee pot with a circular base designed so that it could be settled into the sand. It had a clay handle and a long narrow spout into which twigs were inserted to strain the coffee grains. The pot stands now on the dresser and I hold it some-times, its globe of smooth red clay sitting easily into the palms of my hands. And when I hold it, I see the waters of the Nile.

I had grown to love the Nile and often walked along its

banks in the evening when the faithful, kneeling on the decks of the river boats, bowed to Mecca and the setting sun flamed across the sky. 'Which one do you like best?' Warsama asked, waiting anxiously for my reply. 'The Blue Nile,' I said and he nodded, pleased. The White and Blue Nile curve into each other at Khartoum which, in Arabic, describes the curve of an elephant's trunk. I preferred the Blue Nile because of its busy liveliness. At the moment, it was flowing fast because the dams had been opened upriver to cope with the winter waters flooding in from Ethiopia.

We had lunch at the Hotel Africa. Warsama left me to perform his ablutions and, while he was gone, the waiter brought a large silver tray covered in a grubby looking tray cloth. The cloth was brown with a tattered lace border. Sitting in the middle of the cloth was a mound of meat, the hot, spicy smell which rose from it making me hungry. The waiter returned to my table: 'Eat,' he said, encouragingly. 'Eat. It is ready.' There were no knives or forks and I guessed that though fingers were the correct implements it was clearly going to be a very messy job. Then, as I looked at the cloth, I wondered if in fact it *was* a cloth. It curled up at the edges in a crisp sort of way and the decorations embossed into the cloth might have been bubbles. Could it be, no, surely not, it couldn't be part of the meal? The harder I looked, however, the more I started to think that perhaps it was. But how could I find out? Did I really want to be the sort of foreigner who ripped off bits of the tray cloth to stuff in her mouth? Surreptitiously, I tweaked at a corner of the cloth and it came away in my hand. I slipped it into the side of my mouth and held it there, cautiously. It tasted a bit like a pancake. At that moment, Warsama came back. 'So, the *zigui* has arrived,' he said and pulling off a large strip of the cloth, used it to scoop up a mouthful of the meat. 'You like it?' he asked. '*Lazees*,' I said, attacking the tray cloth with relief.

A veil of red, night-time dust hung over Khartoum. Growling cars appeared out of the fiery glow, then disappeared back into it again without trace. A large building loomed up on our left. 'Our political prison,' Warsama said casually, negotiating a bend. Together with Rashid, a friend of his, we were off in search of *arak*, the local brew distilled from potatoes. Rashid, world-weary, glitzy and high on learning, had been out of the country for six years, studying economics. His head buzzed with all the ideas he wanted to talk about but it was fast-food conversation, spiced up with Lenin and Marx.

'Marxist-Islamism is the answer to Sudan's problems,' he pronounced from the back of the car. 'To the world's problems, in fact.'

'Socialism maybe,' I said, 'but how does Islam fit into the equation?'

'There is no problem. Islam contains the concept of socialism. It embraces socialism.' Warsama listened but said nothing.

We made our way into a souk on the far side of town, parked the car and picked our way through a shamble of narrow alleyways bordered by low square houses, their smooth walls of red mud baked hard by the sun. Warsama knocked on a green wooden door set into a wall and we were ushered into a small courtyard in the centre of which was a tree, light from a lamp hanging in it flickering through the leaves. Round the tree sat the family. 'They say you and

I must go to the house of the headman, to get the *arak*,'
whispered Warsama. 'Jamilla, the daughter, will show us the
way.' The headman's mud house was small, tucked in at the
end of an alleyway, a candle glimmering in the small square
window. Warsama did the deal, handed over the money and
we took the bottle back to our hosts. A meal had been laid
out while we were away: *ful*, fresh bread, yoghurt. Two
glasses were brought out, one for me and the other to be
shared by everyone else. I objected to this arrangement.
Why should I be treated like a *howadja* (a foreigner) when
I was among friends, I said. (*Howadja* originally meant the
man with the hat on, the busybody colonial official. Now,
it means simply a foreigner.) My point was taken, the second
glass put away and the remaining glass filled to the brim
and passed to me. I drank lightly before handing the glass
to Rashid but there were loud shouts of encouragement: I
must drain it before passing it on. The *arak* tasted musty,
neither pleasant nor unpleasant, but here, among friends,
on my last warm night in Khartoum, I would happily have
drained every last glass passed to me. Rashid got drunk very
quickly and I noticed him watching Jamilla who, at fifteen,
was tall, beautiful and somehow distant. 'She'll be sold into
prostitution,' he told me under his breath. 'It's the only way
her family can make some money.' Jamilla sat by her father,
getting up every now and then to get glasses, a jug of water
or to pass food around. I felt defensive on her behalf and
wondered if Rashid were right. I hoped not.

'Prostitution?' I said. 'Well, nothing new in that. Some
young women students in England work as prostitutes to
raise the money for their course fees.' I wasn't sure if I was

making this up or not but I wanted to dent his complacency. He looked at me in amazement, then shook his head: 'Capitalism!' he laughed mockingly – and fell backwards off his seat.

I tried to limit myself to two more glasses – *arak* is strong when your defences are down – but more *ful* and bread appeared and the bottle kept coming round. Warsama, as a fairly devout Muslim, didn't drink. Islam frowns on alcohol and in my hotel the proprietor used non-Muslim waiters or refugees desperate to earn some money to serve it. Jamilla came and sat beside me.

'What are you studying at school?' I asked her.

'At the moment, English, history and science but when I go to university, I want to study engineering.' Engineering!

'Great,' I shouted courtesy of the *arak*. 'Well done.' She smiled at my delight.

'My father is trying to find the money to pay for my studies and my brother, who's working in Egypt, will also help.'

'You hear that,' I called across to Rashid. He was wrong, out of touch, had been away from his country for too long. 'She's going to go to university. She'll be an engineer.' Stuff that in your smug pipe, I wanted to add. Rashid tried to regain ground: 'You must tell your mother to give you a room especially for yourself in which to study. It's unhealthy to live and study in the one room.' Jamilla listened politely. 'And if you need anything, any help,' he continued grandly, 'let me know and I'll see what I can do.' But she had no need of Mr Big. She had her family and had already planned her life.

Warsama and I sat by the Nile one last time. A breeze, gentle and warm, blew through the night. It was 2 a.m. and in six hours my plane would be bearing me away. The dark waters flowed fast below us, onwards, downriver, to Egypt and the Mediterranean. Warsama, knowing my sadness at leaving, took my hand: 'You'll come back,' he said. 'I know you will.' '*El hamdhu lilah*,' I replied. But I never did.

CHAPTER THREE

Flashpoint on the West Bank: 1982

The man crouching down behind the wall at the corner of the street had hate in his eyes: 'Hitler was kind,' he hissed, 'compared to what you people do. Get away from here.'

But I was desperate for his help and shook my head. '*Le yehudi*,' I told him, in Arabic. 'I'm not Jewish. *Anna min Irlanda*. From Ireland. These are my friends. We're working with the Palestinians. We've got to get off the street quickly because of the curfew. Please help us. *Le yehudi*.' I pressed myself back into the shop doorway and closed my eyes. The Israeli soldiers were forming up to come down the street towards us, guns in position. The curfew had already begun.

I'd spent the morning trying to make something of the language lab at Hebron Poly. It was cumbersome and outdated but the Director wanted it used. 'More students will enrol,' he said, 'when they know we have this equipment.'

The Director was small and rotund, dressed in a suit but

without a tie which gave him an unexpectedly rakish, rather sexy look. In his welcoming speech, he'd said he hoped to exploit our energy and that maybe this would be mutual. He further hoped that his students would be enabled to gain from our generous endeavours. 'We will put at your disposal everything to meet your requirements. We have photocopier, paper, library. We even have blackboard and chalks.' And he smiled sadly at us. I'd wrestled all morning with the plugs and the knobs, with the back and forth buttons of the console, hitting the trip switch with a sweeping brush to restart the system when the power fluctuated, trying, all the time, to ignore the sound of the muezzin, the blaring car radios, the shouts in the street below. Round about noon, a couple of dull booms momentarily distracted me. A supersonic aircraft, perhaps. I supposed the Israelis had them. The noise of the traffic seemed to grow louder, the car horns more insistent. There was a strange, unsettling sense of urgency in the air. I tried to concentrate on the recalcitrant tape deck and had just thrown down the useless manual in fury when the door burst open and the Director hurried in. His bald head was shiny and his face was sweating.

'You must leave immediately,' he said. 'There has been a shooting at the Islamic College.' He took off his spectacles, wiped them with a handkerchief then put them on again. He no longer looked sexy.

'What's happened? Has anyone been killed?' I asked.

'I don't know. Maybe many people.' He was agitated. 'Quick, take your books. You must go back to Jerusalem. We cannot be responsible for you here. Someone will take you as far as they can and then you will have to walk to the bus. For us Palestinians it is dangerous but for you, it is all right. They will see you are foreigner.'

'Who will see?'

'The soldiers.'

There were four of us in the group, just arrived in Hebron. The other three were newly graduated from Cambridge and had volunteered to teach English to the Palestinians. I was there because, after seeing the refugee camps in Sudan, I wanted to learn something about the Palestinian camps on the West Bank so that I could write about them. That, ostensibly, was my excuse though really, after Khartoum, I just wanted to hang out with Arabs again and see if I'd picked up anything from the Arabic lessons I'd been having with my Syrian teacher, Abdel Nabi. I knew I hadn't really learned a lot but Abdel Nabi's love of his own language had transmitted itself to me and I wanted to learn more. I'd gone with him, one evening, to hear the Palestinian poet Darwish reading in London. The room was packed with Arabs. They perched on window ledges, sat on the floor, stood on the stairs. Most of them Palestinian, they clapped and applauded Darwish, clustering round him in order to reach out and touch him, while I hovered on the edge, an outsider. That night, however, I decided to get myself to the West Bank. How I would do it I didn't know. Allah, no doubt, would take care of the details.

As indeed he did for, by chance, I read about the work done by volunteers recruited by a University-Palestinian educational charity, based in Cambridge, was interviewed by them, found to have the right attitude, the necessary qualifications and, most important of all, the cash to pay my airfare to Tel Aviv and back. A briefing in Jerusalem was followed by a bus ride to Hebron, a major flashpoint on the troubled West Bank. This morning was my first day at work. We looked at the Director in dismay. Returning to Jerusalem was out of the question. All our things were in the flat provided for us by the Red Crescent (the Arab equivalent of the Red Cross). I had my passport with me, as always, but the others had left theirs at the flat. It was this that proved to be the clincher: 'We've got to go back,' I told the Director, 'to get our passports.' Reluctantly, he agreed to take us part of the way and hurried us down the concrete stairs of the Poly and into his car. He drove fast and nervously and when he saw a barrier at the top of one street, manned by Israeli soldiers, braked hard.

'You must get out here and walk. I can't go any further. It is too dangerous. Quick, please go.' Apart from the soldiers, the street was deserted: an Israeli army patrol with a loud hailer had already been round warning everyone to be inside their houses within fifteen minutes. The soldiers at the barrier shouted at us, indicating with their guns that we should back off. Were we such a threatening sight, four anxious women with books and folders hurrying towards them looking for help? Accustomed to talking to heavily armed, blacked-up soldiers at checkpoints along the Northern Ireland border, and usually finding them ready to exchange civilities, I approached the Israeli soldiers: 'Where is your officer?' I asked in my best Lady Bracknell voice. One of the soldiers, in an upturned bushwhacker hat, shouted something at me. 'No,' I called back at him, 'off-i-cer. Your *officer*. Where is he? We have to go to our flat. It's just up that road behind you.' And then I added, by way of being helpful: 'We are from Ireland.' It was a magnanimous if undemocratic inclusion of my three English companions but simplicity was paramount, I felt. In any case, I was the only one carrying a passport and that clearly said Irish. The soldier came forward with his gun across his chest, using it to push me away. Mistaking us for Palestinians, he was trying to herd us off the street.

According to the Director, you had three minutes to scatter before they started firing and we had one minute left. Edging from doorway to doorway we reached the corner of the street and encountered the man hiding behind a wall. 'Jews!' he spat at us. Persuaded that we were not Jews, Akram grabbed my arm and pulled me down an alley and in through a side gate. From there, we clambered over walls, passing from one back garden to the next until we reached his house. On the vine-shaded veranda, a group of people were sitting quietly, stunned by the violent events of the morning. They told us what had happened. Someone, a crazed Zionist apparently, had burst into a classroom at the Islamic College and raked it with gunfire. Two teachers and two students had died instantly. Their bodies and those of a dozen or so injured had been ferried in cars to the local Arab hospital. Our flat was right beside the hospital to which all access had been closed. Even people coming to donate blood to the injured had been turned away. 'That is deliberate,' said Akram. 'They want as many Palestinians as possible to die.'

The garden, overflowing with courgettes, melons, quince and grapes, was like the Garden of Eden and all afternoon I sat imprisoned in it while a military helicopter circled overhead. Everyone had a story to tell, of uncles who had been tortured, sisters abused and men forced to close down their small businesses.

The stories were told and retold and by late afternoon I felt drained of sympathy, embarrassed that I had no more left to display. All I could do was sit and listen. 'I can't go out of my house or speak to my friends,' said Akram's neighbour whose business enterprise had failed due to successive curfews. 'I don't have a good job. I ask for a passport, permission to start a new business, permission to import some things – little things like batteries – but always I am told wait. Come back next week. It's like ploughing sand.' He looked at me helplessly: 'I sit at home all day, like a woman.' Occasionally, the conversation lightened.

'What do you like to do?' asked Akram.

'Play poker.'

'It's a game?'

'Sort of. A card game. Of skill. We play for money.'

The businessman was shocked. 'For money? But that's unfair. Perhaps some people don't have as much money as you.'

'It's usually the other way round.'

'You are Gentile?'

'No, she's Irish,' Akram told him.

At nightfall, we climbed back over the garden walls until we were within shouting range of the hospital barricade. There, a courteous Israeli officer, speaking with an English accent, escorted us to our flat. He was sorry, he said, for the inconvenience, but hoped we would understand. The curfew was imposed across the whole of the West Bank. Shops and business premises were boarded up, schools and colleges shut. In Hebron, the mosque was closed and the muezzin's call was silenced by day as well as by night, though there was little chance of sleep: loudspeaker patrols gave out warnings three and four times during the night, telling people to stay off the streets. Life went on, of course. People shouted to each other from adjoining rooftops. Neighbours handed food to us over the garden walls. Someone, managing to get to the bakery undetected, brought us back some bread. The Red Crescent ambulance returned with fruit from a nearby village and distributed it via the back garden network. By the end of the week, the foot patrols were easing up on their vigilance. Once they'd passed, people hurried along the street to disappear in through a neighbour's door although they never dared to make a run for it across the street. Anger simmered close to the surface but fear of the consequences of acting on it held it in check. The Poly Director sent us some food and from the family opposite we received an invitation to supper. We should come, the message said, provided there were no patrols about.

Azad, the father, was the family philosopher. A thin, bespectacled man who looked and behaved like a teacher, he was, in fact, the owner of a small factory which made headscarves of the sort worn by Arab men and made famous by Yasser Arafat. 'Keffiyeh,' Azad explained to me carefully, 'from the French coiffure.' The young son of the house, Hassan, was eighteen. His dark eyes were soft and gentle, the beseeching look in them such that one day someone would surely give him his heart's desire, whatever that turned out to be. Each night, at bedtime, Hassan took his father's hand, pressed it to his lips and then forehead: a courtly gesture of filial devotion, performed with teenage insouciance. Azad was proud of his family. 'I am happier than a king,' he told me, 'because I have a house and family. I live for my sons. I give them my life and my work, the food from my mouth. As we say here: without people, heaven is nothing.' He didn't mention his daughter.

Some of Azad's memories were not good, especially those of the Palestine Police: 'The Israelis are bad to us but so too were the English. For them, we had to stand in the heat of the day, all day, until people dropped to the ground, sick in the sun. Why? Because they wanted us to betray our own people.' However, he didn't allow these feelings to get in the way of his love of the English language, his knowledge of which he liked to demonstrate at great length. We had occasional learning sessions which were supposed to be an English/Arabic exchange but I rarely got a word in edgeways – in either language.

'Today, I will teach you the parts of the body,' Azad said. 'So, first, we have the shoulder, the arm, the hand and,' gesturing grandly, 'lo! the wrist.' He paused for dramatic effect then hurried on: 'Now the breast and the back. And what is this? It is the hip.'

'Excuse me, could I just ask . . .'

'When I go to buy meat, I look for the hip of mutton. And this (pointing to his shoe) is my foot. I don't, of course, mean the shoe but what is *in* the shoe.'

'Of course. But how does one say . . .'

'And now: yesterday and today. Today, I am drinking, he is drinking, you drinking milk. Mary! Drunk! You have drunk coffee. But wait! I have not yet drunk coffee.'

'I wonder, if, suppose, one wanted to say . . .'

'And now: knowing. When I know you, I say how are you, but if I do *not* know you, I say what do you do?'

*   *   *

The young doctor treating babies at the Rehydration Clinic had studied medicine in London.

'Everyone knows about Hebron,' he said, 'but there is another way to say it: in Arabic, it is El Khalil.' I tried, too, to remember to say El Quds when talking about Jerusalem. El Khalil/Hebron was – and remains – a West Bank flashpoint for a variety of reasons. One is that the tomb of Abraham, which is sacred to both Islam and Judaism, is located here and the large mosque, Abraham's Mosque, is a place of pilgrimage for both Jew and Muslim. A second reason is that an informal Jewish settlement had grown up here. These settlers, ultra-orthodox Zionists, were easily recognizable because the men had side-locks and the women wore headscarves to cover their shaven heads. Their small compound was in the middle of the Arab quarter, guarded by a rabbi and with an Israeli flag fluttering overhead. Another larger settlement, Kiryat Arba, on the other side of town, had modern-style houses, shops, schools and a synagogue. Both had walls thrown up around them, topped by barbed wire, turning them, ironically, into ghettos.

After a week, the curfew eased and people were allowed out of their houses but only during daylight hours and along designated routes. The muezzin was once again heard, hawking and clearing his throat into the microphone before the pre-dawn call to prayer. We finally ventured out on to the streets, accompanied by our minder, Hassan. At the bottom of the hill, a bus had broken down. At its windows, nervous youths in skullcaps peered at us through their spectacles. Standing by the bus, on the pavement, was a rabbi and beside him a young man with a pistol stuck in his belt.

75

Then I noticed that he held in his other hand a larger firearm and that there were three other young men, also armed, standing at each corner of the bus, guarding it. They looked tense and it was soon clear why: a crowd of young Palestinians had gathered on the pavement opposite the bus and a low hum of excitement was starting to develop. Nothing you could put your finger on, but unnerving. Hassan hurried along, intent on getting us out of this potentially dangerous situation. Then, as we turned the corner, a police car arrived and the crowd melted away. When he was sixteen, Hassan was taken in by the police and held in a cell one metre by two. They wanted him to sign a piece of paper saying he'd seen some boys throwing stones at the soldiers. He refused. He was handcuffed and had a bag put over his head but after forty days they set him free. Victoria, his mother, wept. She'd thought he was dead.

Back at the flat, there was the usual crowd of people waiting for us. Some wanting lessons in English, some wanting just to talk. Others wanted to poke about among our belongings to see what we had. A few wanted to argue. This last was tiresome but it was an informal way of teaching English. Assad wanted to know why you had to apologize when you were late: 'Is it my fault that there is a traffic jam? And why can I not ask people what old they are?' he complained. 'How else will I learn?' And was it true, he wanted to know, that there were no churches in Russia and that English people did not give wedding gifts? Assad was only eighteen but already had some very fixed ideas. Young men in England – a country he had never visited – had too much freedom, he told me. They should dwell at home and listen to their fathers. We dealt with the word dwell and moved on to the whole question of freedom, which was a concept close to everyone's heart. Assad held the floor. He didn't like to smoke or drink, he said, or stay late in bed. Nor did he like killing: 'I won't like to shoot anyone,' he said, 'even Jew. Only soldier.'

With the curfew easing off, Victoria and Azad had a bit of a party. Our flat was a purpose-built block of concrete but their house and garden were a delight. Within the gate was a courtyard shaded from the sun by overarching vines, light from the hanging lamps glimmering through the purple grapes. Victoria was baking bread in the outside oven, sliding in trays of loaves to cook on the open flames. I sat with Hassan and his father while the women hovered in the background preparing a meal which, as always, was more like a feast: fresh-baked bread, water melon, stuffed courgettes, saffron rice with what looked like bits of liver and an orange-coloured soup that tasted cheesy.

'As I was saying,' said Azad, who started all his sentences this way, 'as I was saying, this soup is grilled milk.' Later, I drifted over to chat with the women. The old grand-mother, wearing a long dress, her head covered by a scarf, sat cross-legged on an armchair. A cousin looked politely at my cheap, mock-gold ring. She herself had plenty of the real thing on display, earrings, bracelets and four teeth.

'It is given by her husband, in case he dies and she has no money,' explained Mariam.

'And the men?' I asked.

But Mariam shook her head: 'The Koran forbids men to wear gold.'

'But I've seen men wearing gold rings.'

She nodded: 'White-gold is allowed.'

'Well, I don't have any gold – white or the other sort. I'm too poor.'

The women laughed politely at what they felt must surely be a joke, though later, when I hitched up my jeans and my brass Guinness belt with the harp on it came into view, they craned forward to look at it.

Azad joined us: 'Cars. Do you make cars in Ireland?'

'No. We don't have car factories. We import them.'

'What do the men work at?'

'A lot of them work on the land. Or used to.'

'Just like Palestinians.'

'In a way, yes.'

'No rich people?'

'Well, no, not really. The ordinary people aren't rich.'

'Just the bad people are rich?'

'Yes, that'd be the height of it.'

'The height of it?'

Later, her mother persuaded Mariam to perform for us and so, tying a scarf round her hips she started to dance, rotating a hip, jutting out a foot, touching hand to eye in languorous gestures. When her father came into the room, however, she faltered. 'She does not like to dance in front of her father,' Victoria whispered.

Just before the party ended, the wrought-iron gate suddenly opened and a rucksacked woman in her mid-thirties came in. 'Whose house is this?' she asked, in an American accent. I pointed to Azad's family group and walking over to the old grandmother, she took her hand, touched it to her lips and then her forehead, the gesture causing a stir among the family. None of us had dared to do that. The stranger introduced herself as Belinda, an

American working as a teacher in London. She had come to join our group and I took an instant dislike to her.

A week later, the end of the curfew was announced and everyone walked round saying *el hamdhu lilah* to each other. Or *lilah*, for short. I said it too for I'd got tired of being cooped up all day. The students were restless, exams were coming up and they were losing valuable time. I settled back into the Poly and on the first morning was asked to go to the Caritas hospital down the road in Bethlehem, to do some English teaching with the nurses there. On the way, I called in to the bank to buy some shekels. The bank – full of old men in long white gowns and keffiyehs, feeding worry beads through their fingers – was busy and noisy as a souk, which, of course, was what it was: a market for money. I flagged down a taxi going to Bethlehem. Taxis come in two sorts: service, pronounced serveece, and special. The first means the car is public and the driver can cram in as many people as he can. Special means private. Mine, a customized Mercedes with a red and gold fringe round the sun visors, was a service. A verse from the Koran, in brilliant holographic colours, was propped up on the dashboard and from the mirror swung a tiny teddy bear, a yellow duck and some worry beads. Outside, fixed to the bonnet, was a black funeral plume – a reminder of the recent killings in Hebron. The radio was on and from it came the mournful wailing of a flute and a voice keening what sounded like a dirge, though equally it could have been a love song. We passed through sandy hills spiked here and there with green fronds: a biblical landscape both of the dispossessed Arab and of the wandering Jew come to rest. Rocks and stone, bleached white in the sun, covered the long low slope of the hillside. Visible on a distant raised piece of ground was an isolated settlement, standing out against the barren land like an abandoned moon city, the buildings stacked up in angular conformity and windows glinting blind in the sun. Ahead of us, a bus pulled over at a junction where a new tarmac road led off to this wilderness. A large sign, giving the name of the settlement in Hebrew, had been sprayed with red Arabic graffiti. The bus stopped but no one got off. Or on. Further along, our service pulled in by a huddle of shops and a sudden sickening wave of smells – body sweat, petrol fumes and cooking oil – enveloped us. A woman waiting at the stop threw a stone at a small, wailing child to stop him following her into the taxi. Beside me, a baby – its hair plastered to its forehead with sweat – woke and started to cry. The father, his few remaining teeth black as coal, held the child's head gently between his hands, talked to him and kissed him and as he did so, the child quietened.

When I got to the cool, white, antiseptic hospital, there were no nurses to teach. They were all on duty. Hot, tired and frustrated I returned to the dusty road and flagged down a taxi going back to Hebron.

'A hundred shekels,' said the driver.

'What? To go back to Hebron? I've just paid forty shekels to get here. A hundred is too much.'

'But this is special taxi.'

'No it's not. It's a service.'

'No. Special.'

I let it go but when he picked up a woman and child and charged them forty shekels, I protested again. And explained I was a volunteer, working for the Red Crescent, at Hebron Poly.

'I too was teacher at the Poly,' the driver said, excitedly, obviously glad to get away from the subject of shekels.

'Why did you leave?'

'Not enough pay. Now, I have taxi – and shop,' he added proudly, though unwisely for he had left himself open.

'So, you are a rich man.'

'I have two children to support,' he protested.

I trumped him: 'And I have three.'

We settled for a fare of fifty shekels and parted friends. I went to the Post Office before going home. Although the curfew had ended, Israeli soldiers were still everywhere. They slouched along the streets in fatigues, dark glasses and long hair, their bush hats tilted at a flamboyant angle: cowboys just arrived in town. There was a group of them outside the Post Office, sitting on chairs which they'd tipped back, long legs stretched out obstructing the pavement. With one hand, they balanced their guns across their knees, in the other, they cupped cigarettes. I asked at the Post Office for a stamp for a letter to Khartoum. 'I will give you one for London.' 'No, Khartoum, please. It's going to Khartoum, in Sudan.' The man shook his head: 'You must send it first to London, then maybe to Khartoum.'

The authorities had banned all post to Arab countries.

'As I was saying,' began Azad, 'we have a story which I will tell you. The lion and the ox decided to share the hunting in the forest: the lion would hunt one day, the ox the next. This was all right until the fox came. To the lion he said, I hear the ox is going to kill you today. Take care. To the ox, he said the same thing. Take care. When the two animals met in the forest, they began to fight and the lion, being the king, overpowered the ox and began to eat his stomach. But when he turned the ox over, the horns of the ox gored the lion and they both died, leaving the forest to the fox.' Azad paused to drink some coffee. 'So, when two men fight, the third man wins. It is better to talk, not to fight. Or, as we say in English, always count to ten.'

I didn't feel like counting to ten with Belinda. I felt like goring her with my horns. I disliked her so much I even came to dislike her tee-shirt. She was tall, with long, dank hair and a pasty-looking complexion. Her worn tee-shirt bore a political message about world hunger and had on it an ascending graph illustrating the increasing amount of food we – the affluent we – consumed each day. Judging by her own emaciated chest, it seemed as if she herself consumed nothing. She had a barren aspect. Belinda pestered me, wanting to borrow my tape recorder but as I was using it for my writing, I was reluctant to lend it to anyone. It was as precious as my notes or my pen. I planned to compile a radio programme from some of the things I had recorded: the muezzin's pre-dawn call to prayer, the ominous sound of the Israeli patrol cars with their loud hailers, the interview with some of the people I had met. I could not afford to risk anything happening to the recorder or the tapes I had already made, so I refused.

Belinda's arrival had brought unease where there had been calm, suspicion where there had been trust. We had all agreed to share rooms in order to leave one room free to work in – or to retreat to when the pressure of visitors became too much. This room she took for herself. 'I never share with anyone,' she said, fixing a makeshift curtain to the window. This was curious as the window, on the top storey, was overlooked by no one. Belinda complained about our erratic working hours and refused to give any extra help to the many supplicants who came to our door in the evenings, begging for an opportunity to improve their English. Though we were volunteers, we were provided with food and accommodation by the Red Crescent and continually received invitations to eat in people's houses. Since we were there and had the expertise, the least we could do, I felt, was to give all we had for the short time we were there. Belinda did not agree. 'We're doing enough as it is,' she said, 'and for nothing, don't forget. Those people in Cambridge could quite easily afford to pay us. It's not as if they're short of money. They have plenty. You should see their budget. Have you ever *seen* their annual budget?' I hadn't. 'Well, believe me, they're on to a good thing back there, while we work our butts off here for nothing. You should ask them about it some time.'

Her remarks left me a little disgruntled. It *was* hard work. The heat was unbearable at times. I often had to hitch a lift on the hot dusty road to Bethlehem, carrying a bagful of books, because the buses weren't running. All during the curfew we had no water and consequently the lavatory stank. Even now, three weeks later, there were interruptions to the water supply. 'The water is *mafish* with us also,' Hassan had said last night when I went across the road to fill a pail from Victoria's tap. Writing up my notes later, by candlelight – the electricity, too, being *mafish* – I considered Belinda's remarks. The constant flow of visitors in the evening was exhausting and their innocent curiosity had become both irritating and intrusive. Added to this was the fact that the man who owned our flat had been doing the rounds, propositioning each of us individually. That wasn't what I'd signed on for. Perhaps the fat cats in Cambridge should be looked into.

Bethlehem was not at all like the Christmas cards. There was no snow and the only donkey I'd seen was a mangy creature hanging around the back of the Rehydration Clinic in Hebron. Manger Square was full of souvenir shops and the crypt was one of the shabbiest tourist attractions I had ever come across. But then, maybe that was as it should be. Jesus, after all, was from a poor Jewish family, similar to the sort of Arab family I saw around me all the time in Hebron. I descended the fifteen steps to the Manger Grotto which was lit by thousands of candles and flickering red lamps. On the walls hung drapes of heavy red leather, embossed and trimmed with brass. A group of pilgrims from the States crowded into the small space. Their voices sounded loud and excited as if they had just come from a children's party. They wore blue and white pleated paper caps with Holy Land Tours, Ohio, printed on them. The guide spoke knowledgeably of the prevailing winds on that 25 December nearly 2000 years ago which was why, apparently, the infant Jesus had to be moved below ground to the shelter of the manger. We stared at the spot on the floor, the exact spot, we were told, where Mary gave birth to Jesus. This then was the famous stable. In the front row, a woman yawned hugely.

Something warned me to start leaving the Grotto ahead of the main herd and it proved to be a wise decision. As I reached the top of the stairs, I heard the fervent voices of the American blue-rinses rising up from the Grotto: 'Oh, Little Town of Bethlehem . . .' Upstairs, the Manger Church was divided between all the various Christian groups, each with its own chapel. The Catholic one was decorated with dust-covered plastic flowers. From the high timbered roof hung heavy, unpolished brass chandeliers and coloured balls. There was no main altar but instead, appropriately – since this story is one of great drama – there was a kind of stage in front of which were strung chains of bright, brass decorations, resembling cheap Christmas baubles. It was a pleasing irony.

Belinda was wearing me down with her importunate requests.

'Of course, Mary is so mean,' she told the others, 'she won't even lend me her tape recorder so that I can prepare some of my lessons. What do you think of *that*?' They looked at me, embarrassed. Young and tired, they had never had a job like this before and felt she was probably right about not doing more teaching than was necessary. About the tape recorder they didn't know what to think. *Was* I being mean, I wondered. The others looked at me and said nothing. I handed over the tape recorder: 'But I'll need it back tomorrow, mind.' She gave it back to me the next day and it failed to work. 'What are you asking me for?' she blustered confidently. 'You think I did something to it? Is that it? You think *I* broke your tape recorder?' The others were disconcerted. We never used to have arguments of this sort. Later, I found that the tape I had made of the muezzin and the army patrols was missing. No one knew anything about it. 'Perhaps those kids took it,' said Belinda, her face open and innocent. 'I told you you shouldn't get so friendly with them, letting them wander about the place.' No one ever wandered into Belinda's room because she kept the door firmly closed. It was a no-go area, even to us.

'As I was saying,' intoned Azad, 'our ancestors wrote fables which have now come true. For them, the truth was already there, but in their minds only. In our fables we had magic carpets which took us everywhere. Now, it has come true: men can walk on foot on the moon and I can travel to El Kuds without putting my foot in the ground. In the fable, Aladdin rubbed his magic lantern to produce the genie while I can pick up the telephone and ask for anything I want. In the fables, people said: Open, Sesame while now I can turn on the television and see the wonders of the world. Our ancestors were wise . . .'

Oranges come from Jaffa. Everyone knows that, Fawzal told me. Her family used to own an orange grove in Jaffa, until it was commandeered by the Israelis. Now she lived in the refugee camp in Bethlehem. The camp was made up of one-, two- or three-roomed dwellings, constructed from concrete blocks. Packed tightly together, they were a ready-made slum of uniform squares. The 'streets' were wide enough to take only one car. In some places, they had a made-up surface. In others, the surface was broken up completely, with an open drain running down the middle which itself was broken in places. Water came from stand-pipes. There seemed to be only women and children around. The men were away working in Jordan, the Gulf or in prison, Fawzal explained. Some, I guessed, were fighting with the PLO. When the children threw stones at the Israeli patrol cars, Fawzal said, the army came and arrested some-one, though not necessarily the culprits. They came to Fawzal's house three days ago because they had been told her young brother had thrown stones. The armoured car rolled in around midnight, towing a cement mixer. The family were given ten minutes to move everything out of the only bedroom. Then the soldiers filled the doorway to the bedroom with concrete blocks and cemented them in place. I could smell the still-drying cement. The mother hadn't had time to get the electric clock off the bedroom wall so that all that was left of it now was the wire disappearing back in through the blocked-up door. As we came down the steps of the house, the stench from the outside lavatory filled our nostrils and I felt embarrassed for Fawzal but as we walked along the street it followed us and I realized the stink came from the whole camp.

Fawzal brought me to her neighbour's house. 'They're from Jaffa too,' she told me. 'They came to this refugee camp twenty-three years ago.' The soldiers had arrived here too, also in the middle of the night and worked until three in the morning blocking off the front doorway. Now the family lived on the vine-covered veranda, with all their possessions under an awning. Across the road was a two-storey house belonging to the camp leader. 'He is paid by the army,' Fawzal whispered. 'He tells them which houses to go to.'

How to henna your hair: mix the henna with tea and put on hair. Leave for eight hours, until dry. Rinse and then wash with olive oil.

How to dry grapes: wash them in a mixture of washing soda and olive oil. When the water gets dirty, replace it. Lay the grapes out in the sun to dry for two to three days, depending on how hot it is.

I learned about the grapes and the henna from one of the women at Noor's wedding. Noor was seventeen, her bride-groom twenty-seven. The business end of the wedding had been sorted out a few months ago by the two fathers. Now the women had gathered to give Noor a good send-off before her husband came to take her away to Jerusalem. All day, they cooked, drummed and ululated. Then, one by one, the guests got up to offer a wedding dance to the bride. Eventually called on to do my bit, I worked out it would be quicker and less painful to get it over and done with and started wriggling my cumbersome hips to the rhythm of the drums. After two or three minutes – a decent interval, I felt – I signalled to the drummer to stop but instead found myself whirling faster than a dervish on dope: the drummer had interpreted my signal as an instruction to up the tempo. All day, Noor, in her long wedding dress and veil, sat on a chair flanked by two plastic orange trees, the whole lot set up on the kitchen table so that from her new position of adulthood, she could look down on us, bored, her gum-chewing jaws moving mechanically. When her husband and his entourage arrived to take her away, car horns blaring, she looked sadly at her mother and wept.

I'd got to know Noor's teacher, Fatimah, a fiery politico who'd taken a maths degree at university in Cairo and who had organized a teachers' strike, demanding better pay. The strikers had won, getting their pay increased from £100 a month to £150, but afterwards Fatimah had been moved to a remote, ill-equipped village school where she could do less harm. She remained unrepentant and when I visited her at her mother's house, I noticed a picture on the wall. It was of Leila Nablisi, a seventeen-year-old school student who had been shot by an Israeli soldier. Fatimah saw me looking at it. 'You see what we are up against,' she said, handing me a glass of water, 'you cannot get back stolen land without a gun.' The picture showed a beautiful young girl lying prettily in a field of multicoloured flowers, her blood staining the green grass. But there had been no field of flowers where she had died: escaping from the soldiers, she had run into a building where she had been cornered on the concrete stairs and shot.

Azad went to the mosque but when Victoria, throwing a voluminous white gown over her head, knelt to pray at home, everything went on around her as usual. The children stepped over her feet, the TV chattered away and Azad continued to talk to me. I felt a bit embarrassed as if I had inadvertently caught someone doing something private, like sitting on the lavatory. I wanted to look the other way. At the Poly, I noticed, the men waved the women away and then got out their prayer mats. Though no one prayed in the streets here the way they did in Khartoum.

Hassan's cousin gave birth to a baby and I went up to the hospital to see it the day after it was born, to the same hospital that the dead and wounded were brought to on my second day in Hebron. That seemed a long time ago now. The cousin lay on the bed which she shared with another mother, both of them taking it in turns to be tired. While I was there, the whole family piled in to see the swaddled infant which was lifted up, held out, handled, its cheeks pinched – and not yet twenty-four hours old. Later, it was placed on the bed and unwrapped. We all leaned forward to look at its male tackle, on display for the first time. 'Allah!' I said in admiration, which raised the laugh

89

I hoped it would. A boy child was especially welcome as the women felt that for every man killed, they had to bear another child to replace him. Having babies was their war effort.

I had a whole weekend off so I took a service taxi to Jerusalem and, passing through Damascus Gate where the policeman on point duty held a cigarette in one cupped hand while directing the traffic with the other, found a small Arab hotel right in the middle of the souk where I hired a mattress up on the roof. Without telling my Arab hosts – they would have been offended – I went to have a swim at the pool of the King David Hotel, which shares with the Europa in Belfast the distinction of being the most blown-up hotel in the world. The tree-lined pool was surrounded by bright yellow and blue deck chairs, the accents were all American. A little girl was lifted on to a chair to be admired by doting adults. She was a miniature woman, dressed in a black bikini, with gold earrings and hair piled up on top of her head. A woman, body fat stuffed into a one-piece swimsuit, shifted a cigarette from hand to mouth in order to lift the child down again. A waitress brought a tray of drinks to the table beside mine and put it down. There were two women sitting at the table. 'OK, thanks,' said the older woman, 'but next time, bring back the blue room chit. OK?' The waitress looked at her, smiled, collected the tray and went back to the bar. The younger woman picked up her glass: 'Grandma, she doesn't speak English. She just doesn't speak English.'

At the Central Bus Station I queued up to buy a ticket to Gaza. The American backpacker in front of me was looking for help getting to the airport:

'Where's the bus stop for Ben Gurion?' he asked the man ahead of him.

The Israeli, trying to make sense of the American's accent, played for time. 'Ben Gurion?' he repeated.

'Yeah, him,' said the American.

I got to the counter and asked for a ticket to Gaza.

'Gate or city?'

'City.'

'Why do you want to go there already? No one goes to Gaza.'

'I'd like a ticket for there, please.'

'There aren't any buses to Gaza.'

'So how do I get there?'

'You'll have to go to Ashkalon and change to an Arab bus. If there are any.'

'Thank you.'

I could have gored her too with my horns.

At Ashkalon, I had two hours to fill in while waiting for my Arab bus and decided to walk across the road to the packed beach. Children screamed and parents harangued them. Men oiled their wives' backs. Bronzed young men in tiny yellow trunks ping-ponged without pause. It might have been Benidorm except for the soldier in fatigues, a gun slung over his shoulder, weaving his way through the beach umbrellas and the brown bodies. An American woman was rounding up her family to go back to the hotel. The umbrella had to be taken down, the beach mats rolled up, the cooler bag repacked, the towels collected. 'Already?' asked the husband as he came out of the sea, hands raised in exaggerated amazement. 'You mean, we've done all this just for five minutes on the beach?' 'So,' she shrugged her shoulders, tilting her head, 'what does it matter? C'mon. We can go to the pool at the hotel.' The husband threw his hands up in despair. The accents were American but the gestures unmistakably Jewish. As they left the beach, the children tripped over me, scattering sand on my book. The parents apologized.

'Please, it's all right. Don't worry,' I said, using a surfeit of politeness to conceal my irritation. It took a bit longer to admit I had been concealing from myself the fact that I disliked them simply because they were Jewish. Hebron was claustrophobic and I'd allowed myself to be infected by Palestinian hatred.

On the beach at Gaza, there were empty bottles, scraps of paper, old car tyres. And people's homes. A man and his sick daughter were living under large sheets of cardboard, the top one bent to form a roof. I ducked my head low to get in. They used to have a tin house, also built on the sand, the father told me, but the soldiers came and knocked it down with a bulldozer because it was built a few feet beyond some invisible line they had been forbidden to cross. Standing outside the cardboard house, I opened my note-book and seeing it, an old man came over to me, a dried up little man in a crocheted skullcap and a soiled djellabia. 'Tell everyone about this because it must never happen again,' he said. 'Write it down and tell everyone.' So I wrote it down.

And then, before I too made my way to Ben Gurion, I walked up the road to Yad Vashem, the holocaust memor-ial in Jerusalem, walking over the fragrant pine needles on the road passing, on the way, a melancholy traffic sign indicating a dead end. The sun was hot but a wind blew through the tall trees making a soft shooing sound which urged me forwards. It was peaceful and quiet at Yad Vashem except for the thump-thump of a jackhammer working away across the valley, where, on a lower hill, another ghost settlement was going up. The memorial building is a square block standing on huge rocks that seem locked for ever into the ground from which they rise making it certain that they will never again be moved. A young man sat unmoving, his back to the wall of the memorial. When I left Yad Vashem two hours later, he was still there, his position unchanged.

Inside the memorial building was a small gallery which looked down on the eternal flame set into the marbled floor, surrounded by the names of the death camps: Ponary, Babi-Yar, Ravensbrueck, Westerbork, Breendonck, Transnistria, Buchenwald, Treblinka, Sobibor, Klooga, Stutthof, Theresienstädt-Terezin, Jasenovac, Mauthausen, Auschwitz-Oświeċim, Majdanek, Dachau, Bergen-Belsen, Drancy, Lwów-Janowska, Chelmno and Belzeċ.

Beside the memorial stands the Holocaust Museum consisting of a series of rooms leading one into the other. The first room is easy, containing some printed facts and figures, one or two photographs. Things I know already: first-hand descriptions of the ghetto, the knock on the door, the separation of children from parents, the railway journeys. The notes left behind. The death camps. As my eye moves from image to image, the camera lens focuses more sharply, refining each picture: the graves . . . the grave . . . one particular grave . . . The people are lined up looking down into the pit which they themselves have just dug. A tall thin man puts his hand on the head of his small son: 'Don't be frightened,' he tells the child. 'We are going to heaven.' Beside the man is his wife, their baby in her arms. She holds the baby to her breast. The man takes his son's hand in his as gunshot rakes the row of people. The infant flies out of its mother's arms, surprised mouth opening in a last gasp for life. Limbs jerking, the man and the little boy pitch forward into eternity. I saw this happening. But can't remember if I read an account of it or studied a photograph of it. There are lots more photographs, some blurred, some faded. The passageway through which I have to pass to reach the next section narrows, hemming me in. It turns a corner. There is no other way but on, leading to what I don't know . . .

1999. I am writing this in Annaghmakerrig, a lovely old house set in woodland in the border county of Cavan. Formerly the home of the stage director, Tyrone Guthrie, it is now a centre for writers, musicians and artists. From my window, I can see the leaves turning to gold, the swans quiet on the lake, but as I reread my notes, nothing seems real. I can't write about these deaths isolated in my room, a carpet under my feet, the central heating warming me. Suddenly, a rainstorm hits the house and I run to get my boots, my raincoat. To escape outside. Hurrying along by the lake, my hood down so that the rain streams across my face, I slosh through the fallen leaves and realize I am running away, again, from Yad Vashem. It is the final picture that I cannot face, an exterior picture taken by a camp photographer. A group of women are running towards the camera, their thin bodies naked, skin drawn tight across their hip bones, pubic hair dark against their white skin, their mouths open in a scream. Their arms are raised as if breasting a tape. The ones closest to the camera are young.

Perhaps they are the ones who can run fastest. One of them, no more than a girl, is pretty. I can see this in her short, dark curly hair. I look hard at the photograph, at the remnants of the women's breasts, at the secret place between their legs, at the terror on their faces. Naked terror. I look for a long time. I am the camera. I am the person behind the camera, focusing on their shameful exposure. Unlike the tall thin man and his son, I don't see these women fall. They are there still, running into the horror ahead. For ever. I see them.

CHAPTER FOUR

A Phone Call in the Night

I had a book I wanted to send to a friend in Lesotho, a novel I'd promised her a long time ago. I stopped the car at the Post Office in Horton-cum-Studley not far from Brill and took the parcel in to get stamps for it. 'Leave it on the counter,' said the woman, 'and I'll see it gets posted.' I'd heard that the new people who had taken over the Post Office were from Zimbabwe. A white couple they were, who probably didn't want to stay there after independence. I thought of telling the woman I'd visited Zimbabwe but didn't. I was in a hurry and, in any case, it was probably a different Zimbabwe from the one she'd known. As I was driving away, I heard a shout. The woman was running out of the Post Office, waving. As I stopped, she opened the car door and threw the package on to the passenger seat: 'We can't take that. We're not allowed take parcels for Lesotho.' Puzzled, I took the packet to the main Post Office in Oxford and posted it from there. Years later, reading Gillian Slovo's autobiography, I discovered that all mail in and out of Lesotho at that time was scrutinized by the agents of apartheid, in the hope that it would reveal something of the activities of the ANC, many of whose members had sought refuge there. I guessed the woman from Zimbabwe knew something about Lesotho the Post Office in Oxford didn't.

I hadn't met any ANC people while I was in southern Africa. In fact, I'd never met an ANC member in my life, at least, that I knew of. My only political activity in relation to South Africa was to boycott Outspan oranges. I was slightly more active when it came to events in Ireland: I joined the Northern Ireland Civil Rights Oxford Committee. This dangerously subversive group met regularly in a room at Blackfriars, the Dominican Priory, and did such things as raise money to give holidays to children living in Belfast. Occasionally, some of us joined whatever march was taking place to protest at police brutality or the use of rubber bullets in Northern Ireland. Once, we even organized our own march. It was not well attended. 'If we had one more person,' said Mick, 'we'd have enough to occupy that telephone box over there.' Then one day, Herbert McCabe, our mentor, drinking companion and, coincidentally, member of the Dominican community, had some bad news: 'The Prior says he's terribly sorry but could we possibly hold our meetings somewhere else. There's been another stone through the window of the Priory.' I shivered: I had never been so close to violence.

There were other things to get out on the street about too. Ian, long before I knew him, had been on the first Aldermaston March. Later, we both joined CND, and later still, I mucked in with a lot of women, rattling the fence at Greenham Common. I even managed to smuggle myself on to the base at Greenham, disguised as an evening class teacher. When I wrote about it all in the *Guardian* a Member of Parliament complained about so-called security on what was the most militarily sensitive base in the country if not Western Europe. Being a member of CND was seen by many as highly suspect. Disarming ourselves of nuclear weapons, we were told, was a weak, lily-livered response to Russian aggression. It was traitorous not to *do* something. Otherwise you were just throwing in the towel. But I had travelled the road to Damascus and had had a vision of the horror of the nuclear holocaust. It had happened in a small church hall in London where a flickering, black and white 16 mm film about Hiroshima was being shown. People came in from the dark wintery night flapping their umbrellas and shaking their raincoats before sitting on the hard, metal seats. I felt as if I were in a Graham Greene novel. (Ironically, it had been Graham Greene's brother, Hugh Carleton Greene, Director of the BBC at the time, who decided it would be upsetting for people to know too much about what might happen after the bomb and had banned the showing of *The War Game* on TV.) That night, though, in Balham, I saw the shadow of a man burned into the steps of the City Hall in Hiroshima and knew I didn't want to be part of that horror.

But in the small Buckinghamshire village of Brill (population 2000) our mild CND activities, meetings, a poster in the window, that sort of thing, were being monitored and one evening there was a knock on the door. It was the men from the Civil Defence, a Dad's Army organization that gave lectures in village halls about what you should do when you heard the four-minute warning. Apparently, we were considered enough of a threat to the security of the state to warrant a lecture all to ourselves. They were decent men, the Civil Defence people, worried and concerned that we seemed incapable of appreciating their arguments. The Russians were waiting to pounce, they told us. They were already in the country, lying low, and would stop at nothing. There were Communist spies everywhere – and the two men looked round the room for signs of espionage.

Disheartened, they departed, leaving behind their leaflet which said that when the siren sounded – by arrangement with the local volunteer fire service – we should stick black paper over the windows and hide under the kitchen table to avoid the worst of the blast. It didn't say what to do next. There had been other unexpected visits. Two uniformed police called to the house one evening, a week after the Bloody Sunday shooting in Derry, in 1972. They'd had a phone call, they said, from someone in the village who told them I might be able to give them some useful information. 'Where were you on the afternoon of Friday, 28 January,' asked Plod, notebook in hand. 'At college,' I squeaked, caving in immediately. Uniforms terrify me. After they left, I remembered that I hadn't been in college that day at all. One of the children had been ill and I had taken the day off. 'Give me the phone. I've got to ring them up and confess I was lying, otherwise they'll come and arrest me,' I said. 'Quick, what's their number?' Ian sighed at my foolishness. He had an endearingly old-fashioned view of the police, seeing them as kindly, if slightly dim, people who would see reason if spoken to clearly and politely.

'Don't ring,' he counselled. 'If you contradict what you've already said, you'll only confuse them.'

On another occasion, a man arrived at the front door – these calls always seemed to happen on dark, wet nights – and asked, pointedly, if he could speak to me alone. Ian withdrew and I brought the man into the kitchen where I was making the supper. He was a reporter, he said, from a Reading newspaper, and he had been told that when a party of tourists was being shown around Chequers the previous week, an unauthorized Irish woman had been detected among the group and that I was that woman. Why, he wanted to know, had I gone to Chequers? I ushered him out of the house – the children, after all, would be home soon, hungry for food – but phoned the paper to check if they had a reporter of that name. They did, they said, though I forgot to ask what he looked like. Round about the same time, two men arrived at the house and asked to come in. They were telephone engineers, they said, come to disconnect our party line. Ian let them in and they fiddled about with the phone and then left. 'But we haven't been on a party line for five years,' I reminded him when I got home.

It was all mystifying though not as mystifying as the gap that seemed to be developing between two old friends with whom we had shared many an inebriated weekend, while our respective children – more adult than their parents – cooked the meals, washed up and steered us home from the pub. Those days seemed to have disappeared into the past. Trevor and his wife Jan were never free to meet up, were busy with this and that and, most ludicrous of all, were unable to come and stay because they couldn't leave the dog. Finally, I confronted them.

'It's because of you and your activities.'

'My activities? What on earth have I been doing?'

Trevor looked uncomfortable: 'It's just something we heard.'

'What *are* you talking about?'

It seemed that an acquaintance of theirs, whose father had some connection with the Kenyan police, had been trawling through police files there, and my name had come up on the screen as someone to be watched. The acquaintance, interestingly enough, was from Northern Ireland. Derry, Chequers, Kenya – all places I had never visited, though I had to admit that the venues were becoming more and more exotic. Trevor was defensive: 'You have to look at it from our point of view. The places you've been to. *We* don't know what you get up to.' I had, I suppose, what might seem as a suspect profile: travelling to southern Africa (the ANC), to the West Bank (the PLO), frequently commuting between England and Ireland (the IRA). Added to that, there was Polisario (the guerrilla army in the Sahara), membership of CND, my activities at Greenham Common and numerous visits to the USSR – the last to research a travel book on the former Soviet Republic of Georgia.

Yet I was as pure as a snowdrop in February. I lived good, which is why I won at poker. The most illegal thing I have ever done was to secrete in my luggage a minute amount of *dagga* which my nephew had obligingly acquired for me in downtown Johannesburg. For my personal use, for my personal use, I repeated to myself on the eleven-hour flight to Heathrow so that the mantra would come quickly to my lips when I was arrested in London, as I knew I surely would be. But there were no sniffer dogs, no body search, no stepping aside, please, for one moment and may I see your passport. It was almost a let down. The passport, of course, was always a give away. Dark green, adorned with the gold harp, it alerted passport controllers the world over. 'You a member of the IRA?' asked the official cheerfully, on the Caribbean island of Dominica. 'No,' I said stiffly. 'No? Man, that *bad.*'

Leaving London for Israel, it was checked and rechecked. 'You know why I'm doing this?' asked the grim-faced young official. 'Yes, I know.' In fact, I knew so well I was terrified about getting on the El-Al plane in case someone had already put a bomb on it. As we went down, would I remember to say *el hamdhu lilah* for, in the Islamic tradition, everything that happens is the will of Allah, and must be accepted instantly. No deals, no promises to be good from now on, no climbing over women and children to get to the escape shute. 'Yes, I know,' I reassured her. In fact, for going to Israel – although I didn't tell her this – I had acquired a second passport. A business passport, it was called, issued by the Irish Embassy in London valid for one year and for use only in Israel. To have an Israeli stamp in my regular passport would have made it difficult when I later wanted to get into an Arab country. To go to any of those countries, I would revert to my main passport which bore no record of the Israeli visit.

Of course, like lots of Irish people living in England in the 1970s and 1980s, I had the usual problems of suspect phone calls, unexpected visits, bomb threats. One of the phone calls I might well have brushed to one side like all the others (which came mainly from foolish village boys) had it not been for my encounter in Hebron with Belinda. The phone had rung in the middle of the night and, as luck would have it, was on my side of the bed. I reached out for it in the dark.

'Yes?'

I could hear party sounds in the background. Or was it a white noise intended to confuse?

'Yes?' I said again. 'Who's that?'

'Hi.' The voice was female, the accent American. 'Are you going to be there tomorrow?'

'What? I can't hear you. Who's that?'

The caller sounded hyped up, excited, as you might be at two in the morning, at a party.

'Are you going to carry a banner for us tomorrow?'

'*What?*' I couldn't make out what the woman was talking about.

'A banner,' she shouted above the noise. 'At the march.'

'I don't know what you're talking about,' I said. 'I think you've got the wrong number', and hung up. But I did know what she was talking about. There was to be a major march through London the next day, ending in Trafalgar Square, organized by the Troops Out Movement, a group that had clashed many times with the police and which had strong Republican connections. Someone was checking up on me. Testing me at a time, the middle of the night, when I might be off guard. Someone who knew me and knew my phone number, even though it was listed under Ian's name. Or was I simply being paranoid? I talked about this, years later, with Donald Woods, the banned South African editor, now dead, whose story, and that of the Black Consciousness leader Steve Biko, was the subject of the film *Cry Freedom*. 'You know,' he told me, 'you get to think you're mad, suspecting everyone. And some things seem just too bizarre you can't imagine anyone thinking them up but they do. In the end, I found so many bugs all over the place that it just wasn't worth worrying about.'

When I got back from Hebron, I thought about that phone call again and about Belinda. There were a lot of things that didn't add up. Or, to put it another way, a lot of things which now *did* add up. Was it a coincidence that she had persisted with her demands until she got hold of my tape recorder and had then given it back to me, disabled? Was it a coincidence that my tape had disappeared at the same time, the tape which had my voice on it, commenting on events in Hebron? Looking back, I marvelled at the skill with which she divided our small group, sowing seeds of doubt among us regarding the validity of the charity. It was a skill born of experience, of that I was sure. But the biggest question of all remained: when she first arrived in Hebron, a lone woman coming to work with the Palestinians, how had she managed to get through the Israeli army checkpoint, in the middle of the curfew. And at night?

CHAPTER FIVE

Home is Where the Toothbrush is

The large atlas lies on the kitchen table, in a pool of warm light, opened at the page where Asia blends into Europe. As I stare at it, the boundaries of the table, of the kitchen, of Dublin itself, melt away into the darkness and I am in Georgia, land of Colchis, of Jason and the Golden Fleece. And of Medea, who, having helped the handsome adventurer get the Golden Fleece, was ditched by him for a younger woman who, like himself, was a Greek. Driven first by despair and anger, Medea purged herself of everything to do with her former husband, killing her two children by him in a final act of revenge. With my finger, I trace the line of the Phasis river which Jason sailed up from the Black Sea. Then I locate Poti, the place where he had his first fatal meeting with the local princess – and feel a journey coming on.

I get up from the table and cross the room to switch on the kettle to make a pot of coffee. The sharp snap of the switch breaks the spell and the little kitchen comes into focus. The uneven floor tiles, the corner cupboard with the coffee pot from Algiers on its shelf and beside the pot a set of tiny coffee cups that I'd managed to bring back from the Netherlands intact, in my bike panniers. On the mantelpiece sits the tiny Buddha given to me by a visiting lama. Beside it, two silver candlesticks from Brill and the old clock which has never worked. On the wall is a poster advertising the Russian gypsy band Loyko, which I've written about, a photo of myself in the Sahara, scarf wound round my head and face so that only my shades show, and the Russian calendar permanently opened at the month of August showing a portrait of the Russian poet, Anna Akhmatova. Next door is my small study with desk, bookshelves, futon and piano – a tight squeeze. On the wall, photos of Freya and Deirdre at a wedding, each of them with Ian's blond hair, both dressed for the festivities in funereal black. A photo of Russell (also with his father's hair but curly this time) at his cousin's wedding in Kerry, aged seventeen – a cool, teenage Bogart in trench coat and bow tie.

Stuck upon the wall is a photo of the Brill cottage garden, hazy in the summer heat, hollyhocks and golden rod lining the vegetable patch, the hundred-year-old Victoria plum heavy with fruit. And a photo, too, of the house in Corkerbeg which, seen through the trees with logs stacked outside, looks like a Viking homestead. Donegal – Dún na nGall, the fort of the foreigner. On another wall is a picture of Pushkin with *his* curls, and beside it, a miniature of the wife who was taller than he was. A large sash window looks straight out on to the street. Opposite are the swing doors to the pub with steps up to them where men occasionally pause, take a comb from their back pocket and carefully do their hair before going in. Sometimes, people step outside to talk into their cell phones, a finger in their other ear as if searching for wax. Once, two brothers barrelled out, punching each other wildly, their mother trying to intervene. Another time, a man rushed down the steps and hurried up to the corner of the street where he met a woman coming from another door of the pub. They talked urgently, kissed passionately and returned by separate doors to, I assume, their respective partners.

If I want to be rid of all these distractions, I simply close the shutters. The clanging noise of beer barrels being unloaded and rolled down into the cellar never distracts but merely rings a bell somewhere in my unconscious, telling me that it's Friday.

Because I travel around so much – Dublin, Oxford, Donegal and the wider world – people often ask: 'Yes, but which is your real home?' Rarely getting a satisfactory answer to that, because there isn't one, they rephrase the question, trying to help me: 'Well, where do you spend the most part of your time?' 'Hard to say.'

And it is hard to say, for each place has its own attractions, irritations and uses. In Dublin, I have the canal to walk along, the willow trees which line it are bare in winter but form a tunnel of greenery in summer. In the summer, too, young boys swim in the lock and swans congregate close to it. Pubs put tables and umbrellas out on the pavement, pretending they're in Paris and, mystifying perhaps to visitors, hang out flags in support of whichever teams are playing the big, county GAA matches: yellow and green for Donegal, two shades of blue for Dublin, red and white for Derry and Cork. All of them a great and joyful expression of tribal support. Diplomatically, the pubs display the colours of both warring teams.

Dublin is a mixed bag of some one million people most of whom don't come from Dublin at all but are blow-ins from Limerick, Laois, Kiltimagh or Skibbereen. At weekends, the pubs empty as the majority head away off to their own towns or townlands, leaving only the locals to argue among themselves about what a true Dub is. Brendan Behan knew. 'It's someone,' he said, 'who doesn't go home for Christmas.'

In Dublin, I'm surrounded by twenty-four-hour shops, restaurants that stay open till four in the morning, wine bars till six and cafés that are open round the clock. There is a gym two minutes away and along the street a small cinema, the stuffy smell of caramelized popcorn in the auditorium a reminder that the air vents haven't been opened in a long time. Sounds of the city seep through my shutters. Bus brakes screech, church bells toll and police sirens whine as outriders shepherd visiting politicians, peacemakers and heads of state from airport to meeting and back to airport again. President Clinton has visited the neighbourhood *twice* and once, stopped at traffic lights on my push-bike, I managed to wave, personally, to Yasser Arafat as his cortège sped past. He waved back. In the pub opposite, even, a Rolling Stone has been seen, socializing. Dublin is a European capital, frenzied and frantic, absorbed with itself. In it, I am energized but when I want peace and quiet I stay at home, reading by the fire or poring over atlases at my kitchen table.

I saw this house only once before buying it and that was over Christmas when it was packed with the tenant's visiting parents and other seasonal visitors, the contents of cases spilling out on to the floor, beds occupied by strung-out revellers and dirty coffee cups littering the kitchen table. Even the Christmas tree was wilting. A month later, I bought the house without either seeing it again or having a survey done. I am, a solicitor friend told me, the client from hell. What drew me to it was the upstairs living room which runs the width of the house. With a mirrored over-mantel, full-length red curtains at the windows, a red velvet chaise longue to recline on or the rocking chair to sit in, this is a winter room, one in which to pull the curtains, draw the chair up to the turf fire, light the candles so that they flicker in the mantelpiece mirrors and, glass of wine to hand, settle in for a night's reading. The bedroom is simplicity itself: a double bed, a small oak desk, a chair, a lamp and two minute cupboards. The walls are white and bare, the only luxury a soft sheepskin rug on the wooden floor. It is a sparse, undemanding sleeping cell exactly to my liking.

It was after one of my trips to Oxford, when I was sitting at the kitchen table having a cup of coffee with Julia, a friend, that the talk turned to marriage – other people's. A good friend, John Wain, writer and one-time Professor of Poetry at Oxford, had separated from Eireann, his Welsh wife. The Wain boys and our children had had some good times together as well as having a few things in common since both fathers were writers and both mothers Celts. The four parents, too, had had good times, mostly consisting of talking and drinking. Ian and I had a rule to avoid eating in the Wain household as far as was polite: plates with left-overs were put down on the floor for the dogs to finish and the subsequent washing up arrangements were always a bit uncertain. When we first got to know them, Ian, noticing the overflowing packing cases in the hallway, thought they must have just moved. 'Have you been here long?' he asked. 'About ten years,' replied John. Eireann worked sometimes at the Bodleian Library, making hand copies of old books on request. Some of these could have been photocopied but Eireann couldn't bear to bend back the old pages. It was a painstaking task, performed with the true devotion of the bibliophile. Compared to it, housework came a poor second.

When John left Eireann for another woman, she was hugely unhappy and when she visited me in Brill, I found her going round my bookshelves turning all John's books to the wall. It was a dramatic gesture but the pain was clear for all to see. Then they got back together again. 'I couldn't bear to see her so unhappy,' John told me. They had a year or two together before she became ill and died. Within twelve months, John had remarried – not his previous lover but a new one. Freya and I called unexpectedly to see them one Sunday morning in Oxford and found all was changed. There was another woman's hand on the teapot. The knives were in the knife drawer and John's pyjamas, I had to assume, were in the drawer marked pyjamas. (Eireann had never been a Mrs Ogmore Prichard.) And though guests were expected to lunch, we were not invited to join them. In the old days, two extra bowls would have been selected from the dirty pile in the sink and we would have been offered whatever was going. Sitting at my kitchen table with Julia, contemplating the oddness of the married state, I recounted all this and heard myself sounding affronted.

'What a mess,' I said, pouring us both another glass of

wine. 'He leaves her and makes her terribly unhappy. Then he goes back to her and as soon as she's dead, he goes and marries another woman. I *mean*.'

'What?' Julia was unyielding.

'Well, the whole thing.' I wriggled a bit, knowing I was heading for the quicksands of self-knowledge. 'Anyway, I just couldn't take to the new wife.'

'Why?'

'I don't know. Just something I couldn't put my finger on.'

'Why do you think you feel so strongly about it all?'

'I don't know.'

'I do.'

'You do?' I wasn't sure I wanted to hear.

'You did to Ian what John did to Eireann.'

'I didn't.' I was immediately defensive. 'I didn't marry again.'

'You left him though.'

'Yes, but not for another man.'

'No, for something much worse.'

'What?'

'You left him for a dream.' She'd said it and there was no unsaying it.

'Have you never seen the similarities?' she asked.

'No,' I lied.

Ian and I had been together for twenty years, twenty good years. By then, however, I needed other horizons while he was content with his. Eleven years older than me, he had done all his travelling as a young man. Marriage and fatherhood came when he was thirty-three, the same age as Jesus was when he was crucified, I often reminded him. By then, he had published two books and a number of his radio plays had been produced by the BBC. Other successes followed. He was commissioned by the BBC to write a radio play to celebrate Churchill's eightieth birthday and he did so, focusing on Churchill's ancestor, the first Duke of Marlborough. BBC television commissioned him to write a play in the *Elizabeth R* series. He chose Elizabeth's death scene, with Glenda Jackson taking three days to die, standing up. He became the *Guardian*'s first radio columnist and later radio drama critic for *The Listener* and while he had the reward of seeing his name – Ian Rodger, writer and broadcaster – in the national press, in academic publications and on the spines of books, I stayed at home, the country wife, simmering, waiting my turn. I had always worked, of course. No one married to a writer, with three children to support, can afford not to. I ran courses in child development, wrote the odd piece for *The Irish Times* and the *Irish Press* as well as for Irish radio. I taught English and Italian at night school. And revelled in the exotic stories Ian brought back with him from London.

Although I'd earlier lived in bedsits all over Earls Court (thirteen in all) this other London was miles removed from what I'd known. The BBC drama department, in those days, was full of writers and poets who the Corporation was happy to let loose on its listeners. Some of them came to stay in Brill and with them came a whiff of the life beyond the village green. Harry Craig (H. A. L. Craig), producing one of Ian's radio documentaries, brought a tale about Caitlin Thomas. Once, while he and Dylan were sitting in the house in Laugharne, discussing a radio project, the curtains leading to the kitchen were pulled back quietly and there, visible only to Harry, stood Caitlin in the nip. It was all he could do, he said, to keep his mind on a higher plane. After a few moments, the curtains closed again and the nude show was over. I longed to be a woman like that but we didn't have the right curtains. Once, Ian came home with another story – these were always recounted offhandedly as part of the main narrative, making them seem even more interesting – about an actor who subsidized his earnings by visiting a man who liked him to undress, stick a feather up his bum and make cock-crowing noises. The old boy paid handsomely and the actor shrugged it off: he had to earn his money, somehow, while resting. I devoured these stories with relish and longed to be part of it all but on the only occasion I went to the BBC for a run-through of one of Ian's radio plays, I spoiled it all by worrying about the babysitter. Caitlin Thomas would never have bothered about a domestic detail like that.

Then with the children approaching adulthood, I went to Bradford University and got a taste for travel. And the more my world widened, the narrower Ian's became, as if there was some ratio being acted on, some relationship between shrinkage and expansion. But this disjunction in our lives was, I felt, the test of a true marriage. We had had the good times – twenty years of them – and now we were having the bad times and I was determined to stay with it. To ease myself through this difficult period, I bought a white sofa from Habitat and decided to take a lover. Neither, of course, was the answer. Unless I was on my own, I could never be this other person I knew I was. I was living in the shadow of a writer when I wanted to be one myself. It seemed like the reasoning of a sulky teenager and, at times, that's exactly what I was. But remembering Donne's words: 'The keys to my prison are in my own hands,' I accepted I had to act.

Reading somewhere that you should discuss the leaving of a partner with three people, a friend, your bank manager and a solicitor, I did just that. My choice of friend might not have seemed wise. He was a gay, New Zealand lapsed-Catholic psychiatrist given to cottaging around Piccadilly. But we had all spent some riotous nights together and he knew both Ian and myself well.

'You think you can't live with Ian any more?' he asked.

'It's not that. It's that I can't live with myself any more.'

Hearing myself speak the words, I knew it was time to go and I set about finding somewhere to live in Oxford. It would be a respite break, I told myself. Later, we would come back together again, regroup, relate to each other differently, make another pattern from the pieces of the kaleidoscope. But eighteen months later, Ian was diagnosed as having motor neurone disease. Five months after that, he died. I returned to be with him in Brill for those last months.

CHAPTER SIX

Saying Goodbye: 1984

The summer of 1984 was long and hot. People started to take the weather for granted, planning picnics in advance, leaving windows open all night, investing in garden umbrellas. Experimenting with Martinis. For parts of the country, however, the heat was of a different sort. In the north of England and in Wales, mounted police charged striking miners and their supporters: Margaret Thatcher's capitalism was operating at its crudest level, setting the people against each other.

Summers in Brill always had a timeless quality to them. Built on a hill, the village supported a seventeenth-century windmill, three pubs and a fine Elizabethan manor house. From the back of our house, which once belonged to Ian's grandmother, Nellie Rodger, the land dropped away steeply and, in the distance, the Chilterns shimmered in a haze of blue. A small side gate led to the field called Well Close where Nellie used to get her water, the water carrier charging her two pennies for a double yoke. In the course of his digging – he was an enthusiastic gardener – Ian found lots of flints, some of which dated from the Mesolithic period, proof that people had lived there 6000 years ago. The Celts had certainly settled on top of the hill, as its name attests. Not understanding the meaning of the Celtic word *Brae* (hill) the Saxons had subsequently named the hill Brae Hill which was later shortened to Brill.

Nellie's house started life as a lean-to attached to the pub next door, The Swan. It was really little more than a hovel of which there were many in Brill at that time – simple dwellings which people erected on any bit of land they could lay their hands on. In fact, the deeds of our house, dated 1611, record that: 'the said hovell was [shortly after] rebuilt and turned into the cottage which it now is'. In 1959, Nellie died and a year and a day later, Ian and I came to the house, now called Ferndale. It was our first real home. In those days, Ferndale had an outside lavatory, one cold tap and a stone sink in the kitchen. The interior walls were wattle and daub and the flagstones on the floor discarded gravestones. The huge inglenook fireplace had a seat set into it with a niche cut into the wall as an elbow rest. Above this niche was a smaller one for keeping the salt dry.

Nellie's family, coming from yeomen stock, were sensible people who filled the house with sturdy oak tables, useful grandfather clocks, lead-lined linen chests and mono-grammed silver. Later, the sturdiness was reined in and delicate pieces of furniture started to appear: a deep red rosewood cabinet, an ormolu clock, a Georgian armchair with fine, curving legs. After the Georgian and Victorian period came the Edwardians, with photographs on the wall of Ian's father and uncle – Lancelot and Claude – two little boys with long blond ringlets, dressed in lace dresses with satin sashes. In time, Lancelot became Lance and Claude, emigrating to Australia quickly, and sensibly, changed his name to Fred.

The house in Brill was full of surprises and enchantment, a perfect place in which to bring up children and indeed all of our three children were born in it and each added to it. Freya, born on Mother's Day, brought spring into the house, arriving with the daffodils and bluebells and the first days of open windows. Twenty months later, she woke in the middle of the night and started to sing, something she had never done before. In the adjoining bedroom, Ian and I listened to her with a mixture of pleasure and apprehension. If she didn't go back to sleep soon, there could be problems for I had work to do. For an hour she sang, in the dark, her small voice happy and without care. I know now, though at the time I didn't, that – a recent arrival herself – she was singing another new life into the house: her sister, Deirdre, was born a few hours later, her birth a special gift on my birthday. The last baby to arrive, Russell, was born on Michaelmas Day, sharing his birthday with his maternal great-grandmother. This baby, and he still has a leisurely take on life, was ten days overdue and so desperate was I for him to arrive that I drank a mixture of Guinness, milk and castor oil and then got down on my knees to polish the wooden floor. When the labour pains started next morning, at 6 a.m., Ian phoned the midwife and, getting no reply, went to her house in the village. Stones thrown up at her window failed to wake her and finally the doctor was called. Russell was born shortly afterwards, completing the family.

Living in a sixteenth-century hovel had its charms but also its disadvantages. Nothing fitted, neither doors nor windows. Draughts gusted down the chimney and when a door slammed the whole house shook. There was also the question of who else we might be sharing the house with. One evening, Deirdre, aged about ten, came into the room where I was sewing to tell me she could hear loud breathing. At first, she'd thought it was her brother hiding under the table, trying to frighten her.

'It's in there,' she said, pointing to the dining room. Unable to hear what she was hearing, I opened the door. 'It's stopped now,' she said. But when I withdrew, she heard the breathing again. A few years previously Ian too had heard sounds in that room, the room in which Nellie had died. When he came home from the pub later, I told him what had taken place. He frowned and looked thoughtful and next day went to the village graveyard to check something on his grandmother's grave.

'I have news for you,' he said on his return. 'Yesterday was the anniversary of my grandmother's death.'

In Brill, that last summer, the red opium poppies came into full bloom as they always did for Ian's birthday in June. Two months previously, in the windowless room in an Oxford hospital, a doctor in a white coat and a red tie had told me Ian was suffering from motor neurone disease and had six months to live. I'd known for a long time that something serious was wrong. Ian had always been an energetic person but over the last year he'd taken to resting a lot, putting his feet up, stretching out in the garden, sitting when normally he'd be digging the vegetable patch, rushing to the post or attending to some fault in the car. He'd become clumsy as well, dropping his coffee mug, letting the newspaper slide from his fingers. Added to that, he seemed to have lost touch with his writing. The diagnosis, therefore, explained everything. Motor neurone disease occurs when the brain ceases to send messages to the muscles which consequently weaken and become useless. The brain itself continues to function normally. As soon as the doctor broke the news to me, I experienced an unexpected lightness in my mind. Now that I knew what the challenge was, I could start to deal with it. But there was another feeling too, something to do with the doctor, a puzzling one which, unable to handle it at the time, I pushed to one side. Next day, seeing the doctor a second time the feeling rushed to the surface before I had a chance to suppress it. This man, with his concerned manner, his dark hair and red tie, I had found attractive, even as he was telling me of the impending death of my husband. So bizarre and unexpected was this feeling that I chose not to analyse it, knowing that I would conjure up some psycho-biological theory – excess adrenalin or displacement activity perhaps – to cloak what was a simple, if inappropriate, charge of sexual chemistry.

We had agreed, the children and myself, that we would care for Ian at home for as long as we were able. Hospital was not an option since he hated anything to do with uniforms or regimentation – a throwback, perhaps, to his public school days. But there was little caring to do for he was a stoical person to whom discomfort was an irrelevancy. Each child found their own way of coping. Freya, back from college in Manchester, and unable to watch her father's slow, inevitable decline, busied herself, uncharacteristically, in the kitchen. Deirdre, home from France, sat and chatted to him or simply sat. Russell, who of all of us had spent more time with Ian since I had left, had learned to understand his distorted speech and was always called on to interpret when friends and family found it hard to understand what his father was saying. All through that summer, friends and neighbours dropped in bringing books for Ian to read, tempting him with tasty bits of village gossip or with specially cooked food which, increasingly, he found difficult to swallow. A lifelong friend travelled from Newfoundland to see him, one last time.

'Why are you in England?' Ian asked and Robert, unable to say he'd come to say goodbye, said he had come to pay a visit to his father. It was a sad exchange, so much to be said that couldn't be spoken.

It was Robert who had asked me if Ian and I had talked about euthanasia, a sensible query under the circumstances for it was clear that this terrible illness could, at some point, become unbearable. But Ian and I had never even discussed his impending death. In the hospital, when he diagnosed motor neurone disease, the doctor had advised me to wait a while before telling Ian he had six months to live. 'He's very sick, with little resources to call on just at the moment. Let him deal with the illness first.' A friend who headed up a hospice gave further support: 'He's an intelligent man. He probably knows already. But wait for him to speak first. If he wants to talk about it, he will, in his own time. Let him have his space.' But only once did Ian touch on his condition. After visiting an acupuncturist, who, it was hoped, might give him some relief, he said to me, with tears in his eyes: 'I'm not getting better.' I put my arms round him, knowing it was true. The only person who adopted an impersonal attitude to the whole thing was the bank manager. Ian's overdraft was running into thousands and I called the bank to explain the situation. 'This is ridiculous,' said the manager, sternly. 'He must put his affairs in order.' But like discomfort, money too, to Ian, was an irrelevancy. His writing had always been an end in itself and when, months after the event, a cheque arrived from the BBC or from a publisher, he viewed it with delighted surprise rather as Early Man, I imagined, must have enjoyed making love and then been surprised, nine months later, with the arrival of a lovely child. Babies and cheques were a bonus.

Ian did, on one later occasion, make an oblique reference to his death. A very close friend and a fellow writer, Denys Val Baker, died and Ian was determined to go to his funeral in Cornwall. The prospect of such a long drive was terrible, for his body now was fragile and his intake of food minimal. Nevertheless, we drove to the funeral and attended the send-off, which consisted of carefully chosen readings and music, with a little bit of jazz at the end to cheer us all up. Driving back to Brill, Ian seemed to fail and we had to stop many times to give his poor body some respite from the shaking it was getting in the car. And so weak did he become with each hour, that I had to face the possibility that he might die on the journey.

The presence of death liberates people from the restraints of having to conform to acceptable behaviour. On my own, trying to sustain him as best I could, I decided that, should he die beside me in the car, I would keep driving till we got to Brill. All I wanted was for both of us to be safely home. Next day, rested, he said how much he'd liked Denys's send-off. 'No religion,' he said. 'It was a good way to do it.' And I knew then that that was what he wanted for his own farewell.

And so the summer passed. The Victoria plums ripened and the golden rod grew tall along the garden path. In the last week in August, Ian caught a chest infection and we called our family doctor. 'How long?' I asked him. 'Maybe a week.' But that evening, lying on the couch, he seemed to slip in and out of sleep. A light beading of sweat lay on his forehead. I held his hand but his eyes remained closed, the pulse in his neck growing weaker, becoming, eventually, nothing more than an intermittent fluttering of life. Watching it, I saw a tide go out to a distant horizon and knew that it would not be coming in again. Two nights earlier, we had made peace with each other and he was ready to go.

The director of the crematorium had been full of helpful advice. Since we were to carry the coffin ourselves, he suggested, we should ask the undertaker to fix two sets of handles on each side, one for each of us. Did we want the cross left or taken away, he asked. Taken away. And the candles? They should stay. Did we want hymns? Music of any sort? Since one of Ian's most powerful radio plays had been about William Blake, we decided we would all sing 'Jerusalem'. The director nodded approvingly: 'Ah, yes. The jam butty song. It's what the Women's Institute sing after tea at their meetings . . . Be sure to pitch it low,' he added in an aside to the organist. 'If it's too high everyone has to stand on their toes to sing it. We're not all pooftas.' We timed the walk down the aisle and decided on our speed. When we reached the top, the director showed us how to raise the coffin slightly to ease it up on to the rollers. From there on, it would be a push-button job. I noted how long it had taken us to walk down the aisle and how much time was then left for the rest of the ceremony. Each cremation was allotted twenty minutes and in deference to Ian's dramatic timing skills, I was determined that this last drama would not overrun.

The day of the funeral was bright and warm with September sunshine. We picked a large bunch of golden rod from the garden to lay on the coffin and added to it some trailing grapevine that Ian had nurtured. Labour Party comrades sent a wreath of red roses. The sun continued to shine as friends gathered outside the crematorium. Everyone was there, Labour and Tory, punks and priests, clergymen and cousins, young and old. I had made out a card detailing the running order for speakers, songs and music and had given it to a friend to deal with. His job was to sit beside the organist and when the final song, 'Carrickfergus', was reaching its last verse he was to nudge the organist who would then press the button hidden discreetly near the keyboard. This would start the curtains opening and set the coffin moving forwards on the rollers. Everything went according to plan. We carried the coffin down the aisle to the music of Planxty's majestic composition *The Pride of the Herd*. (It was only later I learned that this was a piece commissioned by the Irish Milk Marketing Board to accompany a TV commercial.) Richard Imison, Script Editor for BBC Radio Drama, spoke of Ian's contribution to radio, his many plays, his devotion to his beloved Brill. An old college friend spoke and had a run at a joke or two. A drinking companion from the village upset my carefully timed programme by writing himself in a part, leaning on the lectern as if he were leaning on the bar of The Sun, waiting for his pint to be drawn. I spoke of Ian's commitment to socialism, to the village and to his family. I wanted Freya, Deirdre and Russell to know that each of them was an expression of our love. And then that great love song, 'Carrickfergus', came rolling towards us:

> And now I'm gone and my days are over,
> Come Molly ashsthoreen, now lay me down.

With dry eyes, for I had done my mourning months earlier, I watched the coffin for the first sign of Ian's final leaving. 'Carrickfergus' was drawing to a close. The button should have been pressed by now. The music finished and there was silence. A long, contemplative silence. Then, mercifully, the crimson curtains began to part, the coffin to move forward. Later, I discovered that the friend chosen to prompt the organist had failed to turn over the card on which was written the final, most important instruction.

That day, the three dramatic unities of time, place and action were uppermost in my mind for I wanted to complete what we had started all on the same day. Which was why, as the Jameson was still being drunk and the coronation chicken being eaten, Freya and I returned to the crematorium to collect the white plastic container – not unlike a Cerebos salt jar – in which Ian's ashes were held. By evening, when the survivors had shrunk to about twenty, we walked through the village to the windmill to scatter them on Brill Common. 'What you do,' one of Denys Val Baker's daughters advised, 'is put your hand into the container and just throw them to the wind.' Which is what we did, one by one, a group of silent people, standing by the windmill in the fading light of a warm autumn day, taking part in this final farewell. One of Ian's oldest friends from boyhood days, a large, awkward man, plunged his hand into the Cerebos salt jar and in a wild and loving attempt to send the ashes high up into ethereal eternity made such an ungainly movement with his arm that the grey-white ashes returned from whence they had been thrown. A few years later, he published a poem in which he expressed his feelings with the grace that had eluded him by the windmill:

So, under the brooding windmill tower,
beneath its sails' quiescent shadows,
we scattered your ashes on common land.
On that brilliantly clear day
one should have observed the frontiers of the universe
from that common's microcosm.
Life should be more
than a handful of dust in the wind,
grey granules of ash in a white plastic pot
in which my fumbling hand touches the last of you,
grasps the elusive handful as a ringed bird released
down a small eddying breeze the direction of grief
in a puff of feathery grey, then falls to the ground,
its end invisible as a rainbow's base . . .

Early the following morning, I went on my own to a spot high up on a plain overlooking the Vale of Aylesbury, which Ian was convinced was the site of the famous battle in which Alfred had repulsed the Danes. There I scattered some more ashes. Later, we laid some around the old plum tree. And still there were ashes left in the container. So much and all of it fine as dust. Then, the first New Year after his death, I went alone to Corkerbeg. At midnight, many years after the New Year's Eve when on the stroke of midnight, in a rainy, blustery Cornwall, he had asked me to marry him, I scattered the last of Ian's ashes in the Poet's House.

Ten years later, a small brown-skinned girl would construct a swing out of a bit of rope and a cushion and, her arms thrown wide to embrace life, would swing merrily over the spot where her grandfather's ashes lay.

CHAPTER SEVEN

Stars in the Sand: 1988

The cook fished a knucklebone out of the stew and threw it across the sand to Khandoud who cracked off one end, sucked the marrow from it and then, gouging out the hole, blew through it to get rid of any remaining debris before filling it with tobacco and lighting up. I'd taken a dislike to Khandoud when we first met a week ago. He was large, with a loud voice and given, it seemed, to boasting. 'I can eat three bowls of rice and chicken,' I heard him tell the other Saharawi in the desert outpost we were holed up in, 'then eat five kilos of bananas and still feel hungry.' Bravo, I thought sourly. I'd been waiting three days to hear whether or not I was to be taken up to the front and was not well disposed to loudmouths. I'd first heard about the Saharawi in Oxford, when Barbara Harrell-Bond – a redoubtable anthropologist, dedicated to working for and with refugees – had involved me in a conference on refugees she was running. She was a bully, everyone agreed about that, but no matter how much she asked of people, it was never as much as she demanded of herself. I would have walked through fields of fire for her. Almost.

The Saharawi are a desert people of Arabic origin who live in what was formerly known as Spanish Sahara. When Franco died, however, in 1975, the vultures moved in: Morocco from the north and Mauritania from the south, each of them greedy for the newly named Western Sahara's rich deposits of subterranean phosphates. As part of its drive, Morocco organized one of the most successful public relations exercises of the 1970s, the Green March, when thousands of its citizens were brought together to march into the desert. The Western media was full of it: these were the people who would turn this barren emptiness into a fertile land, we were told. They would green the Sahara. Flower power, they called it. It was an imaginative idea but it had one major weakness: the desert was not empty. It was home to around 250,000 Saharawi, many of whom had settled along the coast and in towns in the interior. Some still plied their nomadic camel trade along routes that for centuries had been used to bring salt down from Tindouf to Timbuktu. So desperate were the southerners for the life-sustaining mineral that they were prepared to pay for its weight in gold, pound for pound.

Mauritania eventually dropped out of the war but the Moroccan army continued to attack the Saharawi, harassing, torturing and finally napalming them until, fleeing across the desert, they were offered a safe haven just over the border in Algeria, not far from the desert town of Tindouf. There, they made a temporary home of sorts, building four tent cities in the sand with streets named after those in the original cities back home. The Saharawi, the 165,000 of them who were now refugees, had taken their homeland with them and, one day, they believed, children, who had never known their parents' birthplace, would return to it familiar with its layout and its street names. Thus, these children, displaced and stateless, were sent to wait out the war in the ante-room of their parents' dream. That was thirteen years ago and they were still there. The Saharawi fought back, of course, forming a revolutionary army called Polisario, and sending emissaries all over the world to seek support for their beleaguered people. Polisario, too, had its own ideas to promote. They had, they announced, dispensed with money. As a society in revolution, they believed in the common good which was why everyone worked for nothing. In return for their services, they were given clothes, food and bedding, all provided by political supporters and humanitarian agencies.

At the Oxford conference, I met the Polisario representative, a small, dark-skinned man with sparkling eyes and curly hair. Living in a capitalist, consumer-driven society, I was intrigued to hear of this society which had no need for money. 'We call ourselves the sons of the clouds,' he told me, 'because we have to drive our herds after the rain clouds.' It was pure poetry and my head swirled with images of camels, clouds and desert landscapes. 'Maybe I could travel to your tent cities and find out a bit more about the Saharawi,' I said. 'She means she thinks you're cute,' said Barbara, sweeping past with a party of conference delegates. It was another four years, however, before, in 1988, I took a plane to Tindouf, 1400 kilometres south-west of Algiers and put myself in the hands of Polisario. Now I was sitting under a thorn tree, exhausted and sick with the heat, the sight of Khandoud tucking into the marrow bringing on another attack of nausea. It was 4 a.m. when I'd been shaken from sleep that morning with the news that it had finally been decided: I was to be taken up to the front after all.

The world is scarred with walls: the Great Wall of China, Offa's Dyke, the Berlin Wall, Hadrian's Wall. There are walled cities and walled gardens, boundaries and barriers. Some walls are Janus-like, keeping the enemy out while at the same time imprisoning their guardians. When the Western Sahara desert war broke out, the Moroccans brought in heavy, earth-moving machinery and threw up a double defensive wall of sand, which now runs through the desert for 2000 kilometres until it reaches the Atlantic Ocean. Positioned along the wall, every few kilometres or so, are companies of Moroccan soldiers and installed on top is a sophisticated electronic-eye surveillance system, a neat little number costing 200 million US dollars and manufactured in the States. Everyone has had a part to play in this theatre of war. I'd seen ammunition, which had originated in the UK, the USSR and the USA, some of it, no doubt, recycled more than once and occasionally within Arab states themselves. When Egypt supported the Camp David Agreement, the Moroccans made their disapproval clear. To win them back again, and restore trading relations, Egypt provided Morocco with weapons for its war against the Saharawi. Every time the wall was extended, Polisario celebrated. It enhanced their self-image as a force to be reckoned with. Irreverently, I saw the wall snaking through the desert, getting longer and longer, its length a measure of Polisario's manhood. Now, finally, I was to see it for myself.

In the pre-dawn chill, I made my way to the latrine where my bowels emptied with fear: wars are not my strong point. Yesterday, I was given a form to sign stating where I wanted my body to be sent to in the event of my being killed. The Irish Embassy, in Rome, I'd written. It seemed as good a place as any. I'd been told not to bring anything with me but surely there were some things I'd need? I made a mental list. Notebook and biro, certainly. My long, all-enveloping Oxfam skirt, which was useful both as a pillow and a towel and for going to the lavatory under. No money, obviously. But anything else? A lavatory roll? In my current condition, definitely. And? Craven treachery invaded my mind: yes, my passport. I would take that with me so that, should I be captured, I could show the Moroccans that this war was not one of my making. That I was merely an innocent bystander. I was not on anyone's side. The cock was crowing for the first time.

As the Land Rover moved away from the outpost, the sun started to rise, a perfect sphere balanced on the firm line of the horizon. It was orange and lovely and as yet gave no hint of the fiery torture it would later inflict on us. There were seven of us altogether: Shadeed – my minder and source of all information – the cook, the driver, Khandoud and two other soldiers. None of them was certain how far it was to our next liaison point. Or perhaps they simply chose not to say. 'Be prepared for a week,' was Shadeed's only comment. Khandoud rode shotgun on the wooden ammunition box, his khaki shirt open to the waist, the tail of his long scarf, or *shesh*, flying out behind him in the wind. The need for a *shesh* had quickly become clear. In the early days of the war, sunlight glinting on the windscreens of the Land Rovers made them easy targets for enemy planes. As a safety measure, therefore, the glass on all of them had been removed. This meant that, riding up front beside the driver, my face took the full blast of the grains of sand that came flying through the air sharp as a thousand needles. Within minutes of wrapping my *shesh* round my head and face, however, the wind whipped it into an ungovernable mess. Glancing back at Shadeed, I followed his example and clenched the end of it between my teeth to hold it in place. Wrapping the shesh correctly was an art and no one did it better than the driver. In fact, no one did anything better than the driver. Despite this being a military outing, he was the only one among all the soldiers with a watch and its gold band glowed among the dark hairs on his wrist. His face was covered in pockmarks but his mouth, with its gleaming teeth – straight and regular – was perfect in its formation, as if drawn according to careful measurements. His lips were the colour of a purple plum that you could sink your teeth in to and he wore his long black *shesh* wound round his whole face so that only his eyes were visible though even those were concealed behind dark shades. I found it hard to stop looking at him.

Only 25 per cent of the Sahara is made up of sand dunes. The part we travelled over was the *hammada* – a great rocky plateau known for its barren aridity. Over thousands of years, the soil had gradually been eroded by wind and during the process of evaporation, the residue of salt – and there are large deposits of it in the Tindouf region – had crystallized, causing huge cracks in the denuded rocks. Sandstorms regularly whip across the *hammada* but, without any dunes to cling to, the sand itself never settles. To the Saharawi, this place of refuge was as bleak as it was barren. By 10 a.m., we had climbed high up on to the *hammada* and found it strewn with blackened stones. The heat thundered down on us from all sides, bouncing off our faces, the metal of the Land Rover and the barrel of the Kalashnikov resting, at the ready, on the dashboard. The scalding black stones, I later learned, were really a sort of plant. At night, their surface is covered with a desert dew which by day evaporates, leaving behind a film of iron and manganese oxide. It is this film that gives the stone its gleaming coat of black enamel. Driving across the *hammada* was like passing over the surface of a mirror out of which shone a thousand burning suns. Above, there was no sun, only a white sheet of blinding heat.

Around noon, the driver stopped the Land Rover by a small, stunted thorn tree, depositing Khandoud, myself and the cook before setting off to liaise with the next checkpoint. I sat in the shade of the tree, taking deep breaths and trying to restore peace and calm to my overheated mind. Khandoud, however, was in his element, riding the rays of the sun as a surfer might ride a wave.

'You'll get used to it,' he promised, squatting down beside me. 'You'll have to. Maybe we'll be here a long time.'

But I felt out of control, nervous about entrusting myself to a group of people I didn't really know. 'What happens if the Land Rover doesn't come back?'

'We look at the water and decide how many days we can live.'

'And food? Have we any food?'

'Enough for five days. After that, we eat each other.'

I'd started to warm to Khandoud. He was a gentle giant,

without guile. When the war had broken out, he'd been away from home, reading for an economics degree in Barcelona. Now he was a soldier, with a wife and four children back in one of the tent cities.

'We have to fight, for our children and for our homes.'

'Is the desert now your home?'

'For the time being.'

'Have you ever been lost in it?'

He looked at me in amazement: 'How could we be? We know this desert like we know our own bodies.' And then proceeded to tell me a story.

'There were four of us and our truck broke down. The rule is, always stay with your truck. It gives shade and someone will come to find you, if you're lucky. Well, first we drank all the water we had, then we drank the water in the radiator and then we had nothing.'

'No food?'

'No. No food. Nothing. So, after four days, we decided to leave the vehicle and start walking, one each to the north, the south, the east and the west. I kept walking for two days, but only at night when it was cool. During the day, I rested. Then I went more slowly and in the end, when I couldn't go any further, I lay under a tree, my mind gone. That day, they found me.'

'How?'

'One of the men had got as far as the checkpoint and a truck had come to look for us. They started out from our truck, the one that had broken down, and they kept driving round and round in bigger circles until they found all of us.'

I thought of the men combing the sands of this vast desert, searching desperately for their lost comrades, forging on through the heat of the day and the blackness of the night until all four had been found. It was this devotion to each other, I knew, which kept the war going. While we'd been talking, the tiny circle of shade which, when we'd first sat under the tree, had been spread out prettily like a girl's summer skirt, had now shrunk right back to the trunk itself. Khandoud and the cook stretched out and went to sleep but, for me, sleep was impossible. Instead, I sat there, the very breath drained from my body, aware only of the white piston of heat directly over us. When Shadeed and the others returned in the Land Rover, they brought with them the roots of a thorn tree they'd managed to pull out of the ground. The cook got a fire going and by nightfall there was rice and onions and bits of goat meat they'd brought back with them from the checkpoint. Shadeed sat cross-legged on a mat, working intently on his cigarette holder. There were, however, no cigarettes for the tobacco went straight into the holder itself where it was packed in with a small stick. Khandoud, sitting with the rest of the men over by the fire, waved his bone cigarette in my direction. 'You smoke?' he called out but I shook my head and he passed it round the men instead.

I turned back to Shadeed, trying to figure him out. He seemed about forty, though it was difficult to tell. For one thing, everyone wore the same sort of clothes here so that there were no hidden signals I could pick up. In Europe, a man may tell you, by the clothes he wears, of his success, his dependability, his rakishness, his unconventionality, his sportiness, his gender tendency, his trade, his profession, his probable holiday habits. His work clothes may even tell you what day of the week it is. Polisario men, however, all wore a military-style shirt and trousers – a job-lot trade deal they'd done with their former oppressors, the Spanish. Some of the older men wore the traditional *bou-bou* – a long white sleeveless tunic worn over shirt and trousers. The women, on the other hand, wore beautiful, brightly coloured robes often with scarves of a contrasting colour that passed over the head and fell gracefully across the shoulders. I'd met some of them working in the irrigation fields near one of the tent cities and from a distance, they looked like diaphanous butterflies, floating wisps of yellow and pink, orange and purple. Later, I'd been brought to meet a token revolutionary woman. Her huge breasts strained at the buttons of her military jacket, forcing a gap between each one. Her thighs were encased in trousers so close-fitting they looked like tights. I felt sorry for her that she had to participate, so uncomfortably, in such a farce. The role of women in this particular revolution was clearly as traditional as it had always been.

Shadeed flipped over the lid of his tobacco pouch and settled down to smoke and chat. The evening had brought a calming coolness to the desert, a benignness that left me feeling relaxed. I stretched out on the mat, using another rolled up mat as a cushion to lean on. Shadeed was starting to transmit: 'Every Saharawi has two mothers: the one who gives him life and his other mother, the earth. From her, we take our soul. Without her, we are nothing. A man without land is bereft, a stranger, an outsider. And without each other too, we are nothing. Unity, you see, is very important to our people.' He paused and I knew what was coming next. 'Why is it,' he asked, 'that *your* people are so divided? Why have you not driven the English out?'

'Well, some people have tried to but mostly the nation is divided about what is the best way to do this. In any case, many people just want to get on with their lives, with or without the English.'

'While their own people are suffering?'

'I'm afraid so, yes.' I had the option of slinking away into a rat hole. Ireland, a country that had fed off its reputation for promoting justice and freedom, had been found wanting by a tiny nation of 165,000 people who were prepared to stand and fight for these very things.

'The problem is, Shadeed, that when you explain to me about the Saharawi and *your* struggle, you always end by saying it's simple. That's a phrase you could never use about Irish politics. Simple it's not. Anyway, there are some people who think that only a political solution will work, that no good can come of violence.'

Shadeed nodded, patiently: 'Well, of course, yes, talking is always better than war but if you are being bombed and driven from your home?'

'Well, that's happened in Northern Ireland, too, you know.'

'So what good is it to talk only?'

'Because there, the fight is out on the streets. The wrong people are being killed.'

Once you get to talking about killing, words take on a different currency. Who could ever say which was the right and which was the wrong person to kill? Besides, it is no longer only soldiers who are killed now but civilians, 85 per cent of whom account for all war casualties. Khandoud, hearing Ireland being mentioned, looked across from the fire: 'Bobby Sands,' he roared. 'Very good man. I want to go to Ireland, to see his grave. I go and stay with the IRA, the way you stay with Polisario.'

'You might get arrested. It's an illegal organization.'

He looked crestfallen.

'You could stay with me in Dublin, though.'

'Is that in Belfast?'

'Sort of.'

The cook had spread more mats out on the sand and when I managed to carve out a smooth resting place for my hip I lay down to sleep. The men continued to sit talking in the glow of the fire. Every so often, someone threw a piece of wood on it and the sudden upwards shower of sparks illuminated their dark faces. Above, the sky was brilliant with light. Lying on my back, it seemed as if the whole glittering firmament was hurtling down on top of me and I closed my eyes against the weight of the stars. The sight of them was more than I could bear. Although it was dark, the air was still warm and I lay without a cover. Later, though, when the men got up from the fire and came over to stretch out on the mats, I felt Khandoud carefully lay a blanket over me.

The Spanish, when they first colonized this part of the world, brought water with them although there is, in fact, lots of water under the desert. Accessing it and then conserving it is the problem. I'd been told that once I'd got out into the desert proper, I shouldn't be too choosy about what I drank. But I was always thirsty and very occasionally I'd had to beg the cook for an unscheduled drink of unboiled water which came brown and gritty and sometimes had a few ants floating in it. But I didn't like doing that. The others could go for hours without drinking and since the water was rationed, I knew I should too. Now, though, the thirst had made me ill. I spent the day in a bleary sweat. Shadeed sat beside me, trying to distract me.

'What is Ireland like? How many seasons do you have?'

'Two.'

'Two?' He sounded surprised.

'Yes. Hot and cold. Unless you count the one in between which makes it three.'

Then I shook my head. That didn't sound right at all. I got the cook to give me a little water, boiled this time, to which I added a few spoonfuls of sugar. It looked and tasted awful but I felt it was the right thing to do. I was worried about the seasons thing and wondered if I'd been correct about there being three. What if there were four? But if it was four, what could the other one have been? Hot and cold was all right because that was what everything was – extremes. You had hot and cold, wet and dry, dead and alive, with the intermediate one as a bridge. But was there another one? My head throbbed and I gave up thinking. While I was sipping my water, Khandoud looked at me and suddenly doubled up, grabbing his stomach and making guttural retching noises, his tongue hanging out and his shoulders heaving. I looked wildly round for the cook. This was more than I could cope with. When I turned back again, however, he was upright, hands in his pockets, smiling. Words sometimes failed him and his demonstration of being sick was merely a show of solidarity.

When we stopped at midday, a bird started up suddenly from nowhere and settled on a thorn tree. 'The desert dove,' whispered Khandoud. Quietly, in one smooth movement, the driver picked up his Kalashnikov, raised it to his shoulder and, without pausing to take aim, shot the bird. Khandoud spread out its wings and showed me the display of soft delicate feathers – grey and white – underneath. Then he borrowed my penknife to cut them off before plucking the rest of it for roasting. There were quite a few birds pecking round the thorn tree, pretty, glowing little things decked out in pink and orange plumage, the perfect camouflage for the desert. In fact, there was far more life in the desert than I had expected to find. The thorn tree, especially, was a model of survival. Standing alone, battered by wind and sand, starved of moisture, it nevertheless gave off a faint smell of damp wood that made me feel lonely and, as I looked closely at it, I saw that each branch was composed of a feathery spray of minute, bright green leaves. Among them, a delicate white moth flitted, light as lace, nonchalantly avoiding another tiny, buzzing insect which was darting from leaf to leaf.

We spent a lot of time sitting round in the desert, doing nothing, waiting for an escort truck to see us through to the next checkpoint. Or just waiting. One afternoon, with nothing to do, the men set up a target practice, using discarded food tins. There were always plenty of those around. The cook, when he'd emptied a tin of beans into his stew, simply hurled the tin as far away from camp as he could. In fact, it was easy to see where the previous lot of Polisario soldiers had been by the pile of discarded tins and the used mortar cases. The cans were piled up one on top of the other at regular distances and everyone took shots at them. The best shot was always the driver. At one point, the Kalashnikov was offered to me. I'd never fired a gun before and wondered what it might be like to do so but the sickness in my head and the shooting of the desert dove brought a rush of nausea which prevented me from even touching the gun. The soldiers laughed. It was what they expected, after all, from a woman.

Everything that grew in the desert seemed to be thorny and prickly. The cram-cram was the worst. It ran along the ground just concealed beneath the surface of the sand and the pain, when its needles pierced the soles of the foot, went straight to the brain and back down again. Mindful of these various prickles, therefore, I chose my squatting site with care. One place I found had already been used for peeing. Like Leopold Bloom, desert men do it from a kneeling position and there in the sand was a random collection of tiny craters, each indentation baked hard by the sun, giving the site the look of a miniature moonscape. This morning, in the dark chilliness of the pre-dawn, I stumbled across the camp to my bush, passing the cook who was poking sticks into the fire. Up in the thorn tree hung a lump of lard. On another branch were two socks and a pair of binoculars. Below them, a goat's stomach swung to and fro like a pendulum. The rest of the goat had been eaten the previous night and none of it is wasted: the stomach is used as a water carrier, the leather is cured and fashioned into bags and tobacco pouches and the bones, sucked dry of marrow, become cigarette holders.

Suddenly, water was in abundance: we had made our midday halt at a couple of artesian wells, the first I'd seen in the Sahara. These wells are fed by clean, cool water running underground from the Atlas Mountains. The stop brought about a burst of activity. The driver drew up a bucketful of water to put into the radiator. 'The car, the camel and the man are always thirsty,' he said in an uncharacteristic rush of words before sloshing another bucketful over the tyres. Khandoud stuck his head in a bowl of water, roaring like a lion when he came up for air. I asked the cook if I could have some water to wash in. I was becoming offensive even to myself. For answer, he emptied the bucket over me and so delirious was I with relief that he started to do it again until Shadeed restrained him. He had slightly overstepped the mark, it seemed.

We were just sitting down in the shade, waiting for the water to brew up for a glass of tea, when a herd of camel appeared in the distance. There were about fifty in all and, driving them, two men in turbans and striped djellabiyas. As soon as the herd got near the well, the men split the animals into two groups, allowing just five or six at a time up to the well. The camels were surprisingly docile about this arrangement and a quiet word or a touch from a stick was all that was needed to keep them in line. The droughts that swept across the Sahel had brought the camel economy to its knees. Between 1946 and 1950, the nomads' herds were decimated and less than twelve years later, another drought brought a further 60 per cent reduction. In 1975, a camel count showed there were only 63,000 camels left. After that came the war, the bombing, the napalming and the evacuation of people from the desert and a further decrease.

A camel can drink two hundred gallons of water in ten minutes and the herdsmen had their work cut out for these creatures were thirsty and once they had started to drink were not always ready to stop. The procedure was simple and hygienic: a leather bucket was lowered into the well and, when full, was emptied into a large truck tyre that had been sliced in half to make a drinking trough. This allowed four or five camels to drink from it at a time. They drank steadily without pause, their huge soft lips working like rubbery disposal units. The waiting camels, their coats reflecting the different shades of the desert – sandy brown here, speckled fawn there – were held back by the soft but persistent shoo-shoo of the herdsmen. Two camels, I noticed, were used as pack animals, carrying each man's baggage, which amounted to little more than a bedroll, a pot and a *querba*. When all the animals had been watered, the herdsmen joined us for tea, bringing with them a steaming gourd of fresh camel milk. The gourd was offered to me first and I drank the frothing milk, closing off my mind to its lukewarm taste. By the time it went its rounds and came back to me again, however, the milk was dotted with red dust, particles of sand and tiny desert insects.

'You like it?' asked Khandoud, his generous moustache now tipped with white.

'Hmm. Quite good.'

'*Very* good,' he corrected me, energetically thumping his heart and rolling his eyes heavenwards, then firing an imaginary rifle in the air. When he saw my puzzled look, he added: 'Very good for making love and war.'

Our meeting with one of the last remaining camel herds took place at a well that was also a temporal crossroads. The nomads were moving through the desert like ghosts in the shadow of the past while the Polisario soldiers were hurtling towards an uncertain future, leaving behind a trail of red dust and diesel fumes.

Overhead, the sound of a plane was lazy in the blue sky but I detected a slight wariness in the way Khandoud swiftly climbed a nearby pile of stones to try to identify it. It was easy to forget that we had now crossed over into enemy territory. 'Probably Moroccan,' he said, 'staying up high so that it can't be attacked by Polisario.' The tiny plane droned on across the sky, remote in its own element. Khandoud called me over to look out across the desert towards Smara, a pre-colonial city held dear by the Saharawi. Built in 1889, close to the River Saquia al Hambra, twelve wells were sunk and numerous palm groves planted during its creation. It was on a camel route, and partly because of that it grew to be a splendid centre not only for commerce but also for Islamic studies. Its architect was Ma es Aininn, a powerful sheik and respected Koranic scholar as well as a member of one of the main Saharawi tribes. In 1913, however, Smara was ransacked by French troops, assisted by a rival tribe out on one of their *ghazzis*, or traditional desert raids. The dome of the sheik's council hall, together with his library, was destroyed. It was a terrible loss.

We gazed across the sands, looking towards the mountains and beyond to El Ayoun, the capital of Western Sahara and Khandoud's birthplace. When the war started, all his family had fled. His sister had been imprisoned seven years ago and was now presumed dead. 'Did you come out into the desert much, before the war?' I asked him. 'Yes. A lot. To stay with friends. There were towns here, you know, but they were destroyed by the bombs.' We sat up on the pile of stones, contemplating the land spread out before us, each seeing something different. Khandoud was looking towards home, his exuberance and love of life tempered by the inner fire of patriotism. There was the cook, always smiling but not too involved, busy about Martha's business and today wearing a torn tee-shirt with the Polisario flag on it. There was Shadeed with his serious manner and academic approach to the war. And there was the driver, on his own as usual, cutting a careful pattern on to his twig toothbrush with his penknife. Then there was me, in a *shesh*, looking out on an alien land for which these men were prepared to die. I could think of nothing I would be prepared, ideologically, to die for. I could, I suppose, have been killed by a stray bullet in South Lebanon or found myself in the wrong place at the wrong time in the West Bank. I could even have had my neck broken while being dragged about by an overzealous policeman at Greenham Common but these would all have been 'accidents', the result of bad luck even and not the result of systematically exposing myself to danger because of my ideals. It is men who tend to be the victims of that sort of thinking, not women.

Someone like Khandoud, for whom Bobby Sands was a hero, would find it hard to understand why I would not be prepared to die for my country. But then, machismo and nationalism are often to be found in bed together.

Khandoud wanted to know how I had got to Tindouf.

'Cycled down through France and then got a boat to Algiers and then a plane.'

'You must be strong,' he said and thoughtfully leaned across and felt the muscles in my thigh which, fearful of being thought weak, I surreptitiously tried to flex.

'The worst worry was coming into Algiers. They wanted to know the registration number of the bike but in Ireland they don't have registration numbers.'

'What did you do?'

'Wrote down my home phone number.'

'Well, you don't have to worry about any of that here.'

'No, I have my ticket back already sorted out. Everything is in order.'

'You've already bought your ticket home?'

'I have, yes.'

'It's paid for?' His voice was accusing.

'Yes, why?'

'How can you be certain you'll go back? You could get killed out here in the desert.'

I realized then we were discussing not my travel arrangements but my taking of things for granted, my flying in the face of Allah's will.

'Of course,' I added hastily and untruthfully, 'not everything is booked. If I leave here I will go to Algiers and then to Marseilles. *Insha' Allah*.' Then I made a further mistake.

'Are you afraid, if you have to go to the wall?' asked Khandoud.

The last time I'd been asked that question, I'd said no. This time, I decided to be truthful.

'Yes. I am.'

He seemed puzzled and looked to Shadeed for linguistic assistance. I hadn't, it seemed, understood the question and he rephrased it.

'If you go to the wall with Polisario, will you be afraid?'

This time, hidden in the question was the clue to the appropriate answer.

'As long as I am looked after by Polisario,' I said, 'then of course I am not afraid.'

And Khandoud's face relaxed into a happy smile of relief.

We sat up on the pile of stones for longer than we should have done. Shadeed climbed up to join us with some books he had brought with him, history books, but Khandoud waved them away. His place of study, he said, was the desert. 'Here, we learn about hope and the revolution.' I left them arguing and climbed down to sit on my own in the shade of the thorn tree. The sky was blue but streaked with flimsy white clouds, thin as muslin. On the ground beside me, I noticed a slight movement: a spider was scurrying across the sand, glittering in the sun like a tiny piece of silver filigree. Occasionally, there floated past on the air tiny puffs of white fluff covered with yellow pollen dust. These were seeds, carried on the wind, destined to waft along until their minute barbs hooked on to something and they settled, to produce a tiny leaf or flower. With them, though it may have been my imagination, came a fragrance that I had not enjoyed since I'd been travelling in the desert.

We spent so long sitting and chatting that the driver, determined to get us to our next destination without losing time, pointed the Land Rover at the horizon and drove for five hours, stopping only once. It was uncanny, the way he negotiated the blank surface of the desert, heading in one direction for hours at a time before suddenly swinging in another direction without any visible signs to help him.

'How on earth does he do it?' I asked Shadeed. 'There are no road signs and he doesn't have a compass. Nothing. If it were at night I could understand. Then he could navigate by the stars, but by day across an endless vista of unchanging sand?' Shadeed smiled gently: 'There are stars in the sand as well, you know.' And, of course, he was right. It was simply that I was unfamiliar with the language of the desert. The stony ciphers were illegible, the great sweeps of sand as mysterious as the brushstrokes of an oriental artist. Everything spoke to me here but to no avail for I was unable to read. During our one stop, I stood beside the cook as he unpacked the tea tin and saw a bullet lying at the bottom of it. Then, just as we were packing up again, Khandoud and the cook began prancing about on the sand, whooping and driving the butt of their rifles into the ground: they had found a snake. Once it was dead, Khandoud picked up its curving body on the barrel of his rifle and hurled the bloody mess out across the sand. Death was never very far away. Just before darkness fell, as the Land Rover rattled along at high speed, we noticed a couple of figures against the darkening skyline. As they made their slow way along, following some invisible route, it became clear that our roads would cross. Here, in this huge unin-habited place, with a thousand paths leading to a million destinations, that we should cross paths with a couple of nomads! 'A coincidence?' I said to Shadeed but he shook his head. '*Le. Allah.*' Allah had a role to play in everything.

The couple were a man and wife, both young, making their way from one place to another – I never found out where – each with a camel and accompanied by a donkey, a couple of goats and a thin dog with brown and white markings. These Kabyle dogs are common around here and are used to guard the tents. The two camels were loaded high with blankets, pots and large water drums. The couple wore sombre clothes, the woman in a brown jumper and a long skirt of the same colour and with a black scarf wrapped round her head and face. The man was dressed in a skinny 1970s type shirt and flares. They reminded me of the old travelling tinkers – in the days when the word denoted their trade as repairers of tin kettles and pots – making their way about the roads of Ireland, carrying with them their few possessions, the sky above them their roof, the hard earth their bed. The woman would have continued on her way had Khandoud not called out to them to ask, on my behalf, if I might take a photograph of them. They both stood for a moment and then the woman moved off with the animals. But when the man dallied behind, ready to exchange a few words – for when had they last spoken to anyone, I wondered – the woman called to him sharply and he left us.

When we set up camp Khandoud and the others lolled by the fire but, in the manner of passengers in a transit lounge, looking up from time to time, listening, turning back to the conversation again but with one eye on the clock, which in this case was the moon. When it started to go down, we would begin our night march across the desert to the wall. Over to the west, mortars flashed across the night sky, their booms echoing among the dunes. 'Moroccans and Polisario,' said Khandoud carelessly, 'talking to each other.' The front was only a kilometre away. Three hours later, we set out, first in a convoy of jeeps and finally on foot, only five of us now, in single file. There was a new man in charge, Abdelahi, a troop commander wearing a white scarf knotted at his neck. 'You remember what I told you,' he whispered into my ear and I nodded: 'Yes. No talking, no noise, do exactly what Khandoud does.' He patted my arm.

We set off as if walking into an ocean, plunging deeper and deeper into the dark night. At first, we walked on sand, through tufts of grass that tugged at my legs and ensnared me. Then the surface changed to stones, sharp little stones that skittered away from my feet, their clatter ringing out like alarm bells. Khandoud was directly in front of me. Ahead of him marching at a brisk pace were two young soldiers, neither more than twenty. Behind me, Abdelahi. Everyone except myself had a rifle over their shoulders. We were to walk as far as the wall, then along it and possibly over it, if there were no Moroccans about.

Stars flooded across the sky but the light of the moon was starting to fade. As it moved down towards the horizon its sharp edge, previously the colour of cold steel, turned a buttery yellow. And as it lost its divinity, so the stars surged into prominence, shining like chips of crystal. Why had I not noticed all this last night, or the night before? Why had I not cherished the still beauty of it when I was safe and at peace? I looked up at the sky laid out like a lost love affair. Was that the Pole Star? And the remnants of the Plough, the first constellation I had been taught to recognize? And Sirius, where was that?

We had been walking now for an hour – or was it two? There was no way of measuring time or distance in this world without boundaries. An unsafe world. I remembered my babies, each one, flinging out spindly arms in sudden panic at finding themselves outside the womb, lost in space. And the wise midwife who showed me how to fold the child's hands across its tiny chest and hold them there, steady, in memory of those nine safe months, now lost for ever. If I threw out my arms now, what would there be? The blinding darkness of the limitless desert. I fixed my eyes on Khandoud's head and then, suddenly, it wasn't there any more. A tap on my shoulder and I turned without lessening speed. Abdelahi pointed out to the left where a dark shape loomed – the wall – and then he pushed my shoulders forwards until I, too, was walking crouched down like a hunchback to get below the beam of the electronic eye. Stealthy as footpads, we marched on. The moon had gone now and for the first time I noticed that the starshine seemed to throw a faint sprinkling of light on to the sand.

Suddenly, without warning, Khandoud threw himself on the ground and I thudded down beside him, catching as I fell a glimpse of a white light in the sky, coming at us from the direction of the wall. Beneath me, I felt a loud thumping against my chest as if it were a heart buried deep in the desert that was beating and not my own. Without moving my head, I opened my left eye and saw that the light had grown brighter – a white light, a flare – illuminating the desert. We lay, shrinking away from its glare. I closed my eye again, my mouth dry. There was no sound, no movement, only the silent light, penetrating my closed eyelids. This wasn't where I wanted to be. In a pub, perhaps, or a shop or with my children but not here in an alien place, in the middle of this forgotten desert war. I saw my white legs mangled, turning red as blood soaked into the sand.

If they shoot, the bullets will catch my outstretched legs. They'll hit me first, before Khandoud. My body is shielding his. But why? He's the soldier, not me. I have no real concern for the Saharawi and Polisario and all their crazy talk of unity and freedom and the motherland. If I get through this one, next time I hit the ground, it will be to the other side of Khandoud. This is his war, not mine. The cock had crowed for a second time.

Khandoud got to his feet and started marching again.

Ahead of us, the wall rose up and suddenly we were there. As long as we stayed huddled together, tucked into its base, we were safe. Abdelahi took my arm: 'If you listen, you'll hear the Moroccans talking on the other side of the wall . . . Shh, listen! They're talking about changing the guard.' I listened and heard the wind drumming through the night and my answering heartbeats. 'Can you hear them?' asked Abdelahi. 'Yes,' I lied. We scrambled along the lee of the sandy wall and started to climb up its steep side, at an angle, like a boat tacking into the wind. Then we were up and slithering down the other side for at this point there was a double fortification. Abdelahi signalled me to follow him, crablike, up the second mound. A stone ricocheted away and he turned back sharply, signing me to go carefully. Then on and up, so fast that I feared I would lose him in the dark and he, perhaps thinking the same, reached back and took hold of my hand, squeezing it twice: OK? At the top, another fall of stones and he squeezed my hand again, a rapid squeeze, hard and urgent: Shush!

Up on the rampart, we came to a small circular construction of stones, a lookout post. I peered down into it and saw the ghost of a Moroccan soldier crouched there, his presence more real than the voices of his comrades I had failed to hear. He sat, silent and still, looking out across the dismal sand, a lost man guarding a land that was barren and devoid of human life. I thought of all the men living out their lives, like this, on foreign soil – the Roman soldier on Hadrian's Wall, the young squaddie standing on a bleak border road in Northern Ireland, rain dripping from his cap, a city boy with the terrible smell of cow dung in his nostrils. Then I was on my face again, head pressed into the sand, a rock grinding against my ribs. For a second time that night, the sky was lit up. Abdelahi squeezed my hand twice: OK? And lifting my *shesh*, whispered into my ear: 'The bombardment has started again. They'll go on all night. Look!' The darkness of the sky was ripped apart as a mortar sliced through it. Then the wound closed and there was nothing – until the next mortar and the next. Then they came, low and deadly, tearing across the sky. From somewhere behind, tracer bullets dotted the blackness and I burrowed down into the sand.

Another squeeze: Come! And we were slithering back down the sand and over the top again and down the other side. Then two squeezes: Wait there! And Abdelahi was gone, crawling across the sand to the two young soldiers who were standing guard. 'Look,' Abdelahi whispered, back again and smiling, 'up there. Orion's Belt.' High over us, the stars glittered, scattered across the sky like seed broadcast by a careless hand. And beside Orion's Belt, shone the most perfect circle of stars I had ever seen, each one clear as a drop of water. Walking back, with Khandoud in front of me again, I knew then that this was his world, not mine. That his world was one signposted by the stars and paced by the moon. That his family was the Saharawi and that for each one of them he could find, at the moment he needed to, the heroic strength to die:

> That something in you, like a bird,
> Knowing no cage's bars,
> Courage supreme – an instant dream
> Of a mind beneath the stars . . .

For me, there were no heroes, no driving compulsion to emulate heroic deaths. There could never be a place for me here for I would seduce all men, every son and every husband, tempting them away from a brotherhood that gave them their masculinity in return for the promise of their blood. For when soldiers pay the blood debt, it is the blood of their mothers that they spill upon the ground.

We marched back across the desert, Abdelahi going up front every so often and bending low so that he could look back and check the silhouette of his troop against the sky, counting to make sure we were all there. The two young soldiers marched on bravely, straying sometimes so that he had to call them quietly – Zit! Zit! – and point to the stars, edging them back on course again. They were his pupils, his young camels, and he checked them as gently as the nomads had their herd. There are some who say that the whole wall exercise is a farce, that there are no Moroccan soldiers on that part of it. That the nightly bombardment is a mock-up. That the long drive through the desert is merely a circular route, coming back to where it started. That the journey through the desert is a public relations exercise to manipulate the media and sympathetic politicians. 'Is that true?' I'd asked Shadeed and he'd smiled: 'That's something you have to decide.' 'No it's definitely not true,' Barbara Harrell-Bond once told me. 'I took a compass and map with me to make sure we didn't go round in circles.'

When I woke next morning from my sleep on the jagged stones of the desert, Abdelahi was waiting. He had a speech to make. He explained that Polisario had sent out a patrol earlier in the evening to draw the fire of the Moroccans and make them withdraw from the observation post we had gone to see. He said that soldiers had also been sent out to clear our path of enemy mines. Then he thanked me for coming: 'You are one of us now,' he said and put his arm round me, the embrace of the desert. 'You were very brave,' said Khandoud, thumping me on the back. He, whose death I had earlier wished. 'For your wife,' I said and gave him the contents of my pocket: a needle, a spool of thread, a box of matches and a packet of diarrhoea tablets. He smiled politely. My token gift had broken the bond between us. Better that it had not been given.

Three days later, flying back to Algiers, I looked down on the smouldering desert. The throbbing plane was taking me back to another world and, as always, I would have difficulty working out which was the real one. This time, the feeling was even more intense for I was a pilgrim returning from the Saharawi land of dreams.

CHAPTER EIGHT

Fathoming the Scraws

I felt displaced after being in the Sahara, belonging nowhere. The bike journey down through France had taken a month. Each night, I'd crawled into my tiny, coffin-like tent and called it home. I'd been adopted off the street by an Algerian family, welcomed and looked after by them until I could get down to the desert. Once there, I became the property of Polisario, taken to wherever they decided, when they decided. I had no responsibilities. The outward journey through France, across the Mediterranean and on to the desert had been gradual but the return was swift. Travelling on an overnight TGV, I covered in one night the distance I had taken a whole month to do on the bike. Back in Ireland, I didn't know what to do with myself. My £1000 W. H. Davis bike with its hand-built frame, its narrow, elongated 'lady's saddle', its tyres with the raised metal tread running along their centre making punctures virtually impossible, was wrong for the bumpy, potholed streets of

Dublin. In any case, it was stolen almost as soon as I returned. To ease the loss, I decided to go up to Donegal.

Winter in Donegal was a season of constant activity: squalls, gusting showers, gales and downpours. The distant mountains faded behind a net of muslin rain backlit by watery sunshine. Sometimes, for days on end, they were swallowed up altogether by ravenous clouds. Run-off water rushed down through drains and ditches, foaming impatiently when its exit was blocked by leaves and twigs. Rivers tumbled across rocks, tannin turning the water to gleaming copper. Ditches shone with wetness, the weeds bent double from the weight of droplets on them. The wind roared through the trees and the roof creaked. Hailstones hurtled down the chimney, exploding on to the hearthstone like tiny, demented demons. The turf fire glowed, needing only one poke to send the flames singing up the chimney.

Outside, on cold clear nights, stars littered the sky and the smoke hung silver in the still air, like an angel reluctant to leave its charge. Occasionally, there was a hoar frost when a thousand glinting ice shards, each one separate and perfect, formed an inch-thick layer on the branches of the trees and the silent cattle exhaled clouds of warm breath across the fields. From my kitchen window I watched the Atlantic rain clouds gathering over the mountains opposite. When first the mountain top and then the whole mountain itself became shrouded by a cloud, I knew I had ten minutes to get to the turf pile and fill the basket or gather the clothes in off the line before the rain hit the little house. The squalls came intermittently but the ten-minute cloud interval was constant.

There is always a danger with a thatched roof that a high

wind might get under it and lift it right off. At the onset of winter, therefore, the straw ropes holding it down had to be tightened and wound securely round a corresponding stone to anchor them. When Atlantic winds gusted round Corkerbeg the house felt sometimes like a tent and sometimes like a small boat anchored in a wind-tossed sea. It was a good place to ride out a storm. The weather reminded me of desert living. In one of the tent cities, I'd noticed one day that everyone was hurrying out to hammer down tent pegs and pull tight the guy ropes: a sandstorm was on the way. It blew for two days. Fine grains of sand, fluid as water, seeped in through the cracks of the wooden shutters and leaked under the doorway. They got between my teeth and under my finger nails. When Shadeed opened the door to come in, his turban unwound in panic and a cloud of red dust spread across the surface of the table. He had to put his shoulder to the door to close it again.

Corkerbeg, in the Barony of Bannagh, in the county of Donegal, was once a townland of more than ten houses. By the time I found it, in 1975, only two were still occupied.

Once a trim three-roomed cabin, the house I bought had become, like the others around it, a derelict ruin not even fit to keep cattle in. The thatched roof had fallen in and with it the tangle of wire that held the thatch in place. Enmeshed in the wire itself were the seven put-puts the owner had dumped when they ceased to negotiate the lane. Weeds grew tall on top of all this, reaching up to where the roof should have been. Only three walls remained standing. My intention had been to rebuild the house, installing some modern conveniences, such as electricity and a shower, while leaving the spirit of the house as intact as possible. The big job would be the roof. 'Put a good slate roof on that house,' I was advised in the pub in Dunkineely, 'or better still, pull the whole thing down and build yourself a bungalow.' I put up with the jokes, the shaking of heads, the pitying looks of the locals and went about getting the thatch done. No one around had ever thatched a roof from scratch, though that didn't prevent them all from giving advice on what to do. The first thing, it seemed, was to get the scraws up.

The scraws – Ian calculated we needed seventy in all – were strips of grass-topped earth, about an inch thick, eighteen inches wide and cut long enough so that they would reach from the eaves on one side, over the roof and down to the eaves on the other side. They had to be cut from ground that had no rushes growing in it otherwise, when the rushes withered and fell out, they would leave a large, gaping hole. Once the seventy scraws were cut, they had to be rolled up like enormous swiss rolls and put in a corner of the field to dry out for a couple of months, briars and branches thrown over them to stop the cattle getting at them. The next stage was to put each one in a wheelbarrow and trundle it down from the field to the house. There, we inserted a good strong stick through the middle of the swiss roll, placed two ladders up against the wall of the house and, with each of us holding one end of the stick, hefted the scraw up, one step at a time, for they were enormously heavy. It all came down to balance. Should the scraw suddenly unravel as they frequently did and tumble back to the ground, we would both be left up our respective ladders holding an empty stick. When that happened, there was nothing to do except climb down the ladder, roll up the scraw again and repeat the exercise. The most difficult part of all this entailed unrolling the scraw *up* the sloping roof until it reached the apex, where, with luck and a bit of gravity, it would tip over and roll down the other side of its own accord.

There was a lot of discussion in the pub as to whether the scraws should be put on the roof grass side upwards or downwards. Drinks were bought, consumed and bought again while the argument racketed along the bar counter. Whichever we chose – up or down – we would offend someone, confirming each camp in their opinion that we didn't know what we were doing. We chose upwards. Thus, for one summer, we had a grass-roofed house from which one or two purple irises proudly grew. It was a miraculous sight. Inside, however, was another matter. For a year after the scraws had been in place, worms were continually dropping down from the roof into our cups of coffee. *Live* worms. The following spring, it was the thatcher's turn to put down a layer of rushes and then, on top of that, the main thatching of straw.

Nature is not kind to Donegal. Its land is rocky and inhospitable and it gets more rain than any other county in Ireland, apart perhaps from Kerry. Thatching is not done in the Norfolk style where only the ends of the straw are exposed to the weather. In Donegal, the thatchers lay out their bundles of straw on the roof so that the whole length of straw gets the full blast of the wind and the rain. You used less straw that way but it had to be redone on a regular basis. The straw, some of it rye, had to be specially grown to a certain height, cut by hand and then flailed to get the ears off it. It was the poor man's way of doing things – and my way. Ian and I were poor but happy as we worked on the house, levering huge dense stones into place in the outside walls, creosoting the thousands of laths on which the scraws would be laid, scouring the countryside for lintels big enough to support the large, open fireplace.

In Killybegs, I went into the Fishermen's Co-op to get some rope to tie the thatch down. 'How many fathoms?' the woman asked and I was stumped. How long was a fathom? 'It's the height of a tall man,' she explained.

Ian reinstated the half-loft, which was a feature of Donegal houses whereby a platform was built in the main room, reaching halfway across. This loft space was used for extra beds or storage and was reached by climbing up a ladder. As living conditions improved, the loft would be closed in, a door inserted and proper stairs built.

Sleeping in a tent during those summers while the work was in progress, we used candles to read by, got our water from the well in the top field and spent a lot of time in the pub. They were hot dry summers, too hot with the earth splitting open and the dry grass crackling like electricity under our feet. Freya and Deirdre went down to the river to wash their hair before going out to dances in Glenties and Ardara that lasted until dawn. Russell built bonfires, climbed up on the roof with us and helped the boys chase the girls.

Once, when a couple was making nooky in the back seat of someone's car, the posse thought it would be fun to tie up the car, securing all four wheels to nearby trees with ropes – then standing back to watch the fun as the driver attempted to take off. As it wasn't my car, I thought it was fun too.

Notes from a Donegal diary

Micheal: 'There's a beach beyond Teelin and when the moon is full, if you go along during the day, very quietly, you'll see bubbles in the sand and if you're very quick you put your hand down into the sand, quietly or the two sides will close and cut your hand sharp as a razor. You take the razor fish and put them live into boiling water with a bit of salt and they're very good.'

Crabs' toes: 'Put them in the fire and they sing and all the juice runs out and you give them a tap with a hammer and then use a spoon to get out the meat.'

May: 'When there's a death, no one goes to work on the day of the funeral who lives within sight of the dead person's house.'

A neighbour's grandmother made some shirts when she was a young girl. She made six, one for her father and one for each of her five brothers. Her father grew flax, which when cut had to be steeped before being made into linen. The girl cut out the shirts and stitched them all by hand. They were bleached and put out to dry on the bushes. Next morning they were gone, stolen. The father never grew flax again.

June 1992: An electric storm. The turf cutters said the lightning ploughed a furrow through the bog. It put out all the bulbs in a neighbour's house and blew the phone off the wall.

1993: Biked from Donegal town to Dunkineely. Had a toasted cheese sandwich at the pub and then a magical ride out to Corkerbeg, the last rays of the sun lighting up the mountains, the moon rising over the hill and the mist swirling in the valley. The air smells of turf smoke, dung and decomposing blackberries – a sweet Donegal combination.

Gossip 1: 'That man's so randy, he'd fuck a bumble bee in a roll of barbed wire.'

Gossip 2: A woman, thinking Marie was a Protestant, confided in her, 'I'm a bit worried. My daughter is engaged to a Catholic.'
Marie clucked sympathetically, 'Sure, my daughter is as well.'
'*Is* she?' asked the woman. 'Ah well. They're not all bad.'
'No,' said Marie, 'some of them are all right.'

1996: Got off the bus in Dunkineely. A blustery evening but warm. Or rather, not cold. The sun was brilliant, just starting to set. I couldn't take my eyes off it all the time my neighbour was talking. Eventually he noticed what I was looking at. 'That's the sun,' he said, and nodded in a satisfied way as if he, personally, was responsible for the glorious light show.

1997: Unbelievably, there was an Orange parade in Dunkineely, 'with a massive police presence' someone reported wryly. Then, a week later, a kerbstone was painted green, white and orange. Three teenagers were taken to Donegal and questioned. The green paint was a bit of a giveaway. It was the same colour as the newly painted front door of one of the boys' grandmother.

The father of one of the boys had, apparently, been a bit of a lad too and when he was ten had got in to the local Protestant church and folded away – very respectfully, my informant told me – the Union Jack flag, replacing it with a pair of knickers. He was charged with breaking and entering, it being too undignified to mention the knickers.

CHAPTER NINE

The Pianist and the Poet

1981: The twin red stars shone above the Kremlin and the illuminated Red Flag streamed in the night wind. The words *perestroika* and *glasnost* were not yet common currency. It was an offence to bring a Bible into the country and to take caviar out of it without an official stamp. Everyone wanted to change money. But no one went homeless. People had warm winter coats and strong boots. The Metro was cheap, rents low and phone bills lower. Though the where-abouts of any phone directory was still a well-guarded secret, there were plenty of phone boxes. For the ordinary people, the staple diet was potatoes, cabbage, chicken and porridge. The Soviet middle class – which didn't exist – ate meat. Capitalism was still no more than a dream, though, in a few years, it would become Russia's nightmare. I'd bought two Aeroflot tickets as a twentieth wedding anniversary present for Ian and myself. He had always harboured a wish to stand at Lenin's tomb and there read a poem by his mentor, Hugh MacDiarmid, the Lallans poet who had been an ardent supporter of the ideals of Soviet communism. But the surprise tickets were a double-edged sword: giving someone their heart's desire also takes the dream away from them.

We arrived on 27 December to find the Metro was full of Muscovites with Christmas trees under their arms: they might not have been able to celebrate Christmas but they were certainly going to have some fun seeing in the New Year. Next day, we walked in Red Square, marvelled at the length of the queue for Lenin's tomb and at midnight returned so that Ian could read his poem. We took the overnight train to Leningrad, sharing our compartment and our bottle of duty-free with the car attendant who, when he realized a party was about to start, disappeared to return with a jar of blackcurrant jam which we ate in between drinking the whiskey. The more I drank, the better my Russian became. The attendant and I chatted busily, comparing the size of our families, how much we earned, the relative pleasures of vodka and whiskey. The English and the Irish. As the heavy train lumbered northwards, we stared out into the wall of darkness, hoping to see wolves. The level in the Jameson bottle dropped alarmingly. The attendant started to sing and Ian, donning the railway guard's cap, went up and down the corridor checking tickets. We arrived in Leningrad early next morning and looked for the attendent to say goodbye but his carriage door was closed, the blinds drawn.

The guide on the Intourist bus was full of numbers: this spire is so high, that bridge is so long, so many tonnes of marble were used to decorate that building, x many rooms in this hotel. Bored, I looked out of the window at the city which was still being so lovingly restored. And remembered the two-year siege when people had tried to stay warm by burning their furniture. Hungry, they tore wallpaper off the walls to lick, getting some nourishment from the fish-based paste. The newspapers still carried requests for information about people who had disappeared during the siege. But it was a city far more cheerful than Moscow. People stopped to talk to us, asking where we were from, what life was like elsewhere. In Moscow when I stopped someone to ask the way, they had hurried off without answering, fearful of being seen talking to a foreigner.

On New Year's Eve, we left the party organized for visiting tourists and went out into the snow where, gathered round a huge, brightly lit Christmas tree, Leningradians were dancing – and falling down a lot – to music coming from a portable radio someone had brought along to the party. We joined in the falling down but when invited to continue partying in someone's apartment, declined. It might just have led to trouble, not for us but for our would-be hosts.

It was a bitterly cold February day, when, eight years later, in 1989, I revisited Russia. The Moscow pavements were littered with rocklike humps of grey snow. At one street junction, the path was barred by a mound of ice-covered snow running along the edge of the footpath where the road sweepers had swept it up and then abandoned it to the pedestrians. The only way was up and over. I was on my way to visit the grave of John Field, the Irish-born composer buried in Nemetski Kladbische, the German cemetery. When the first Germans came to Russia, unable to speak the language, the Russians called them the speechless ones – *nemetski*. Now, the word means simply German.

The Nemetski Kladbische was shrouded in snow, the impacted ice on the footpaths tobacco-yellow as an old man's moustache. The woman path-sweeper, of whom I asked directions, grabbed my arm and together we set off on our perilous way around the huge cemetery. Somewhere in the middle of it, we came to the grave and letting go of my helper's arm, I picked my way across the snow on the adjoining grave to read the inscription on Field's:

John Field, born in Ireland, dead in Moscow.

Somehow, the word dead made his end seem even more final. I thanked the woman and gave her the half bottle of Jameson I had been carrying around with me. I had brought it originally for Conor O'Clery, *The Irish Times*'s Moscow correspondent, but he pointed out that his apartment was awash with whiskey since everyone who dropped in from Ireland brought him a bottle, certain there was a drought in Moscow. 'Give it to some Russian,' he said. 'They'll really appreciate it.' So I gave it to the surprised path-sweeper and hoped that, like Field, she enjoyed the odd drink.

The next year, I was in Moscow again. Olga, at the language school, talked to us about Pushkin, opening the book at the page which showed his picture. 'He was of Ethiopian origin,' she said and, as she talked, slowly caressed his dark curls with her long slender fingers. Then she stopped talking and simply looked at him. My previous visits to Russia had been in winter. This time, I was seeing

Moscow at its autumnal best. The trees – and the city has thousands of them – looked light and golden as they started to turn and everywhere leaves fell like rain: lime leaves and rowans, birch and maple.

In the park, a mother rocked a Christmas present in her arms. It was her sleeping baby, swaddled tightly and then tied up with three large, pink nylon bows. Two little girls with her had gathered up a huge pile of leaves and were making a comfortable bed out of them to lie on when a dog came along and pissed on it. The children stood and stared in silent horror. I was sitting on a bench nearby, reading a book of Akhmatova's poetry, when three leaves drifted down and settled on the page. I closed the book, not knowing that in two years' time, when I reopened it, they would waft to the floor, light as memories.

I had come to Moscow to do a Russian language course in preparation for a journey to Georgia, one of the Soviet republics, unaware that it would have been much better for me to learn Georgian since Russian, the language of the colonizer, was hated and despised in the southern republic. Olga was teaching us Russian in a co-operative college in Mytishcha, a town seventeen kilometres outside Moscow. Once a small village – you could see the old dachas through the birch trees – it was now a dreary place, full of broken pavements, tower blocks of flats and shops selling cheap plastic goods. In fact, just like any working-class ghetto built on the edge of any European city, but with one great difference: each day a train on the Trans-Siberian Railway thundered through, taking food and fuel to the distant peoples of Russia's Far East.

Olga was tall, with big bones, a large chest and blonde

hair. She usually wore a sensible skirt and a freshly ironed blouse with a pretty embroidered collar. She had a precise way of purposefully closing her mouth to finish a smile and though the smile was completed, it still remained on her face like a shadow. The finishing of the smile indicated the next stage of the proceedings, though we didn't always know what that was. Yesterday, she finished the business of smiling and then invited us to put questions to her, in Russian, of course. Someone asked her if she was married and she said no. Then she paused, smiled, finished smiling and said: 'But I have a friend', with that special intonation that indicates the friend is more than a friend. *Droog* – it's a word you have to be careful with.

We had classes in the mornings but the afternoons were free and so I spent my month's stay visiting all the places in Moscow associated with Pushkin. Yesterday was warm and sunny and I went to Pushkin Square, bought three carnations and laid them at the bottom of the poet's statue where they blended in with the rainbow of flowers already there. Russians put flowers everywhere but especially in places that have anything to do with Pushkin. I passed a house where he had lived, very briefly, and there was a bunch of flowers laid on the window ledge. However, for Alla, I took, not flowers, but soap and talcum powder, which were what she had asked me to bring from Ireland. Things are in very short supply and people here always take a string bag with them when they go out, just on the off chance they'll see something on sale somewhere. This bag is called an *avoska*: a just-in-case bag. The rule is, if you spot a queue, get into it, just in case. Alla taught literature at the Pushkin Institute. Hers was the first Muscovite apartment I had been in and it left me gobsmacked. Some of the furniture was of Karelian birch, a strange, light-coloured wood, so highly polished that it looked like plastic. It was very expensive and the furniture in her dining room, dark, heavy mahogany, was thought not to be half as good as the birch.

Alla was living in limbo. Her husband had been having an affair with a woman and was dithering between wife and lover. Alla gave him an ultimatum: go or stay. If he went, she would make her own arrangements. 'After all,' she told me, 'I wasn't in the garbage can when he found me.' Before he had a chance to decide, however, he was struck down with a brain tumour. So, since he was about to die, he told Alla she should allow the other woman to visit him at home. She agreed to this but on the second visit, she found the dying man locked in a sizzling embrace with his new main squeeze. This was too much for Alla. 'I will take part in a tragedy, yes,' she told them, 'but not in a farce. And certainly not a *vulgar* farce.' Now he was waiting for the operation. If he recovered, she would divorce him. And if not? She shrugged.

We had meat for lunch, which was a rarity procured specially in my honour and I toyed with it not wishing to reveal that I was vegetarian. I wondered how she got it. She won't queue, she told me, and she won't use public transport. Halfway through lunch, her cleaning woman arrived. Middle-class Moscow did exist after all. Lunch was possible today because Alla's students were all away helping with the potato harvest. In the old days, helping with the harvest was a patriotic duty. Nowadays, you get paid for doing it but the students still hate it. I told Alla about my intention to visit all the Pushkin sites and she said I must go to the house in the Arbat, so I moved it to the top of my list. On the way home, I queued for forty-five minutes for a kilo of grapes. I didn't really want them but I was curious to see how long you had to queue for. Seasoned old women have it sorted: they stand their husbands in the queue while they go off to do their other shopping. Some people pay surrogates to queue for them.

Misha, a friend of a friend, invited me to supper with his family. The old grandmother, who was ninety-seven, wore two sets of spectacles. The steel ones, for reading, she slipped under the main ones when needed. Misha was a musician with an interest, he told me, in 'middle-aged music'.

He was reading Jilly Cooper's *Class* but was disappointed to find that she was not 'seriously funny' about her own class. Remembering my assessment of Alla as being middle class, and living in an English village in which there were about twenty layers of class, I was interested to learn if Misha agreed with me. He did and he didn't. The intelligentsia, he said, are the middle class but academics are a higher class. Class is always a difficult one for social migrants. My paternal grandfather was a constable in the Royal Irish Constabulary and then worked as a nightwatchman for a Dublin brewery. My maternal grandfather was an inspector in the Dublin Metropolitan Police, though his employment records show him as, originally, a labourer. My father went to his Kerry school barefoot, became a dispatch rider with the Royal Dublin Fusiliers during the 1914–18 war and later became a civil servant. 'Don't say Daddy has gone to work,' my mother reproved me. 'Say he's gone to the office.' With a maid who changed into a black frock, little white apron and a lace cap to serve tea, a holiday cottage we could spend the summers in and a head of family who had become a *senior* civil servant, we had progressed from working class to Dublin bourgeoisie, clearly members of the fur coat and no knickers brigade. Ian, on the other hand, came from a long line of public school men and had one or two titles in the family. I had definitely married up.

There was talk around Misha's supper table of the current economic climate. Everyone knew someone whose wages hadn't been paid for months and the joke going round was of the worker who says to the company: 'OK, you pretend to pay me and I'll pretend to work.' Coming back on the *electrichka* train, the woman opposite me was knitting with small precise movements. She had done four or five inches of rib, perhaps for a sweater. Beside her, deep in his book, sat her husband, or perhaps her *droog*. The ball of wool was concealed somewhere in a bag on his lap and fed out between the thumb and forefinger with which he held his book. When the woman needed more, she pulled sharply while he, oblivious, continued to read. Once, she pulled a little too sharply and he looked up and smiled at her. The demanding tug, followed by the wool sliding through his fingers, was a sensuous little love dance performed in public, though perhaps they didn't realize that.

At Mytischa, I stepped out into a damp drizzle. The wooden platform was gleaming with wet leaves and I picked my way between puddles black as treacle. A number of people had already got off and in the distance, in the centre track, a powerful beam shone through the mist: a train was making its slow way towards us. As it drew nearer, the beam silhouetted the passengers, their shadows elongated behind them, plodding doggedly into its cold brilliance like people drawn into their own doom. And as the train rumbled through the station, I saw that the slanting segment of light was alive with a thousand drops of moisture being carried forward as if on a sheet of glass. Then the train passed and the people disappeared into blackness.

The autumn weather was becoming moist and slightly dank. I almost believed I could smell musty mushrooms in the air. Soon it would be time to fly home. It wasn't until my last week in Moscow that I managed to complete my series of Pushkin pilgrimages by visiting Number 53, the Arbat. At the Metro, there was a breakdown: the up escalator had suddenly stopped working. Everyone simply stood, waiting patiently for something to be done for them. Only one person chose to start walking up under his own steam. It's difficult enough for a person with legs to get up and down the escalators but how, I wondered, do those amputees, left with only a trunk, manage it? They congregate at the stations, scooting about on wooden platforms with castor wheels fixed to them, using their arms as paddles. Last night, one – under the influence – had keeled over completely, his trolley upended as he slept the night away, watched over by the other down-and-outs and misfortunates who had made the station concourse their home.

Earlier in the week, I had been to the Mkhat Theatre to see a production of Gorky's *The Lower Depths*, a play about down-and-outs. It was a standard production, efficient, faultless and disappointing. The first time I saw *The Lower Depths* was at the Abbey Theatre in Dublin. Going up in the lift, looking for the Russian director, Galina Volchek, I found myself in the company of the actor Cyril Cusack who had a major part in the play. 'Have you any idea where I might find Galina Volchek?' I asked. There was silence while his face went through his repertoire of expressions appropriate for occasions of this sort: puzzlement, frowning concentration, valiant attempt to understand, dawning realization. He had the floor, after all, with no competition and a captive audience, at least to the next level. Eventually, he gave me an accusatory smile: 'Ah,' he said, 'I think you mean *Madame* Volchek.' Galina, an old friend of mine, had her own theatre, the Contemporary Theatre, on Chistni Prudni Boulevard. I went to the first night of her production of *The Twisted Way* by Evgenie Ginsburg, who survived seventeen years in a gulag. It was a marvellously visual production, with sudden switches from humour to horror and an ending that wiped from your face any vestige of a smile that might have still been there. Galina herself was larger than life: emotional, tough, disdainful, warm and focused. She wore glittery tops and a long, white leather coat with huge shoulders which gave her the slightly sleazy look of an overblown mafioso. I sat in her office while she was being interviewed by a French journalist. During the interview, the phone rang – there were three on her desk – and while continuing to talk she picked up one after another till she located the ringing one. Then she replaced it on its cradle. Volchek had class.

Number 53, the Arbat had been Pushkin's home for only a short period but the Muscovites had made the most of it. The house was light and airy, decorated in French Empire style with magnificent parquet floors, but the furniture seemed to run out after six or seven rooms. One sported only the poet's desk with some pictures on it of himself and his wife, who, people repeatedly told me, was taller than he was. There was a whiff of crematorial decor to each room, heavy drapes, a reverent silence, framed pictures of the poet, which turned them into shrines. In the salon was a grand piano on which rested a picture of John Field, who died in 1837, the same year as Pushkin. I wondered if the two had known each other? The curator took me upstairs to where they had a list of all the people Pushkin had ever met. There was no mention of Field. His picture on the piano, she explained, was merely a prop. She didn't have a picture of the poet either: 'Our people are not interested in Pushkin,' she said sadly. 'Now, all they want to talk about is *perestroika*.'

CHAPTER TEN

Toast of the Stray Dog Café

The Russian calendar on my kitchen wall in Dublin, opened permanently at the month of August, shows a woman with film star legs clad in silky black stockings. She sits on a wooden stool, perhaps it's a piano stool, long slender fingers quiet on her lap. The skirt of her navy and cream dress falls light as silk over her angular knees. The dress is cut low, revealing her delicate collarbones and long, taut neck. A pale orange stole has slipped from her shoulders and hangs in folds around her arms. Her feet are clad in expensive high-heeled shoes trimmed with a band of fawn leather, their gloss reflects the grained wood of the footstool on which they rest. The right knee is crossed over the left so that the foot hangs above the stool, the instep curved, the toe just touching the stool. Her head is turned slightly revealing the curving profile of her face, the distinctive hooked nose, the fringed dark hair gathered at the neck. The woman is Anna Akhmatova, St Petersburg's beloved poet and Russia's greatest. The year is 1914, she is twenty-five and, together with her clever, daring husband, the poet Gumilev, she is the toast of the Stray Dog Café. A poem she wrote at this time gives a hint of what was happening in her life:

> I, quiet and gay, lived
> On a low island, which, like a raft
> Had stopped in the splendid Neva delta.
> Oh, mysterious winter days
> And beloved labour and faint tiredness
> And roses in the wash basin.

It is the final line which imparts the secret: she and the artist have become lovers.

I can't recall exactly when I came to Akhmatova's poetry, but once I started to read her I couldn't stop. Now, on my bookshelves, I have fifteen books either by her or about her. She is the only poet I have ever read whose meaning transcends the medium. That is, I seem to know what she is saying before I have figured out the sense of the words. She speaks directly from the mind to the heart, bypassing the cognitive process. After reading so much of her work, of course, there came the time when I realized I had to visit her grave. In 1988 a constellation had been named after her and the following year I bought tickets for myself and Freya and in January we flew to Leningrad. The painting on my kitchen wall shows a beautiful woman whose grey pensive eyes and enigmatic expression tell something of her inner sadness for, by then, Akhmatova was beginning to realize how solitary her four-year marriage to Gumilev had become. Immediately after their Paris honeymoon – they married in 1910 – Gumilev left for an African safari. He was gone six months. The following year, he was gone again. Loneliness and a certain sadness set in:

> Three things enchanted him:
> white peacocks, evensong,
> and faded maps of America.
> He couldn't stand bawling brats,
> or raspberry jam with his tea,
> or womanish hysteria.
> . . . And he was tied to me.

Four years later they divorced and Akhmatova married, inappropriately, a scientist. They divorced in 1921, the year in which Gumilev was shot by the Bolsheviks on suspicion of being a spy. The Bolsheviks saw Akhmatova as a threat, disliking her use of religious metaphors and the fact that she had taken it upon herself to speak on behalf of the suffering, silent majority:

> I am your voice, the heat of your breath.
> I am the reflection of your face.

It was Trotsky who commented sourly: 'Her god seems to be a very comfortable portable third person with good drawing-room manners, a friend of the family from time to time, fulfilling the role of doctor specializing in women's ailments . . .' An unofficial ban was put on her work and nothing of hers was published for eighteen years.

St Petersburg, built on great windy marshes, was conceived by Peter the Great. It would, he hoped, dominate the Baltic. Wooden piles were driven into the islands on one of which stands the Peter and Paul Fortress where both Gorky and Trotsky were imprisoned. When the Marquis de Custine visited Russia in 1835 he found it a grim place: 'Russia is like a pot of water boiling with the lid on and underneath the fire grows hotter and hotter. Sooner or later there will be an explosion.' It took two uprisings before the lid blew off, the final one Lenin's *coup d'état* of 1917. The post-revolutionary calendar sets the date of the coup as 7 November and any small boy born on that date was called Valodja, short for Vladimir, which was Lenin's name.

St Petersburg was, and still is, a city of writers. By the Moyka river is the house where Pushkin died following his fatal duel. The Tsar had the corpse taken away under cover of darkness so that by morning snow had covered the wheel tracks of the cortège and the crowd was unable to follow the poet to his last resting place. Further into the city, by the Fontanka river is Akhmatova's apartment where, in 1945, the crass Randolph Churchill, looking for Isaiah Berlin, had stood in the courtyard, looked up and yelled out his name, knowing Berlin was visiting the poet but not knowing which apartment to find him in. Berlin, thirty-six at the time and Third Secretary at the British Embassy in Moscow, had been browsing in a Leningrad bookshop and, coming across a book of Akhmatova's, had enquired about her. He was astonished to learn she was alive and living close by. Guided to her apartment, he fell for the beautiful, beleaguered poet, her maturity adding to her attraction. Together, they talked the night away. When he next tried to contact her, a few years later, however, she refused to see him. Churchill's indiscretion had revealed she had been entertaining a foreign visitor, which Soviet citizens were not allowed to do. Years later, talking to Isaiah Berlin in the Athenaeum Club, in London, for a radio programme I was making about Akhmatova, I asked him to tell me what had happened that first night. He smiled. He was then in his eighties and it had all been a long time ago. 'We talked about writers – she hated Tolstoy and admired Dostoevsky. We talked about Russia and England and about ourselves.' It was said that electricity sparked that night between the poet and the diplomat who was more than twenty years her junior. 'Was there any more to it?' I asked. He shook his head: 'People used to think I was in love with her, that we had had an affair. But it wasn't true. She was far too tragic for me.'

Churchill's carelessness had dire consequences for Akhmatova. Buying some fish shortly after her meeting with Berlin, she noticed her name in print in the newspaper wrapping and smoothed it out to read what was in it. Which was how she learned that she had been denounced by the Politburo. Her poetry, the report said, 'is the poetry of an upper-class, overwrought lady – she is both a nun and a whore who combines harlotry with prayer'. In an attempt to silence her, she was expelled from the Writers' Union and her son, by Gumilev, was arrested for the third time.

Akhmatova's city has been renamed many times, St Petersburg, Petrograd, Leningrad and now St Petersburg once more, but to Akhmatova it was always Peter. And to the people of Peter, she was their poet. 'You are the first Englishman I have ever spoken to,' the taxi driver Valodya told me when he dropped me at Akhmatova's former home. Later, when he came to collect me, he brought me a present of a tiny volume of her poetry. She was still the people's poet.

I spent the cold January mornings walking the city with a friend, Valentine, who, in his long dark coat with its astrakhan collar, recalled the elegance of the old city. Listening to him recite Akhmatova's poetry was like listening to a love poem. We crossed and recrossed the bridges over the Neva, while he talked to me of her, of the time when people waited for the knock on the door from the Cheka, the forerunner of the KGB, of Stalin's unstoppable reign of terror, of the days when a dark pall of fear and suspicion hung over the city like a poisonous fog. We walked the length of the red and grey wall of the political prison where Akhmatova had queued with other women to hand in food parcels for her husband. I followed him through the rooms of the apartment she later shared with a new lover, art critic Nikolai Punin, and with his wife and child for the accommodation shortage was so great in Leningrad at that time (1926) that the wronged wife had nowhere else to go. Punin and Akhmatova occupied one room, his wife and child the other and all shared the kitchen. (Later, in 1938, after Punin had been arrested and then freed and after he and Akhmatova had exhausted their love for each other, she said to his wife: 'Let's change rooms back again', and so it was done.) In Moscow, I'd met Lydia Chukovskaya who, as a young woman, had known Akhmatova in Leningrad. The older woman's room was terrible, she told me, with springs protruding from the three-legged armchair, the floor unswept, newspapers covering window panes and wet clothes hanging in the kitchen. But, in the midst of all this, reclining in a black silk dressing gown adorned with a silver dragon, Akhmatova would spend the winter days reading. She read *Ulysses* four times and found it remarkable though rather too pornographic. When a young man came visiting, Chukovskaya was instructed to hang a scarf over the lamp: 'I don't look my best today,' said the great poet, then in her sixties.

Valentine was unable to accompany Freya and myself to Akhmatova's grave at Komarovo but put us in touch with Julia, who, he said, would take us there.

Diary Notes: January 1989

Met Julia today, at a café. She is about thirty, her heavily made-up face prettily framed by a furry hood, making her look like a fairy snow-queen. Her husband is a chemist, researching into Aids. Their daughter Vera is eight. Julia speaks perfect, if sometimes puzzling, English: 'I have been interpreter, spy, editor and now teacher,' she tells me. She feels strongly about women's rights and women's education but when she gave contraceptive advice to her young, female students, the principal put a stop to it, saying it was vulgar. She herself thinks the poet Joe Brodsky, a Nobel prize-winner and protégé of Akhmatova when he was a young man in Leningrad, is vulgar. Her mother-in-law too is vulgar but luckily she lives far away in another town. Julia lives in a two-roomed flat and has had one abortion. She earns 250 roubles (£25) a month, of which one rouble goes to her union, three on rent, seven in tax. She talks non-stop, weaving fact into fiction. She expresses both prejudice and pride in relation to Russia. Is an admirer of all things English. Her reading includes Dickens and Ellery Queen. She quotes from *Hamlet* and, for my benefit, sings 'I'm

Getting Married in the Morning'. Now, at the end of the evening, I seriously wonder if I can endure her company tomorrow when we go to Komarovo.

Freya is unconcerned: she has met up with some students from a college in Minsk. They are from Cuba, Tanzania and Madagascar and appear to be serious drinkers. In the hotel lift we meet two of them. 'Are you interested in high-class music?' one of them asks her and at the next level the three of them exit sharpish. There's a bar on that floor.

This leaves me in the lift on my own, except for a man. I ask him where he's from, first in Russian then in English but he is twice baffled. He turns out to be Finnish and plants a huge, bearlike kiss on my cheek to emphasize his Finnishness. He follows me out of the lift and, as I wrestle with my room key, makes a speech in Finnish and shows me his room number. There is terrible confusion and for a moment I fear I have inadvertently made a tryst with him but then it all becomes clear: he has his key but he can't locate his room. I point out he is on the wrong floor and, solemnly, we shake hands and part.

Akhmatova was born in 1889 – she shared her birth year with Adolph Hitler – and died in 1966 at the age of seventy-seven. Komarovo, where she had the use of a state dacha and where she is buried, is about an hour's train ride from Leningrad. We went to Finland Station to get the train and I bought three red carnations to take to her grave. The *elektrichka* was full and we sat, squashed up three to a seat, small puddles of melted snow forming at our feet. Julia fussed with our bags, hanging them for us on the hooks by our slatted wooden seats so that they dripped down our necks. The train rattled through snowy countryside darkened by a grey sky. The man opposite opened his book, removed the bookmark and settled down to read. Julia talked.

At Komarovo we climbed down from the train, squelched across the railway line and made for the forest. Snow had started to fall as we began our trudge along the track. Two students, coming out of the forest laughing and breathless, stopped to point the way to the cemetery. We had, they told us, picked the worst day for our pilgrimage. They were right: the cold was biting and more heavy snowfalls were expected. Freya and I had strong shoes but we should have had boots. Julia had boots. The students scooted off on their Finnish sledge – he pushing, she sitting – and, turning off down a small track, disappeared into a large dacha set among the trees. When the door was opened for them, a rush of laughter and golden light spilled out across the snow, momentarily melting the gloom and the cold. I imagined the students stamping snow off their boots, being welcomed by their friends with cups of hot coffee – I wanted to follow them. Our destination, however, was the icy land of the dead.

A winter mist, dazzling white, descended on the forest. After half an hour, we came, on the left, to an old wooden house, painted blue and white: Akhmatova's faded clapboard dacha. Small and solitary, it was impossible to reach across the deep snow drifts. I thought about her living there, an old woman, her body grown heavy, her hair grey though with a face still beautiful. Her golden youth had given place to hardship and tragedy. One husband had been shot. Another disappeared. The third died, leaving her to live out a life made terrible under Stalin whose lackeys played a cat and mouse game with her, using her son as bait. His imprisonment, release and re-imprisonment were carefully orchestrated in order to keep her in check. Publicly, she was derided. People were discouraged from visiting her. But still she wrote. Friends learned her poetry off by heart, where the Stalinists could not censor it. Though opportunities to leave Russia presented themselves, she chose not to for without Russia she had no language. It was the breath of her life and her words breathed life into those for whom death was a daily possibility.

Although it was only three o'clock in the afternoon, the light was fading fast, the forest round us darkening, the snow getting deeper. I felt my back grow chilly and shivered. We left the dacha and plodded on until finally we reached the cemetery. The small lodge was empty and the gates stood open. The grave, over to our right, was without name or date as she had requested and was marked only with a black iron cross, one of the arms tilting downwards, in the Russian Orthodox manner. When making my radio programme about Akhmatova, I also interviewed Joe Brodsky who told me how, on the morning of the funeral, the grave digger was drunk and that he, Brodsky, had had to take the spade from him and do the digging himself. Around the grave, the leafless trees were hung with bits of ribbon and tatters of cloth, a tradition based half in religion, half in superstition. I unwrapped the carnations and smoothed the petals, pleased that I had finally got here, all the way from Ireland, and that on this day, at least, there would be fresh flowers on her grave. But, of course, despite the wintry darkness and the forlorn remoteness of the spot, someone had been there ahead of me: in the snow lay a fresh bunch of red carnations. The blinding mist closed in on us as we shuffled back through the forest and the cold had started to get to my bones. My feet felt icy and the tips of my fingers ached. We passed the house where the students were staying. A smell of burning wood filled the air. Lights from the windows shone through the trees and smoke came from the chimney. I thought of them warm inside, drinking, laughing, maybe making love. Was it they who had put the flowers on Akhmatova's grave? Or were they, in their golden youth, filled only with thoughts of today, knowing nothing of the Russia Akhmatova had known?

As we came to the station, the train churned towards us out of the white night, its heavy machinery clanking like a huge medieval engine of power, its one beam cutting into the darkness, the ground trembling beneath its iron wheels. We climbed up into it, leaving the cold, dark forest behind us, leaving the snow to fall silently on Akhmatova's grave, on the red carnations and on the black cross. It would continue to fall and in an hour or two the flowers would have disappeared. Tomorrow, however, there would be another pilgrim, fresh flowers. More snow. And Akhmatova's poetry for ever.

CHAPTER ELEVEN

Working the System: 1990

Getting a visa for Georgia had been difficult. A person free-wheeling around on her own was not something the Soviets could handle. I should join a group, they said, like everyone else. But I'm not a tourist, I explained, I'm a writer and need time to wander about, talk to people. Get lost a bit. Then I should travel with a group of writers, they said. But any writers I knew who travelled to the Soviet Union seemed to do so courtesy of grants and other freebies. I planned to travel under my own steam, literally. In Moscow, the man who might be able to help was Valodja Tushko. In between my language school sessions and my various pilgrimages, I visited him to discuss my planned visit, how long I would stay, where I would stay, what I would do.

'I want to visit the land of Medea.'

'And how will you do that?'

'Well, what I plan to do is take my bike with me and cycle around, as much as I can.'

Valodja was aghast. 'That's not possible.'

'No?'

'But who would be responsible for you? You would be on your own, in a strange country. You don't know your way round Georgia. You can't speak the language.' He leaned forward sternly: 'Who would know where you were? . . . No, no. It's impossible. Someone has to take responsibility for you.'

'Me?' I asked. 'Can I be responsible for myself?'

But this was totally out of the question. Soviet citizens could never be responsible for themselves. It could be the state, the person's union or perhaps the person's employer but there always had to be someone to whom the individual – always a dangerous entity – had to answer. I toyed with the bribe in my pocket – a bottle of Jameson.

'You'll have to find *someone* in Georgia who will take responsibility for you.'

'But this is the thing. I don't know anyone in Georgia. I've never been there in my life. Which is why I want to go there,' I added, hoping the conundrum would intrigue him. It didn't and Valodja walked with me to the main entrance of the House of Friendship. We paused at the door.

'Those women over there are Georgian,' he said and we watched as two dark-haired, queenly beauties descended the stairs in a stately fashion and disappeared through a door. Valodja forced himself to return to me and my problem: 'If you find someone to be responsible for you, let me know.'

'I will,' I said and handed him the bottle of whiskey. There seemed no point in carrying it round Moscow all day. 'Wrong,' said a friend who knew how to work these things. 'You oil the wheels at the start of the journey, not the end.'

I spent a few months researching the Medea legend in the Bodleian Library in Oxford and discovered that, despite having murdered her children, quite a few Georgian women bore her name. There had to be a reason for this.

Dominant groups see everything from one point of view only – their own – and the Medea legend, coming to us from the Greeks, therefore, carried their interpretation of events. Jason was their hero, sent off on his various quests, one of which was to find the Golden Fleece and bring it back home. When he sailed into Colchis, so the Greek version goes, a wild woman cast a spell on him which made him fall in love with her. The woman, Medea, was strange, a barbarian, of course, something of a witch, given to plucking plants from the hillside and making dangerous concoctions with them. But there was no denying that without her Jason would never have found the Golden Fleece. Like many legends, this part of the story has a grain of truth in it: the Golden Fleece was probably a sheepskin used, as they still are today, to pan for gold. In gratitude, Jason took Medea home to Greece with him where they lived with their two sons until he grew bored with her and took up with another, younger woman. Consumed with rage, Medea killed her rival and then, in a final act of revenge on Jason, killed her two small sons as well.

In 431 BC, Euripides entered his play, *Medea*, in the Greek playwriting competition and won it. It is mainly from this play, the only one of twelve entries to have survived, that we know what we do of Medea. But what of Colchis, of Georgia? There, they tell a different story. Medea was the much-loved daughter of the king. She fell for Jason – handsome, exotic, brave – for the gods had put a spell on him to ensure that this would happen, knowing she was the one woman in Colchis who could help him. She did not give him one of her magic-mushroom potions, the Georgians say, and nor was she a witch. But she *was* a healer, going up on to the mountains to collect the herbs and plants she needed for her cures, something which Georgian villagers still do today. As for killing her children, they gloss over that, shrug their elegant shoulders and offer you more of their heady wine.

Determined to explore the whole story for myself, I sold a radio play to the BBC, blew the £1000 fee on a week in Tbilisi during which I hoped to find someone who would be responsible for me and, against all the odds, I did. This allowed me to get my visa, put my bike on the train at the Hook of Holland, change trains in Moscow and travel south, finally reaching Tbilisi two days later. It was 1990 and I had been two years getting there. But once there I discovered, to my horror, that the Soviet Embassy in Dublin had put the wrong exit date on my visa and that I was expected to leave Georgia a month earlier than I had planned to. The man to whom I was sent who would deal with all this – a friend of a friend, all of them Party members – examined the visa, thought about the problem for a bit and then came up with the solution: 'On the day before you are due to leave Georgia,' he said, 'you must become ill.'

'Ill?' I hadn't been planning on that.

'Only a little ill,' he said reassuringly. 'Something small. Maybe a sore throat.'

'I don't like sore throats. How about a toothache?'

'A toothache, yes. That would be quite all right. So, let's say a toothache.'

I waited for the next bit of bad news.

'Then, with your toothache, you must go to a doctor – I will give you his name – and he will say that you are too ill to travel.'

How simple it all turned out to be and what a perfect system it was whereby those who made the rules were also the ones to whom one went to get advice on how to break them. In the event, I wasn't in Tbilisi on the day on which I fell ill but a doctor examined me in my absence, declared me too ill to travel and my visa was extended.

CHAPTER TWELVE

Look How She Beautiful: 1989 and 1992

We travelled with the sun but lost it somewhere over the Atlantic. Later, outside the airport there were black skies, black faces and a darkness sudden and warm. 'Fifty bucks,' the taxi driver says. There's a deafening sound in my ears, a thousand engines whirring and clicking, compressed energy busying itself somewhere in the region of my ankles. 'How much did you say?' The driver looks surprised to hear me shout above the rackety din: he's used to the crickets. I hand over 100 US dollars and get my change in Eastern Caribbean ones. I have arrived in Liberta, the largest village on the small island of Antigua.

Antigua is the first landfall for transatlantic sailors, English Harbour where they dock. Deirdre, her husband Radics and I walk down the track to the road that leads to English Harbour. On either side, in the darkness, I can sense breathing in the undergrowth, creepy things watching us. Suddenly, there's a crash in the bush, a ripping of leaves and a thud, like the descent of a body from heaven. Then silence. 'That's good luck,' says Radics, 'to hear a coconut falling.' I think of George Berkeley. Had we not been there, would it have made a noise? It's toofer night in English Harbour – two drinks for the price of one. The music is deafening and pleasing to the 'yachties', the golden boys and girls who come here for the two Ss: sex and sailing. The girls wear tiny skirts that cover their pert bottoms, almost. The boys are in frayed cut-off jeans. You can tell the Australians: they all have long, brown legs and sun-bleached, shoulder-length hair. The women do as well. When they dance, they do it crotch to pubic bone.

A man in a Hawaiian shirt joins our group, his face shining in the disco light, his teeth slanting outwards at an angle as if someone has tried to open a beer bottle with them. His eyes, set low in his face, are blank and his speech slow. He's police, on the lookout for people smoking ganja. Nobody likes him, especially since he comes from Dominica, a much-loved island in these parts. The problem is, policing ganja smokers is an unpopular job that no Antiguan wants to do. If you're from Dominica, however, where money is even shorter, you join the police and look out for ganja smokers. No one likes you but you eat. We move with the swell to another bar. Someone gives me a cocktail, cold and coconutty. I swallow the cherry without savouring it, lie down on the midnight grass and sleep. Next morning, I wake in a small wooden house in a bed narrow as a coffin. From the other side of the partition wall comes a whisper of sounds: sighs, snuffles, then the padding of small feet. Framed in the doorless doorway stands a small, brown girl with plaits sticking out from her head like tiny, electric shocks. Silently, we stare at each other. We've met before, three years ago, but she won't remember.

1990. Oxford, six o'clock on a frosty January morning.

I'd put the alarm on a chair by the bed to be sure of hearing it. When it goes off, I send it and the chair flying as I hurtle out of bed. Down the stairs, pulling on clothes, the sudden screech of a tripped-over cat sounding behind me through the slammed door. Through red traffic lights, along empty streets and into the dark car park of the hospital. Breathe deeply, I tell myself going up in the lift. Above all, *look* calm.

The birthing room is quiet and dimly lit. Deirdre sits in a chair, eyes closed. Behind her, in the shadows, the midwife waits. Occasionally, she comes forward to listen to the baby's heartbeat. Last night, when I drove Deirdre in, they fixed her up to a monitor. We sat and listened to the steady boom-boom-BOOM, boom-boom-BOOM, boom-boom-BOOM and I saw a white horse, tail flying, galloping free across a landscape that had no horizon: life's never ending journey towards eternity had finally begun. When the contractions come faster, I have to do my deep breathing again, admonishing myself: all she's doing is having a baby. Everyone does it. You've done it yourself, three times.

Deirdre was the middle one, born on my birthday. The difference between then and now is that I made a terrible racket whereas she is quiet and controlled, withdrawn into some private place deep within herself. Her and her baby. I walk over to look at the waiting cot and for comfort touch the tiny electric blanket. The midwife smiles at me. She's young, Deirdre's age and has a ponytail.

Outside, a wintry dawn is starting to appear. There'll be ice on the Isis. Grey January light seeps through the pale Venetian blinds and through the glass window in the door I see people in the corridor going about their business as if the world were still an ordinary place. Surreptitiously, I look at my watch. I have a journey planned to Moscow and have to call the travel agents at nine if I am to get the cheap fare that's on offer. Then, suddenly, there's something to see – a dark segment, shiny as liquorice and purple as a plum. 'The head . . . I can see the head.' My excited voice is loud and out of place in the quiet room.

Deirdre doesn't want to move from her chair so the midwives ready up, down on their knees, arranging the tools of their trade on a white sheet spread out on the floor. 'Hang on a minute,' the ponytailed midwife says, 'till I get my rubber gloves on.' But Deirdre is a now person with a low patience threshold. Hanging on is not her style. With a sudden, slippery whoosh, the traveller arrives: a tiny girl, brown skin bearing the trace elements of slavery, squashed nose the legacy of Africa. 'Are you all right?' asks the young midwife anxiously and I realize it's me she's talking to. Unknown to myself, I've been crying. 'Yes, I'm fine.' We talk in normal voices again. After a decent interval, I head for the door: 'Just going to make a phone call.' The midwife looks round, busy with her bundle: 'Oh, don't go yet. Not until we've weighed her. They'll ask you what she weighed. They always do.' I check the clock. Five to nine. I don't have the nerve to say I'm going to ring not the family but the travel agent. Later in the day, Radics comes to see his daughter and nods approvingly: 'She a good strong girl and she don't cry plenty.'

Five years earlier, only a month after Ian died, Deirdre had been asked to join the crew of a yacht that had to be delivered across the Atlantic to Antigua. She was twenty and had never been on a yacht before. By the time she got to Antigua, however, she'd learned the ropes and after a few years crewing around the Caribbean had settled in Antigua with Radics, returning briefly to Oxford to give birth to Eta.

Soon after my arrival in Antigua, they packed their belongings into a few duffle bags and moved to another house in Liberta. This latest one is like the last one except that our address is now Millionaires' Row. We get our water from a standpipe. The main advantage of this new house is that it has a lean-to construction close by. 'It's great to have a kitchen,' Deirdre says and I don't bat an eyelid. It depends, after all, on what you call a kitchen. The lean-to is made of upright planks of wood topped by a tin roof. Here and there, the planks are missing so that, through the irregular gaps, we have a fine view of the coconut grove and mango trees beyond. We've knocked nails in the planks and hung up pots and mugs on them. The floor is clay, baked so hard by the weather that it can be swept smooth. Once settled in the new house, I go into the capital, St John's, to see if the tourist office has managed to find out anything for me about cargo boats going to Dominica.

The woman behind the counter signals me to sit. Gold jewellery gleams against her skin. Tiny drops of glass hang from her ear lobes. Her fingers are long and delicate, her nails scarlet. She wears a tight grey skirt and a silver-grey blouse. Black, grey and silver – expensive colours. She is the epitome of style but she has bad news: 'There are no boats to Dominica,' she says. 'You have to go by plane. By

Liaaaht.' The second syllable drawls out of her red-lipsticked mouth, long and bored as a yawn. I can't afford an air ticket and, in any case, I want to arrive in Dominica by boat, so, disgruntled, I leave the tourist office and decide to give myself a treat, a glass of arrowroot syrup and iced milk, spiced with ginseng. The café serving this delicacy is run by Dominicans, in a street which used to be named after a pirate. Drake Street, it was called. Now, renamed after a cricket hero, it's Viv Richards Street. Two doors down from the café is his parents' house. Above the porch is a painted notice which reads: 'Yes! God is Good in Earth and Sky.' Viv Richards was born in 1952. He first played cricket for the Leeward Islands when he was seventeen. Five years later, he was playing for Somerset CC and in the same year, he began touring with the West Indies team. In the museum, they have his cricket bat on display. *The* bat. The notice under it reads: '1976. When Viv Richards graduated by wielding his bat like a broadsword and England's captain threatened to make the West Indies team grovel. In 1985, he captained the West Indies team and, in 1986, he broke the world record for the fastest century – in terms of balls received: 56.' Not much grovelling there.

'Any luck?' Deirdre asks when I get back to Liberta and I shake my head. 'There are a few yachts in English Harbour that might be going down that way,' she says, later that evening, as we sit on the back doorstep, watching the gleam of the rising moon shine through the avocado trees opposite. But I don't fancy a yacht. The moon rises over the tops of the trees and I pour myself another Red Stripe. 'No, I think it'll have to be a cargo boat. It may be less adventuresome than a yacht but at least I won't puke.' 'Then you'll just have to go down to Deepwater Harbour and hang about, asking.'

Deirdre's house is a challenge. For a carpet, she's stapled to the floor a piece of cotton that she'd tie-dyed into a bright, orange sunburst. It looks good. Food we keep in a canvas camping larder that I brought from England but, without a fridge, things like butter go off fast so we only buy a couple of ounces at a time. Milk comes in powdered form.

She still has her job at the pizza place and had a day off today but – even though it's Mother's Day – there was work to be done, and without running water it's hard work. On the line hung a full wash of miniature clothes: eleven pairs of small pants, six dresses, thirteen tee-shirts and seven pairs of shorts. They fluttered brightly all day in the breeze like a ship's display of flags signalling mother-love. Last night, I had to get up to have a pee and not able to find my flip-flops in the dark, left my bedroll and padded out in my shoes instead. This morning, forgetting all that, I tipped out my left shoe which acts as my bank for the night. Into it, before I go to sleep, I put my watch, any loose change I have, my biro and my National Health teeth. It was about the safest place to put anything, given I didn't have a bed, let alone a bedside table. This morning, however, I found the dental plate in two pieces – I'd stepped on it during the night. I did a first aid job on it with blu-tack which seemed to work and wondered how I hadn't noticed it giving my heel a bite last night. Maybe my rum nightcap had been extra strong.

Monday: the water is turned off again. There was a sudden, sharp burst of rain this morning, filling the air with midges. The rain made the ground wet and the path muddy and slippery. The *ghaut* (a large ditch filled with the mush of plants and old tree trunks) had filled up too, probably with water that had come down from the hill on the far side of Liberta. If you fall into the *ghaut*, Deirdre says, you'll never be found again. She tightropes across it on a fallen tree trunk but, viewing its slimy green growth with uneasy distaste, I go the long way round. Tuesday: the electricity as well as the water is off.

Eta lives an enchanted childhood here. Chickens come scavenging round the yard. Goats graze down by the *ghaut*. Tiny frogs, the size of a ten pence piece, hop into the house while she plays. To get to the path that crosses the *ghaut*, you have to negotiate the neighbour's donkey. Tiny birds fly in and out of the house, pinching whatever crumbs they can find, their beaks tap-tapping on the floor. Magical sounds fill her world: the creak of bamboo in a ghostly wind, cocks crowing, donkeys braying, night-frogs tinkling like tiny bells in a breeze, crickets clicking, birds singing. In the mornings, she swings in the hammock, under the palm tree, singing to herself, sometimes stumbling back to the house with a fallen coconut so big she can hardly get her arms round it.

There seems to be a lot of religion at her pre-school. I occasionally hear her singing:

> 'I bubblin' bubblin' bubblin' bubblin',
> Bubblin' in my soul.'

I have decided to visit the church at the village of Gilbert's where I'd heard that, in the old days, the Methodists there had taught the slaves to read. And because it's Sunday, with no buses, I'll have to hitch. I make a cup of tea with freshly picked lemon grass, add a few bay leaves, leave it to infuse, then strain it into a cup. To eat, I have a piece of bread and cheese. 'Me want bread too,' Eta says, in island patois, hopping from one foot to the other. 'Please may I have some bread,' I say, sounding dreary as a foghorn, and, dutifully, she repeats the polite, cumbersome phrase. My lift drops me at the turnoff for the dusty track to Gilbert's Church but everyone else has arrived by car, the men dressed up in Sunday suits and ties, the women as if they're going to a wedding – wide-brimmed hats, gloves, pleated skirts, matching jackets, shimmering greens and shiny purples, black patent-leather high heels, white sandals – and hymn books under their arms.

One lone white family sits at the back of the church, but the buzz of excitement comes from a bench at the front where the choir sits leafing through hymn books, leaning across each other to point out the page, signalling to the choir master, waving to late arrivals. And all the while, the pianist plays with great feeling and energy, opening up huge chords, foot busy on the pedals. A piano teacher, surely. Then we all stand to sing and smile at each other for we have the Lord in our hearts.

Where there was only despair at Betty's Hope, the biggest sugar plantation on Antigua, here at Gilbert's there was real hope for, if you were a slave, there had to be the promise of something better in the next life. Nathaniel Gilbert was the man able to offer that hope. Gilbert was the son and grandson of planters. At the age of twenty-one, he was sent back to England to study law and at twenty-six returned to take his father's seat on the Antigua Assembly. Sixteen years later, he was elected Speaker of the House. Gilbert was a rich man – his father had left him £40,000 and a plantation with 300 slaves. But it was an uneasy time for planters and a restless one for their slaves. The Africans outnumbered their white owners by twenty to one but the latter were protected by arms and monstrous laws. Slaves were not allowed to give evidence against their masters. Masters sometimes killed their slaves (penalty: £300) or gelded or dismembered them (penalty: £100). Small wonder, then, that those slaves who could absconded. Such runaways – and they daily became more numerous – emerged as a major threat to the efficient running of a plantation, which depended for its prosperity on a stable workforce. Slave owners therefore were encouraged to shoot runaways with the offer of official compensation since such deaths were considered to be in the public good. In 1748, Nathaniel Gilbert was awarded £60 for having one of his runaway slaves executed. Eventually, the cruelty and injustice suffered by the slaves reached an unbearable point and a leader, King Klaus, rose from among them to lead a famous but unsuccessful uprising. Nathaniel Gilbert was one of three judges who investigated the case and was responsible for sending forty-seven of the insurgents to their deaths.

It was round this same time, while he was on a visit back to England, that Gilbert met with John Wesley, the founder of Methodism. It was a turning point in his life and he returned to Antigua with the flame of Wesley's ideals burning in his heart, determined that his slaves, too, should share in his religious fervour. To this end, he taught them to read – the first white person in Antigua to do so. Educating slaves was strictly against the law and Gilbert had to take them out into the bush to teach them in secret. His activities, however, when they became known, were seen as subversive by the other planters and so unpopular did he become that when he resigned the Speaker's Chair, in 1769, he received no vote of thanks. On his death, two slave women, Mary Alley and Sophia Campbell, took on his work, looking after the church, teaching and keeping the congregation together for a few years until, in 1778, a Methodist shipwright arrived in English Harbour and they were supplanted.

Now, on this bright Sunday morning at Gilbert's, the air is full of song. Hosanna, hosanna, we all sing, to the tune of 'Why Was She Born So Beautiful'. A cool breeze floats through the church. The shutters have been taken off the windows and through them I can see a swaying tamarind tree. The organ swells with joy and lifts our voices to the roof timbers. The choir master hurries across to the piano player, passing into a shaft of sunlight coming through the stained-glass window so that, just for a second, his black, shiny face is radiantly stained red, purple and blue. The lay preacher, an elderly man with white hair and an impeccable, black single-breasted suit, rises to give his sermon. It is Palm Sunday, he tells us, and on that first Palm Sunday, the Lord was going among his people, promising them freedom from their colonial oppressors . . . Beside me, a young girl slips off her lilac suede shoes and dozes through this old story being retold. Slavery and colonial oppression mean little to her. We stand again, to sing of crossing the river to a golden shore. In the distance, I think I hear the murmur of voices in the bush, of slaves dressed in rags, far from home, sick and tired to death, taking solace from the promises of their white master.

Antigua boasts a whole litany of churches: the Deeper Life Revival Church, the Church of the Living God, the Church of Christ of the Latterday Saints, the Seventh Day Adventists, the Pentecostal, the Church of God in Christ, the Moravian, the Pilgrim Holiness Church, not to mention the ordinary old Catholics and Protestants. When I wrote them all down in my notebook, it seemed a lot of Christianity for an island only twelve miles long.

Back in Liberta, I lie in the hammock, looking up at the cool, dreamy clouds. Overhead, the tall, straight trunk of a palm tree curves slightly into the sky, its leaves swaying sleepily in the sun. The weather has been strange, unnerving. I don't know what to make of it. Some days, the sky is filled with rain clouds but the warm wind carries them away to another island leaving Antigua parched as ever. There are no mountains here and no rivers so water is always short. During the worst years, the island had to buy in barge-loads of water from Dominica. Yesterday evening, Eta and I took a walk across the sun-cracked village cricket pitch. Although it's April, it feels like the end of summer. The end of something. Shutters creak and doors bang. Occasionally, at night, rain rattles on the tin roof. Six weeks now to the official beginning of the hurricane season. Deirdre rubs cream on her lips to stop them cracking while we sit on the back step, talking. They don't like ganja here, she says, because it's being brought in from Jamaica. Foreign stuff. Growing your own brings stiff prison penalties but it's still grown. At the local school, the church minister asked the children if they knew what ganja was. They all put their hands up. But when he asked them if ganja was smoked at home, no hands went up.

The heat gets to me all the time, especially at night. I sleep on my lightweight mat, which I unroll on the floor. Then I pull my sleeping bag over my head to protect me from the nightly onslaught of mosquitoes and sweat it out till dawn. Deirdre's pillow is her leather jacket stuffed into a pillow case, mine any pile of clothes I can find, bundled up, wrapped in a towel and pushed under my head. My tiny mirror – the only one in the house – is a treasure. Getting ready to go out, for a bit of fun at English Harbour with some friends – Radics has been away visiting his mother in Dominica – Deirdre peers into it, fixing her hair. She looks good: gold earrings, a red bead necklace, blonde hair shining bright, startling blue eyes (her father's eyes) set in a freckled face. Eta, busy with a book, looks up and catching sight of her mother, widens her eyes in wonder. Pattering across the room to me she shakes my arm urgently. 'Look,' she cries, her small voice filled with excited admiration, 'look how she beautiful.'

Seven in the morning and as I hitch a lift to the airport to make the twenty-minute flight to Barbuda, Antigua's sister island, our conversation proceeds according to form, the driver still under the influence of last night's rum session.

'Where your husband?' he asks.

'Not here.'

'You leave your husband at home?' he shrieks in disbelief.

'Yes. Where's your wife?'

'She got only one leg.'

'Really? What happened to her?'

'Sugar.' Diabetes is a common complaint here.

We lurch along for a bit, in silence, and I try to close my nose to the stink of rum.

'It na good you leave you husband.'

'And it's not good you left your wife.'

'But she only have one leg,' he protests. 'She can't look after me.'

Barbuda is a flat sand-coloured leaf floating on a pool of blue. Water laps its edges and the wind, whistling across its desolate landscape, makes me feel uneasy and unsafe, fearful that at any moment a wave may flow across the whole island and engulf it. It's a short walk from the single-roomed building that is Codrington airport to the rutted main road, its potholes filled with yellow water, thick and gungy as last winter's engine oil. About 1500 people live on this island which measures fourteen kilometres by twelve. Opposite the Post Office, which doubles as the Barbuda Treasury, is the Blood Pressure Clinic. A notice on the wall reads: 'Blood pressure and urine test. Please turn out in numbers.'

Close to the clinic is another notice pinned to a wall: 'Man to man is so unjust: You just don't know who the hell to trust.' Adjacent to the sign is a bank.

I have to send a postcard to a friend. The clerk in the Post Office pulls out a book that looks like a collector's stamp album and turns over the pages for me to choose. I can have whichever stamp I like, he says. Eagerly, he tries to interest me in his own favourite – a likeness of Winston Churchill – but it wasn't what I had in mind. He turns a page and together we stare at the picture of another man. 'I don't know who this man is. You know who he is?' the clerk asks. I peer down at it again. 'De Gaulle,' I say but the clerk looks mystified. There are other stamps, one with a kestrel, an aeroplane, another with a parrot on it. I choose the parrot. 'This the right stamp for a letter to Europe, do you think?' The clerk smiles. 'Whichever,' he says. There are two shops in Codrington and I try both for postcards. The first one has none at all, the second has birthday cards only. No pictures of Barbuda so I compromise by buying two envelopes, writing on one and putting it inside the other and addressing it to Bill Heine, a friend from Oxford and a graduate of All Souls. 'I used to look up at the portrait of Codrington,' he'd once told me, 'when we dined in college, and wonder how that man made his money.' I am about to find out.

Barbuda bangs and clangs like a ship buffeted by winds that seem to strike it from every direction. The sun beats down on the treeless landscape and I look for shelter in a rum shop. To get your drink, you approach a wire cage, order what you want, pass your money under the wire and wait for the drink to come through a little opening in the cage. The chat in the rum shop is desultory. A toothy, unshaven old man gives his glass a top-up from an uncorked bottle on the table and tries to focus his eyes on me. He used to be a sailor, he says, and he's been all over – Puerto Rico, Dominica, St Lucia. He pauses, trying to remember where else he's been. As he spreads his hand on the stained table, I see that it has two fingers missing.

'De fish,' he says, 'dey teeth like my fingers.' He has nobody now, he says, no woman, nobody. And he stares groggily into his rum, feeling sorry for himself. 'When me dead . . . when me dead an' gone, dey know. Dey sorry den.' The man sitting on the far side of the tiny bar nods his head: 'Yeah, that the world, man.' This philosopher is sober and wants to know where I'm from. England and Ireland, I tell him and he leans across to shake my hand.

'That good. That very good. I live in England ten years. Now you go back and tell them you met me.' 'Who shall I say,' I ask politely, sounding like the butler. 'I Hillbourne Frank, that's who I am. MP for Barbuda.'

Barbuda has many problems but its main one lies forty kilometres away and is called Antigua. You can see Antigua from Barbuda but you can't see Barbuda from Antigua and therein lies the rub. Ten thousand years ago, the two islands were joined but now, to most Antiguans, Barbuda is invisible, unimportant, unvisited. The Codringtons, owners of Betty's Hope plantation on Antigua, were granted Barbuda by the English Crown and eventually the island fell into the hands of William Codrington. 'Apparently, *this* Codrington,' Bill Heine had told me, 'had some sort of slave farm out there. He bred them, to stock his plantations. That's where the money for the All Souls library came from . . . If you ever get there,' he'd added, 'send me a postcard.' So I'd sent him the envelope inside an envelope.

West African slave dealers – the big slave states were Dahomey and Asante – had a sliding scale of charges. The best slaves went to those who could pay the highest price – the Arabs. The next best went to local buyers for use as domestic workers. The rest, which sometimes included men and women past their prime, went to the West Indies. To circumvent the charges made by the slave traders and ship owners, the Codringtons came up with a novel idea: they would produce their own slaves. And where better to do this than on Barbuda whose soggy, water-logged land made it totally unsuitable for much else, certainly not for growing sugar cane. It was Codrington, an early advocate of protectionism, who committed the plan to paper noting that

'. . . the value of the aforesaid Island of Barbuda consisted chiefly in its extreme fitness for a nursery for Negroes and that, in this sense, it is not only a source of much profit . . . but also a preventive to the African slave trade.' Genetic farming it's called nowadays. The slaves from Barbuda were used to stock the Codrington estates on Antigua and were strong, tall and well fed. We are proud that we are the tallest people in the islands, a Barbudan had told me within minutes of my arrival there.

The imposing gates to All Souls College, opposite the Radcliffe Camera in Oxford, are decorative wrought iron, painted gold. If you peer through them, you can see the college fronted by an immaculate lawn. Housed within is the famous Codrington Library. In 1601, a Bill was introduced in London that aimed to outlaw the stealing of children and servants and 'the carrying off of them beyond the seas'. It failed to get past the second reading and, one hundred and fifty years later, the Codringtons were still importing Charity School boys to work on their estates. Slavery traded under many dubious names and altruism was one of them. Towards the end of the eighteenth century, when another Christopher had inherited the lands and titles, a law was passed on Barbados, where the Codrington family had its seat, making it an offence for slaves to be taught either to read or write, a bitter irony indeed when set against the fact that the Codrington profits from slave labour were used to establish the library at All Souls.

Here in the rum shop, however, slavery isn't a subject I feel like raising. The wind and the desolation outside have drained my enthusiasm for history. In any case, Hillbourne isn't interested in the past, only the present: 'We want

Barbuda for ourselves,' he says, thumping the bench he's sitting on with his glass so that the rum splashes nervously over the top. 'It belong to we.' The sailor nods topping up his glass. 'To we,' he mutters in agreement. 'No Antiguan man,' proclaims Hillbourne, now in top gear, 'can come here and take our land. It private. They have to have a piece of paper from the government for that and they don't have it.' 'Why do they want Barbuda?' I ask. 'To sell, man. To sell to scamp Italians. They try to, in 1980, was it? I forget. They want our sand. They streets of gold, that sand. They want it to build hotels for they tourists come to see the bird sanctuary so they make more dollars – with our sand. But one day, they gonna see. The day's gonna come when the British will go down here and say: what you mean, doing that? They fight our case, the British. One day, Barbuda gonna be a republic like they Baltic states.' Beside me, the sailor rouses himself. He's been left out of all this and needs some of the limelight. 'What's the longest river in the world,' he asks by way of conversation, pushing his rum bottle towards me. I shake my head. I don't know and anyway I'm on Heineken.

'Let me see, the longest river?'

It's hard to concentrate on my school geography. Hillbourne continues to develop his discourse on the future of Barbuda, a woman tries to buy a bottle of rum that won't fit through the wire cage and when another customer comes in – a rum drunk who steadies himself on my shoulder – the shop seems to have more people in it than feathers round a duck's arse. But the longest river? I can't get my thoughts together.

'The Yangste?' I try but the sailor shakes his head.

'The Ganges?'

'No.'

'I give up.'

'The Niagara Falls,' says the sailor in triumph.

'No Antiguan man . . .' continues Hillbourne, 'can come here without that bit of paper . . .' The Barbudans are lucky to have Hillbourne Frank. If they didn't have him, they'd have no one to put their case. He'd been living in England when the island's only lawyer died and when sent for, returned, leaving his wife behind. Hillbourne and the sailor start chatting and the man behind the wire cage leans his elbows on the counter, listening to the island gossip.

'Can you believe that?' Hillbourne is saying. 'This man, he young boy, walking along and he see this lady and she being attacked by three men and he go to help and they break his neck and all he bones broken and he go to the hospital . . .'

'What hospital?' asks the sailor.

'What hospital? Why it matter what hospital? Some hospital. And there he meet a nurse and she take him home and marry him. Can you believe that? Marry him. Well, it was in the papers so you gotta believe.'

'Where all this happen – in the paper?'

'Man – you listenin' or what? It happen in the States, that's where it happen . . . I tell you, she take him home and marry him.' Hillbourne drains his glass. Silence follows as we ponder all this.

'He work with computers,' Hillbourne adds as a coda.

The sailor rouses himself.

'Me mother know that woman.'

'Yeah?'

'Yeah. That woman Georgia Stein. She name Georgia Stein.'

'Georgie? Not Georgie Stein?'

'Yeah. You remember her? You remember Georgie Stein?'

'Yeah, I do. What happen to her?'

'She die.'

Outside, the wind from the lagoon ripples the puddles of muddy water. The air is hot and, in the distance, I can hear the drone of the plane coming in to land. Hillbourne and I shake hands. 'I'll be back,' I lie and start walking up the track towards Codrington airport, wondering why they still called it after such a family.

There's a house in St John's, Antigua, on Nevis Street, called Coates Cottage. It has two rooms with a leafy, flowery yard at the back. Recently, it's been turned into an art gallery but on the door to the yard is hammered a sign: 'The Barracoon'. This was the place where the slaves were held before being auctioned or delivered to whatever plantation they'd been ordered for. At the bottom of Nevis Street is Barbuda Wharf. The Codringtons landed the slaves from their Barbudan estate at this wharf and then transported them off to Betty's Hope. When I got back to Antigua, I walked along the broken, dusty road from the wharf to the Barracoon, counting my paces. Ninety-four, it took. Ninety-four steps to desolation.

'You want to pass a stool?' Fitzy asked me, looking worried as he stood at the wheel.

'No, no, but if I could just . . . you know . . .' He nodded his head towards his own cabin and turned back to the wheel. The proximity of the skipper and the intimate nature of our exchange had me confused. Would it now seem ill-mannered to bolt the door? I was, after all, only having a quick pee and he wasn't actually looking. I settled for shutting the door firmly and sat nervously on the pan as the water below gurgled and rose alarmingly like a hungry creature reaching up from the deep. 'Thank you,' I said when I came out on the bridge and I meant it. Unsavoury as the skipper's lav was, that of the crew was far, far worse. Not that I was a crew member, merely a passenger, but I did have to share their quarters.

I'd finally drawn lucky while sheltering from a tropical storm under an overhanging roof in the dock area of St John's. Sharing the shelter was Jojo who knew a man who knew another man who had a cargo boat. I stood looking out at the dense curtain of driving rain, at the flapping awnings, the rapidly filling potholes and felt the sun had come out.

'You know the name of the skipper?' I asked Jojo. 'Or the owner?'

He didn't. His mind was on other things.

'You takin' a lover while you here?' he asked casually.

'No.'

'*No?*' He seemed astounded.

'No.'

'OK. Just asking.'

'That's all right . . . So you don't know anything about this boat?'

'You married?'

'Yes.' I resurrected Ian regularly in such situations. 'Are you?'

He was affronted. 'I not married. Not ready yet . . . Why you not takin' a lover?'

'Not ready yet,' I said. He'd walked into his own web.

'Anyway, this boat. You don't know anything at all about it?'

'Know its name just.'

'Oh, you *do*? What is it so?'

'The *Danny Boy*.'

'The *Danny Boy*?' This was my boat. It had my name on it.

'Yeah,' Jojo said. 'It's a famous song.'

'I know,' I said. 'I come from Ireland.'

Jojo looked puzzled. 'What about Ireland?' he asked.

'Well, that's what makes it famous.'

Jojo shook his head. 'Don't know nothing about that. 'Danny Boy' famous because Harry Belafonte sing it.'

Antigua sank lower and lower into the sea as we pulled away and soon it was nothing more than a string of lights necklacing the horizon. The engines thrummed comfortingly as we moved steadily through the navy-blue water. I stayed up on deck as long as I could, postponing going below to avoid breathing in the sickening smell that hung about there – a smell of faeces mixed with rotting vegetables. I investigated my bunk, spread my sleeping bag over the stained mattress and wrapped my towel round the lumpy, sour-smelling pillow. In one corner of the cabin was the curtainless shower, the unmistakable ammoniac odour of urine rising from the begrimed shower tray. It was too filthy even to be sick into. In the galley, Spice – one of the crew members – was cooking something which I guessed was adding to the overall stink. On the table lay half a defrosting chicken, its thawing blood dripping on to the floor. The sink was blocked with dirty cups and plates and a pan of grey, scummy lentils bubbled on the gas cooker. I took my bread and cheese and bottle of water up on deck again and ate them as the fresh night wind blew across my face. The *Danny Boy* had turned out to be a small cargo boat that plied between the islands. When I found it was sailing for St Kitts before heading southwards for Dominica I knew it was my birthday: St Kitts was the first link in the Carib chain that ended in Dominica.

The Caribs – the indigenous people of the Caribbean – were originally a nomadic people from Central Asia who migrated to Siberia and then followed their reindeer herds across the ice of the Bering Straits into Alaska in search of fresh pastures. Later, they moved down through the central plains of North America and sailed the seas until they came to the land mass of South America where they built their villages along the coast and on the river banks, some of them finding safety deep within the rainforests. During the Stone Age a group of them, the Siboney, paddled northwards again to make their homes on the volcanic islands that had erupted out of the ocean bed, of which Dominica was one. The Siboney were followed, around 500 BC, by the gentle, peace-loving agriculturists, the Arawak, who left their homes along the Orinoco and moved northwards among the islands. The Arawak were, in turn, driven further north by the warrior Caribs, for whom the Caribbean is named. It was these Caribs that Christopher Columbus encountered, in 1493, on his second journey across the Atlantic, when he made landfall, naming the island he saw Dominica, because it was a Sunday. Its real name, its Carib name, was Waitikubuli, though he wasn't to know that, of course. There were some of these same Caribs on the island of St Kitts when, in 1623, the latest wave of settlers, the English, arrived.

We docked in Basseterre, capital of St Kitts. The bus, when it came along, was a smart, newly painted twenty-seater called *De Outlaw*. Buses have good names here in the Caribbean. In Antigua, it was usually a toss up between the *Iron Eagle* or *Risky Business*. *De Outlaw* took us up out of the small town, past neat houses with well-kept gardens and to the top of the coast road where I got off. The landscape was sunny and green, the air smelling of summer days, of bread and jam sandwiches, of hay-making time. I felt happy and at home, surrounded by the breathless, yellowy still-ness that lies at the heart of a perfect summer's day. The grass smelled sweet and I took in great gulps of heady air. A pale blue butterfly fluttered down on to a clump of grass. Behind me was the turquoise sea. It was not yet nine o'clock and, with the whole day ahead of me, I sat down on a warm stone to take stock.

Somewhere around here, at Bloody Point, the English, combining with French settlers, ambushed 2000 Caribs and, killing them, divided the island between themselves. For three days, the gorge ran red with the blood of the slaugh-tered. There are many such sites scattered about the islands, places where the plan to kill off the Carib population, once and for all, had been put into action. In Dominica, the site of the killing is still called Massacre.

When I got back to the dock at Basseterre, I found that a cargo sailing boat, with an open hold, had put in. The unloaders looked a wild lot. Some were stripped to the waist and one or two, with a bit of scarlet cloth wrapped round their heads for protection from the sun, must surely have been the crew of a pirate ship. It wasn't the crew that caught my attention, however, but the familiar buff and black wrappers of the cargo: row upon row of Guinness cans, packed into row upon row of Guinness boxes. I got out my camera to take a picture.

'Fuck off,' said a voice, close to my face. The voice came nearer. 'FUCK OFF . . .'

One of the pirates had climbed up on to the quayside and was waving his hands dangerously close to the camera, which I quickly lowered.

'Fuck off,' he said again. An interested crowd started to gather.

'I'm just taking a photo of the Guinness . . .'

'You take a photo I mash your face . . . I mash your fucking face.'

'Look, I simply want to take a photo of all that Guinness.'

The pirate moved nearer and I took a step backwards. But only one step. I wasn't going to give way that easily. The rest of the crew had stopped working, waiting to see what would happen next.

'You take a photo and I mash your fucking face. And I mash your fucking camera. Why you want to take a photo anyway? You think we fucking monkeys, or what?'

On cue, one of the men in the hold began to jump up and down, screeching and scratching his armpits.

'It's not you I'm photographing,' I said, 'it's the Guinness.'

The pirate advanced and my heart thumped as we eye-balled. At any moment, he might indeed mash both me and my camera. Then anger – allied to national pride – came to my rescue.

'Listen,' I shouted at him, 'that Guinness comes from where I come from. That's why I want to take a picture of it.'

Like Palestine, the territory of Ireland is a state of mind. Wherever you go, it goes. Ireland, however, is not all things to all men. To this one, it meant nothing.

'You fucking stop or I mash your fucking face . . .'

The repetition was mindless but anger had rendered me the same.

'Listen,' I bawled, 'just listen. I come from Ireland. If it wasn't for us, you wouldn't have any of that fucking stuff. You hear?'

Nevertheless, I didn't risk taking the picture and was relieved to get back to the safety of the *Danny Boy*. Grateful I had a home of sorts to go to.

We set sail almost immediately and some time in the middle of the night I woke and saw, through the open gangway, a glimmering, incandescent sky. I went up on deck and gazed out over the sea. All around was the Caribbean, made docile by the calming moon overhead. The engine hummed quietly as we moved steadily through waters which parted silently at the bow before closing again to trail us in the moonlight. The windless night was serene as a sleeping infant. Dominica lay ahead. I went back to my bunk and slept.

Chapter Thirteen

Caribs, We Work from the Heart: 1993

On the first Sunday after All Saints, which was the third day of November, about daybreak, a pilot of the flagship cried: 'Largess! Land in sight.'

Account by Chancar, Spanish physician to the fleet of
second voyage of Christopher Columbus in 1493

Wilson beat out a reggae rhythm on the dashboard in time to the car radio. 'First time you come in Dominica?' he asked. 'Yes,' I said, preoccupied. I had to keep my eyes on the road since he wasn't. 'You drinkin?' he asked, taking a swig from his bottle of Red Stripe and holding it up, waiting. I shook my head. As soon as I'd flagged down the car and got into it, I knew I'd made a mistake.

On the dashboard was stuck a little verse:

> You can play with my money
> You can play with my wife
> But when you play with my car, man,
> You fuckin' with your life.

'Roseau not far,' Wilson said. 'We there plenty soon.' As far as I was concerned, plenty soon wasn't soon enough. We had sixty minutes of reckless drink-driving ahead of us.

The *Danny Boy* had brought me safely and smoothly to Dominica where the last remnants of the Carib community lived, the ones Columbus had encountered when, on that Sunday in November, the lookout had sighted a lush, green island powering out of the sea. 'What I could never work out,' Deirdre had said, back in Antigua, her sailor's mind pondering the puzzle, 'was why Columbus turned away from Dominica. After all, they'd been at sea for over forty days and here was this island with mountains, which meant fresh water and they must have been in great need of that. Plus it had trees which meant timber so it would have been a good place to stay for a bit to do running repairs to the boats.'

The mariners certainly found the island pleasing:

> We steered directly to examine the one which we had first sighted and reached the coast, going more than a league in search of a harbour where we could anchor but one was not to be found in all that distance. As much of the island as was in sight was all very mountainous, very beautiful and very green down to the water and that was a delight to see since in our country at that season there is hardly any green. When we found no harbour the admiral decided that we should go to the other island. (Chancar)

The previous year, making landfall further north on Hispaniola, Columbus had encountered the Arawak and traded with them: his currency bits of glass and broken barrels. The Arawak were peaceful, welcoming and gave no trouble. They were, Columbus noted, intelligent and made excellent navigators. However, as the main fleet sailed on past the north tip of Dominica, Columbus sent out a small reconnaissance boat to have a look round the corner at the north-west coast. There, his men saw signs of habitation, shelters and pirogues but, noticing also that the locals were armed with bows and arrows, they sailed back to rejoin the main fleet. When Columbus finally got round to landing on Dominica, he found the Caribs curious but friendly. By the next year, however, wishing to take possession of the island – its water and timber and its abundant fresh fruit were, of course, a godsend – he had a different story to tell. The indigenous people were warlike and dangerous, he reported back. They were extremely aggressive, ate human flesh and would have to be subdued. As he had hoped, the royal order came instructing him to do whatever he thought fit. Thus began the destruction of an ancient seagoing civilization that had been in existence for thousands of years.

I caught the weekly bus from Dominica's capital, Roseau, and travelled up to Salybia, in the Carib territory on the eastern side of the island. Blue smoke rose up from a banana plantation where last year's trees were being burned. From somewhere deep in the forest came the faint thump of a machete. In the distance, the mountainside, dense with green palms shading into blue, was crisscrossed by a thousand secret footpaths. Below, far below, the white foam of Atlantic rollers crashed on to the black, volcanic rocks. In the lee of the mountain, the Carib Chief's red-roofed house stood solitary in a clearing with a fiery flamboyant tree in the yard and a pink oleander bush by the gate. The morning was a quiet time with everyone about their business: Salybia at peace. It wasn't always like this. Every country has its day of tragedy – the day when something terrible happened, something so terrible that simply naming the day is sufficient to evoke the horror. Bloody Sunday, they say in Ireland; 9 April, they say in Georgia; 13 June in Soweto; 19 September 1930, they say in Salybia.

The people of Salybia had been accused of smuggling rum and tobacco, for the rule of British Customs and Excise ran even to this remote part of the world. Or was supposed to. To the Caribs, however, Customs and Excise was a body external to them and they continued to evade the authorities as their forebears had done for hundreds of years. Then, on 19 September 1930, those authorities decided to act. Five armed policemen arrived in a pre-dawn raid, searching for smugglers. Two Caribs were shot. The people, protesting angrily and vehemently, drove the police out of the area. Hesketh Bell, the British Governor sought help and a British naval frigate, the *Delhi*, was dispatched from Trinidad. The frigate fired a series of blanks and flares and combed the coastline with searchlights. The Caribs, intimidated by the lights and the shots, left their houses and took refuge in the rainforest. Marines landed and, working with the police, went through Salybia rounding up suspects. When the Carib Chief went down to Roseau to protest, he too was arrested and divested of his status. Upon investigation, it emerged that the whole operation had been foolish and ill-judged. A trial was held on the island, the police case collapsed and the Caribs were acquitted on all charges. This verdict, however, was overturned by a House of Commons Commission, which found the Caribs morally responsible for the deaths that had occurred. It was a verdict the Caribs were unlikely to forget and 19 September is now Carib National Day.

The lives of all the peoples of Dominica – European, African and Carib – are threads woven into a foreign cloth. The indigenous Caribs were subdued by the Europeans and, in turn, supplanted by Africans taken from their ancestral homes. Although to the average outsider all Dominicans are the same, the two peoples, Carib and Afro-Caribbean, are quite distinct. We are all, of course, clothed in mantles not of our own choosing. When I am in Northern Ireland, my Catholic background puts me neatly in the nationalist slot. In England, my Irish background categorizes me as a Republican. (I am, of course, a republican.) Even the mantles we *do* choose, in the literal sense, may do little to protect us. When Hesketh Bell met the Carib Chief he later presented him as a figure of fun, a dotty old boy in funny clothes, someone rather amusing to write about. 'August, the Chief,' he wrote, 'was clad in an old and dilapidated black morning-coat that shone green in the sunlight, with a pair of white cotton trousers, while, on his head, was precariously perched one of those flat-topped, hard felt hats beloved of church wardens.'

Nearly fifty years later, the travel writer Patrick Leigh-Fermor meeting the then Chief, George Frederick, puzzlingly described him variously as a grandee and a Manchu. In 1964, the TV presenter Alan Whicker travelled to Dominica and interviewed Chief Germandois Francis, a twenty-eight-year-old barber. Whicker finished his television interview with the following words: 'Soon, these bewildered descendants of the warriors who defied Columbus will have retreated from their wretched and pathetic today, and faded away to join their forebears in the Valhalla reserved for them in the history books, leaving only their sea, the Caribbean.' His comments couldn't have been further from the truth and my heart lifted as, thirty years on, I made my way along the path to meet Auguiste Irvince, the present Carib Chief.

The path to his house was narrow, hedged in on both sides by tall, straggly bushes. As the tangle of growth opened out on to a bit of land, I cut across it, skirting a cornfield to follow a track that eventually brought me to a one-storey dwelling set in hard, red earth swept until it was shining. A tall young woman, her long dark hair in two plaits, opened the door, a small child in her arms. Her husband, she said, would be ready in a minute. I found a seat cobbled from bits of wood, where I could sit. It was a pleasant, busy garden. No green grass but everywhere colour and life: gourd and dasheen plants, onions, sweetcorn, coriander, a scarlet cordia tree, purple bougainvillea, a big shady mango tree and, my favourite, the cheerful yellow allemanda. I sat under the mango tree and it was some minutes before I realized it was raining – a soft rain to start with, then persistent and finally a rushing, deluging downpour. A window in the house opened and the Chief looked out. Through the wall of water, I could see him beckoning to me to come in. Auguiste was thirty-one and there was no mistaking his race. Broad-shouldered and short of stature, he wore his black hair in one long plait down his back. His cheekbones, set in a brown face, were wide apart and his dark eyes narrow – the eyes of the Steppes, of the great plains of North America, of the rainforests of South America. Eyes that, over the centuries, have been trained to carefully scan the horizon of the seas for possible enemies. Eyes narrowed against the glare of snow, the gleam of sunlight, the glint of water. Eyes patient but determined.

Auguiste was a grave person, concerned that I should understand what he was saying about his people. His talk was of money matters, grants and the IMF, who got what, where the funds came from. I became restless, looking beyond him, out of the window at the flame trees, reminding myself that the Caribs too have a right to be uninteresting, are entitled to drone. I tried to balance this against history, against the image of a people who had to face up to Europe's greatest explorer, who repelled the most powerful navies of the world, who defended their homes against aggressors not during a single battle or a single lifetime but over hundreds of years. I closed my eyes the better to weigh these facts against the reality of sitting at a table with the leader of that people, who I was now finding faintly boring. The trouble lay not in Auguiste himself but in the subject matter: 'We get an annual grant,' he told me, 'from the Dominican Government. 21,000 Eastern Caribbean dollars. It's not much and we keep asking for more but they always say they don't have it to spare. That sum has to pay for the Clerk of the Carib Council, an honorarium for the Chief and for road maintenance.'

'And it's not enough?' Obviously it wasn't but the room was hot and I hadn't done my calculations correctly – 21,000 EC dollars was about £4000. 'Enough? It's mustard seed.' 'So how do you manage?' 'For me, it's different. I live in a pool of water here. It's the other side of the mountain where the people have a real water problem.' For a moment, he looked tired. It seemed another burden was to be laid on his young shoulders. I changed the subject. The previous day, Eugenia Charles, the Prime Minister of Dominica, had agreed to give me some of her time. She had firm views on the subject of the Caribs and was clearly not prepared to put up with anything that might seem like a challenge to her authority. 'What about this thing the Prime Minister told me about outside men not being allowed in to marry Carib women? Is that true?' Auguiste nodded: 'There's nothing new about that. In our traditional laws, strangers were never allowed in to settle. We spent hundreds of years trying to keep them out. If an outsider comes into the Territory, do we let them have our land, that we have fought for, for so long? No. There's only a little bit of Dominica left to us and we must hold on to it.' He looked hard at me to see if I understood then turned away to stare out of the window. The rain had darkened the earth and left the leaves glistening bright and green. 'It's a problem for us. We want to preserve our race. There are only five hundred families left here now, in Salybia. We have to take care of them.' He paused, thinking. 'Five hundred. Before Columbus, there were millions.'

Then he became restive, stirred by the cause he'd wanted to fight for since he was a small boy and I was ashamed to have thought that what he was talking about was dull. Ashamed to have had such thoughts about a man who has to fight a lonely battle on this small island, a battle for survival, differing from his ancestors only in his methods. He'd always wanted to get involved with his people so, after David (the 1979 hurricane which killed thirty-seven people and left three-quarters of the islanders homeless), he'd got work surveying the damage to trees and crops. Then he went to college in Grenada and when he came back to Salybia, the people elected him as Chief. Then they re-elected him. 'And again? Would you stand again?' He frowned. 'Do you belong to any party?' 'No. The different parties are uncertain what exactly I am.' A smile spread across his face: 'They're still trying to get me.'

The people of Salybia are Dominicans first, and then Caribs, the Prime Minister had told me. I repeated this to Auguiste and his eyes slid away from me, unfocused, as if he were looking out across an unbridgeable gap: 'She hasn't yet recognized us as an indigenous people. We have to educate the politicians. Look, the government has got to see it – we make a contribution to the island. People want to know about the Caribs. You'll read all about us in the tourist programmes . . . Come and see the shy Caribs, it says. As if we were some sort of attraction. Then, when we protest, they say we're backed by Communists.' He folded his hands and put them on the table, firmly. Firm hands. Hurt eyes. One of his small daughters slipped in and whispered something in his ear. Without interrupting his flow of talk, he leaned across the table and handed her a roll of lavatory paper, which she took and ran out again. 'We have to educate ourselves. And how can we do that? In our schools here, the children learn nothing about their Carib culture. Nothing. There are no Carib teachers to tell them about it. We have no policemen. Well, there are Carib policemen in Dominica but no Carib inspector and it's the inspector who oversees things. We want Carib police here who will understand the problems of a young Carib boy who gets arrested for being drunk. We want someone to say yes, but why was he drunk? What is his problem? A Carib's problem is different from a Dominican's. Dominicans think all the time of their African background and now they want to be part of the modern world, with a TV, a car, wearing a baseball cap and looking like someone from the US. A Carib doesn't. He's a quiet person, grows his own food for himself and his family. He doesn't want a car – he goes to work on foot, with his cutlass in his hand. We've always been like that, and have always been here but not the Dominicans. They were brought here from Africa, and now they look on the Caribs as second-class citizens. You're just a Carib, they say.'

I knew that what he said was true because the other day I bought a book in Roseau, a children's book about Dominica, published with UNESCO money. It was thirty-one pages long, only one of which was devoted to the Caribs and their history. Auguiste told his story with resignation. The Caribs wanted little and were given less. I could think of nothing to say. The marginalized seem always to be surrounded by an emptiness, a void over which hovers embarrassment, resentment, sadness and loss. I had heard this story before on the West Bank, in a refugee camp in Sudan, in Soweto, in a prefab council house in Oxford, in a Dublin Corporation flat. The poverty of their desire, John Stuart Mills called it, speaking of the poor and the dispossessed. My biro rested, but only for a moment: Auguiste was relentless. 'No policemen,' he continued, 'no nurses, no teachers. If Carib children want to learn more, they have to go to a secondary school off the Territory and that rarely happens. Teachers from the outside don't help them reach their potential, so they drop out. And take nurses. My wife would like to be a nurse. She *is* a nurse, in her heart, but they want her to have four O levels. O levels! We are Caribs. We work from the heart, not from books.'

I took a photo of the family, the Chief and his son in their bare feet. His wife, leaning slightly to one side, conscious, perhaps, of the fact that she was taller than her husband, the little daughters smiling shyly, the small son impishly. An ordinary family. An historic family.

CHAPTER FOURTEEN

A Dream of Incest

The man came to the young girl every night and, in the dark, made love to her, never letting her see his face. 'You must find out who he is,' the old woman told her. 'Here, when he comes to you tonight, put this juice on his face and in the morning we'll all be able to see who is doing this to you.' So, that night, while they made love, the young girl did as she had been told and caressed her lover's cheek with the juice from the plant the old woman had given her. In the morning, she searched the faces of all the men in the village, wondering which of them it was that had made her body sing. When she saw the man, the one who had the streaks from last night on his face, she shivered. It was her own brother. To hide his shame, the man left the village and made his way up into the sky, to hang there every night, desolate, the marks on his pale moon-face showing the wrong he had done. Below on earth the girl, abandoned by her lover, lay down on the red soil and wept. Some months later, she gave birth to their child, and that is one story of how the Carib people began.

Enacted: *An Act of Parliament for the Annihilation of the Caribs.*
Public notice in Dominica: *Caribs wanted, dead or alive.*
Travellers' accounts: *'The Indians of Dominica are Carib and they eat human flesh and, in their drunkenness, kill christians . . . The way of these caribe people is bestial . . . The man was ill-proportioned and must be of the caribes who eat men . . . A large band of caribes, squatting on their backsides like monkeys . . .'*

Columbus on the Caribs: *'. . . they are very intelligent and when they have got rid of their cruel habits to which they have become accustomed, will be better than any other kind of slave'.*

Prosperous Paris is thirty. His cheekbones are broad, his skin olive and his eyes narrow. His shoulders are wide and strong and his long black hair hangs down his back in a shining plait – a sure sign of his Carib birthright. Tonight, Prosperous is teaching the young people of Salybia a Carib dance, one which he has devised himself. The boys and girls – the boys with long plaits like Prosperous – circle and dip to the beat of a drum. Sometimes, the boys stoop to pick up imaginary bows and, leaning back, fire arrows into the air. The girls stoop also, scattering seeds on the red earth. Occasionally, the drummers utter a cry, a repetitive cry vibrating in the throat, like the call of a solitary bird echoing somewhere deep within the rainforest.

Further along the track that runs from the high end of

Salybia right down the steep path to sea level, there is a church with an altar made from an upturned canoe. Behind the altar is a painting which shows a half-naked Carib paddling his pirogue through choppy waters, under a grey sky heavy with rain. He is travelling towards a land of sunshine and bright flowers, a land over which arcs a rainbow. He is moving from the rainforest that is his home to the bluebird world of Christianity, a world where people go clothed and darkness is seen as evil. The painting was done for the church by a local artist, Faustulus Frederick, a one-time chief of the Caribs.

The Caribs were indeed warlike and put up fierce resistance to the invaders. They were highly skilled archers, able to fire four arrows in the time it took to load a musket, an expertise equalled only by the crack English archers at Agincourt. They used six-foot bows and shafts fashioned from the reeds which grew in abundance and from which Dominica's capital, Roseau, gets its name. The tips of the arrows were first hardened by scorching in fire then dipped in poison from the manchineel tree. The arrowhead was bound to the shaft with a length of sisal but this was loosened just before firing so that when the head embedded itself in the victim's flesh, the shaft could be pulled out again for reuse, leaving the poisoned arrowhead behind to do its work. To increase the power of their weapons, Carib archers tied balls of flaming kapok to their arrows and fired them at the settlers' thatched huts. Small wonder, then, that Dominica was the last of the Caribbean islands to be subdued by the Europeans.

Louis Dupigny is keeper of what is left of the Carib language on Dominica. An anthropologist came to Salybia once to study the Caribs, married Louis's sister and left in his possession a school exercise book with pages curling up at the edges in which is written some notes about the Carib language. It is Louis's passport to scholarship and respect-ability. Nothing much else about him is respectable. He wears a grubby vest with a tear in the middle through which his knotted old navel peers like a third and lewd eye. He jabs a finger at the school book: 'Here, look here. You see this? You know what it say?'

The phrase is a jumble of strange words. Beside it is a translation in English which I read: 'I want to make love to you,' it says. Louis smirks. 'All the English ladies say that to me . . . And look here, at this word, you know what that mean?' His third eye contracts with excitement as he cackles: 'It mean darling,' he says slyly.

Salybia is different from the rest of Dominica. The soil up here is red as rust and, in the evening sun, glows warm as the embers of a fire. Down each side of the road, the earth is banked up and sown with bright flowers – crimson oleander, blue periwinkle, scarlet cordia, purple bougain-villea, pink passionflower and yellow allemanda. The little houses have red tin roofs and neat gardens full of veget-ables: dasheen and gourds, sweet potatoes and peppers. In one, the blue-green manioc leaves run riot over the ground and tumble away out of sight down a hill. Breadfruit trees grow alongside avocado and soursop. Across the valley are banana plantations, the distant leaves varnished electric blue by the sun, their bunches of emerging bananas purple and flagrantly engorged. It is as if the essence of the island – its fertility, its lushness, its very soul – has been distilled in this one corner, guarded by its spiritual owners.

In 1492, the total Carib population numbered around four million. Two hundred years later, there were some 5000 Caribs on Dominica. By 1730, they had shrunk to 400 and by the time the island was finally lost to the English, in 1763, there were 30 families left. Now, there are 2000 Caribs on Dominica, some of pure blood and some of mixed blood. Their territory in Salybia has become their home, as far away and as isolated from Roseau as possible. It is both the forgotten and the cherished part of Dominica. Few people here can afford electricity. There are no street lights, though in an age of light pollution, this is a blessing for most nights are lit by moonlight, stars and dancing fireflies.

When a village water scheme was introduced on Dominica, Salybia was omitted from the plan. It was too expensive, the Caribs were told, too difficult to bring it to the far side of the island. In any case, the politicians said, they had plenty of water what with rivers and the ocean. And so the Caribs continued walking down to Crayfish river, filling up their cans and carrying them back up the hill again. Until, one National Self-Help Day, they took matters into their own hands, diverted the river water into a tank and took it to a standpipe close to the road where the women now congregate to wash their hair, launder clothes and exchange news. 'You stayin' with Genette?' Gloria asks, beating her washing against the rocks by the side of the road. 'She my sister, you know. Her mother my mother.' Later, in the shop, Hester says the same thing: 'You stayin' with Genette?'

'Yes. You know her?'

'Hmm. Her father my father.'

'Oh, so you're sisters?'

'No, different mother.'

I've rented a room in Genette's house. It's a neat little tin and timber dwelling, set into the hillside and surrounded by a garden that climbs back up the hill. The garden is bountiful, full of peppers and callaloo, cabbages and coriander. Up on the slope there are lime trees and a couple of coconut palms. The yard is shaded by a large mango tree. Genette's husband, Vic, fixes things round the house, breaks coconuts, prepares food and keeps the stall at the side of the road stocked with home-grown cinnamon, ginger, gum, castor oil and coconut oil. Three nights a week he loads up a neighbour's truck with garden produce to take down to the market in Roseau. The market opens at six in the morning but Vic stays by the truck all night to make sure his produce isn't stolen. Genette has a job taking water to the men who work out along the road, keeping the drains and ditches clear. The job lasts for two weeks, then another woman takes over. Caribs are used to job-sharing, to living and working on a communal basis. It's their way of life. Tonight, when I got back to the house, after talking with Prosperous, the place was in darkness. The main room doubles as a storage shed and, in the dark, I felt my way round a mountain of coconuts until I saw the gleam of a white cloth spread on the only table in the house. On it, Genette had left some supper for me: fish stew, dumplings and plantains with fresh lime juice to drink.

My bed is a mattress on the floor, set out in a tiny area off the main room, through a doorway that has no door. I blow out the candle and lie with just a sheet covering me, listening to the tiny frogs chiming close to my ear on the other side of the thin wall. Suddenly I am awake, thinking

I hear rain on the tin roof but it's only a rush of current from the Atlantic, drawing a light veil of wind across the cliffs. The air, disturbed as I had been by the fidgety movement, resettles itself. I lie on my mattress, hearing the secret sounds of the night: the urgent screech of a nocturnal bird, the bell-like pipping of tiny frogs, the nervous rustle of leaves as a lizard scurries past, the tick-tick of tireless crickets. A thousand minute rachets working through the night. And then the sudden silence as they pause, listening to me listening to them. What if you could harness this energy, transpose it on to a page, arrange the marks into a pattern – a poem, perhaps, without words. Or better, a piece of music with pizzicato and pauses, grace notes and rests, a mighty chorus of a thousand soloists. Or simply a musical ornament. If you could take the clicks, one by one, and string them together, making a necklace of hopping sounds, tiny as fleas, to wear round your neck. Now, as I plan their metempsychosis, the crickets pause and I'm caught like an eavesdropper, holding my breath, my thoughts left hanging in midair, until they start again and I can relax. Or can I relax? Suppose – heart-stopping moment of death – suppose they stopped and never started again? The Caribs used to think that, when you died, your heart-spirit went up into the blue sky. Now Christianity has come and they have hell and purgatory instead.

When I next wake, it's to the sound of Vic brushing the yard. Shr-shr-shr as his bunch of twigs sweeps the dusty red earth outside. He's up at five every morning to start brushing, working at it for half an hour. Shr-shr – another poem. And further down the village, someone has started grinding manioc, the wheel turning smoothly: whrr-whrr, ticket, ticket, whrr-whrr, ticket, ticket. Yesterday, when I tried turning Gloria's wheel, I lost the rhythm: whrr-whrr, ticket, tocket, whrr, ticket, whrr, tocket, ticket. The birds are up too, hidden deep in the forest, invisible but exuberant. Their call is solitary, meant only for their own kind but I think of them in there, a busy collection of frail bones and feathers, chests puffing, throats filling, each jostling for position on the scale, nudging notes out of the way, extending their own song till their lungs are like tiny, inflated sacks. Thousands of them, darting from tree to tree in their dark green world, out of bounds to humans. Though not the fou-fou. The tiny, nervy hummingbird was hunted by Carib men for its brilliant feathers which they wore in their hair. Parrots too they hunted, lighting a fire of charcoal, gum and pimento under the tree so that the smoke rose to stupefy the parrots which then fell off their perches.

The table and chair – Genette's only pieces of furniture – have been made silvery grey by the first touch of dawn shimmering through the main room. One of her tall sons passes through from the communal sleeping area and goes outside to wash from the bucket of water at the side of the house. Vic's brushing continues, shr-shr-shr. Shr-shr. When I next open my eyes, the sun is shafting across the outer room, leaving a sheen of gold on everything it touches. And then, like a goddess walking through fire, Genette, naked to the waist, passes into its light, her bare breasts, brown and full, unscathed by the flame of the sun-king.

CHAPTER FIFTEEN

Sekunjalo: Now is the Time: 1994

De profundis clamavi, ad te, Domine.
Domine, exaudi vocem meam.

For the group of people gathered together in the Mandela corner of Dublin's Merrion Square it was a grim occasion and as Terence McCaughey intoned the *De Profundis*, I understood, for the first time, its true anguish:

From the depths have I cried unto thee, oh Lord.
Oh Lord, hear my prayer.

It was April 1993 and Chris Hani, a prominent figure in the anti-apartheid struggle, had just been assassinated outside his home in Johannesburg. He was fifty-one and his killers were a right-wing Polish immigrant and a deputy in the apartheid parliament. A piper played a lament and the small gathering, reluctant to disperse, broke into groups to discuss the implications of this terrible murder. Hani was immensely popular with the people and a strong leader within the South African Communist Party. His death, it was feared, would precipitate an outbreak of righteous rage that could well turn out to be more than the dying apartheid regime could cope with. But out of the depths of fear and anger rose hope. Two months after his murder, it was announced that the first fully democratic elections ever to be held in South Africa would take place the following year, in 1994. Which is how I found myself in a town called Burgersdorp in the Eastern Cape, attending a rally to mark the first anniversary of Hani's death. The mourning period was over and, unlike the stricken group in Dublin a year ago, this gathering was devoted to singing, dancing, clapping and toi-toing. In a few weeks, the celebrants would go to the polling station to make their choice.

Soon after the election had been announced, I read a newspaper feature by British MEP, Glenys Kinnock, in which she noted that there would be the need for a large number of international observers at the election. I wrote to her to find out how one became an observer and she replied, explaining that the observers would probably be drawn from the ranks of European parliamentarians. Feeling that there were others who might well do the job as well, if not better, I made more enquiries which led me to Rafique and Frankie Mottiar, mainstays of the Irish Anti-Apartheid Movement. My name was put forward by the IAAM as a candidate to join an Irish contingent of election workers and, to my joy, I was selected by APSO, the Association of

239

Professional Services Overseas, a Dublin-based body funded by the Department of Foreign Affairs.

Burgersdorp, on the edge of the Karoo Desert, is a small Afrikaner farming town halfway between Johannesburg and Cape Town. Although the desert proper lies some distance away, its edges reach out like a visitation from another land, encroaching upon the neatness of the town. The red sand is always a pervasive presence and the persistent wind leaves a layer of dust on tables, cars and clothes.

Election Diary: 14 March

Driving between the small village of Bethulie, where there was to be a polling station, and Knapdaar, where the election officer lived, was like driving across a sheet of silk. The wheels of the car had nothing to grip and at the side of the road drifts of sand lay like a fall of red snow. I drove through this strange landscape for fifty kilometres without meeting another car or seeing another human being.

Our work as election observers is taking us to all the outlying towns and farms though Burgersdorp is the focus of our activities. When we first arrived, I asked how many people lived here and was told 12,000. This seemed a small figure for such a large town but Burgersdorp is made up of three distinct communities, black, white and coloured and once the black township is included together with the outlying farms, the population rises to 27,000.

Eureka, where the observers are billeted, is the coloured township artificially created when, following the Group Areas Act of 1950, many people, reclassified as black or coloured, were uprooted and shifted from one part of the country to another. Across the main road and further separated from Eureka by a foul-smelling river that is nothing more than a slow-moving sludge of human waste, lies the black township of Mzamomhle, where, originally, all non-whites lived. A mile or so down the road lies the white part of Burgersdorp, set out like a little toy town with a town hall, bank, Post Office, church, supermarket and petrol station. Houses here have neat curtains at the windows. Sprinklers keep the lawns green. During the day, the town is busy, the car park full of farmers' bakkies (open-backed trucks), but by six o'clock in the evening, the noisy, shouting, laughing, drinking black people withdraw to their township and the white part of town shuts down. Then it's a lonely place to be in.

I'm renting a room in a house belonging to Charlie, who is a teacher, and his wife Susie, who runs the local play-group. Charlie's big smiling face is black and his hair crinkly. Susie carries her baby tied to her back in a blanket like many African women. But though they both *look* black, they are, in fact, coloured. I'd been trying to suss out Charlie. He's obviously an ANC supporter though he doesn't belong to any political party. This means that, as a so-called neutral, he can always be called upon to chair a meeting or inter-vene in a dispute.

21 March

The Burgersdorp Transitional Council consists of twelve white people – the sitting tenants, so to speak – until the elections decide who's going to run Burgersdorp. The white members sport grey beards and grey hair. Most speak English, though one large-thighed, balding safari-suited man speaks only Afrikaans. On the Council also are sixteen black and coloured people. The older black people are quiet-spoken, polite, respectful. Among the black group are Boswell Simsi and Toto Wonga, two twenty-something teachers from the black township. Unlike the white people, some of whom have come to the meeting in shorts and shirt sleeves, Boswell and Toto are dressed smartly in well-cut suits and ties. Toto wears gold-rimmed spectacles while Boswell is unmissable, his eyes blazing with emotion, his head completely shaven.

The discussion focuses on the out-of-town farmworkers who don't earn much, live in tied accommodation and who are dependent on the farmer to drive them in and out of town at weekends. During the week, if they want anything, they have to buy it at the shop run by the farmer's wife. As observers, we have been worried that voter education has not been reaching the farmworkers. The point being raised now is that because the farmworkers are outside the town boundary, they can't be represented by Boswell and his comrades.

'The boundaries must be changed,' says Boswell, who, flying high on the knowledge that the ANC is going to win this election, is now certain that anything is possible. The Chair demurs: the boundaries have already been drawn up and agreed nationally. Boswell persists, standing up and leaning his hands on the table the better to make his point.

'The farmworkers out there are my black brothers,' he says passionately, gesturing towards the window, 'and we must represent them otherwise they will have no one.' I admire these aspirations, but secretly, as I am 'neutral'. Toto too rises and talks about the way in which the labourers have been exploited. The white group sit impassively through these two speeches. They have learned that silence is one part of discretion. The Chair behaves impeccably but towards the end is irritated: 'Look, if we refer this back that means we're saying we are unable to decide for ourselves.' But Boswell is unperturbed. He's used to being told by white people he can't decide anything for himself and anyway has never believed it.

Defeated for the present, the Chair moves swiftly and efficiently to the next item on the agenda, which happens to be the position of the Chair itself. Toto would like there to be more than one Chair. 'How many,' asks the Chair, a trifle ironically. 'Two? More? You?' Toto holds his ground. He would like to see the Chair rotating – a novel idea in Burgersdorp. Nominations are sought but when Toto is nominated, he declines. Boswell also declines. Eventually Charlie, who has been surprisingly silent throughout the meeting, is nominated and accepts. After the meeting, one of the white men draws me aside: 'You see? They're very difficult to please, these people.' One of the things he finds hardest to handle is the ANC's penchant for democracy: 'We talk and talk and try to reach a decision with them but these people,' and his hands wave about helplessly, 'they can't do anything without consulting with their own people.'

Back home, Charlie explains tactics: 'We always have a caucus before a meeting when we decide who's going to speak. We also choose a sleeper, someone who simply observes and who analyses the meeting afterwards.' He was the sleeper at today's meeting. It's clear that the ANC has done a good job educating its members in the business of politics. 'We are not triumphalist,' says Charlie, 'or confrontational. When I'm chairing a meeting, I always try to get people to reach a consensus rather than putting something to the vote especially when I see we're going to win hands down. It's better that way.'

I'm drawn to Mzamomhle. In the evenings, smoke rises from the open fires dotted round the township and there is always the noise of singing and clapping. It's a magnetic kaleidoscope of intriguing sounds that makes me feel I'm missing out on a party. I'd prefer to rent a room in Mzamomhle but our group leader – a military man – has told us not to venture into it on our own and never ever at night. As usual, I feel restricted, hemmed in, prevented from making contact with the very people we're supposed to be serving. It is a perennial problem for travellers, having to bear on their shoulders the fears and prejudices of others on top of those they've brought along in their own personal baggage. Nevertheless, I persuaded my fellow observer, James, to come with me to a gospel singing competition being held one evening in the black township.

The competition was taking place in a small wooden church where members of the congregation, by making a small donation, were allowed to nominate a hymn that their chosen choir would then sing. My donation was five rand and this, I learned to my horror, entitled me to twenty hymns. The only one I knew was 'Thula Sizwe' ('Be Peaceful, My Country'), a gentle, close harmony number I had grown to like. A discussion was held about this as, strictly speaking, it was a song rather than a hymn. However, in view of my inadvertently large donation, it was agreed I could have 'Thula Sizwe' sung for me. Ten hymns later, we pleaded election business and left. Things weren't always this peaceful in Mzamomhle and the liberation struggle has taken a terrible toll of its people. One church minister, Dinti, lost his son but few people wanted to talk about it. Thaba, a teacher in one of the local schools did, however, recounting the awful story in a monotone dirge: 'Dinti's son was twenty-three and a mob came looking for him. He was, they said, a sell-out. When he was brought to hospital, they found he'd had a spear thrust in him. They'd got plastic dustbin lids and plastic bags and held him down and they'd set fire to him . . . On the day of his funeral, it was raining. The mob said no one except the family should go to it. The grave was dug and filled in, three times. He was a sweet boy. His father was a member of PAC [the Pan Africanist Congress] but who knows what he was . . . The police arrested them. One of the comrades informed. Two of them were put on death row but taken off it. They were released in 1992. One of them is in Cape Town. His mind is not right. The other came back and committed a serious crime – he raped a woman and then stabbed her. Now he's in prison again but it's no consolation to the minister.'

'Were the killers ANC?' I asked her but she couldn't bring herself to say exactly.

'They were comrades but they were also a mob.'

29 March

I'm trying to learn Xhosa which most people speak here. It's one of the clicking languages but clicks are the least of my problems. I have my lessons with Mr Lusiba who is a lay Methodist preacher and also a teacher. We've had some difficulty with family words. You can't say granddaughter or grandson. You must first say grandchild and then define its gender. Nor is there a word for son-in-law or daughter-in-law. When you marry into a family, you *become* a son or daughter in your new family. And, of course, the word sister embraces a multitude of cousins. '*Thula* means calm,' says Mr Lusiba. 'How I calm my baby,' and he cradles an imaginary baby in his arms. '*Isi bhakabhaka* is sky,' waving his hands above his head. 'No man's land. Above that, far up, is *izulu* which is heaven. And *phezulu* means top.' His gestures leave me uncertain as to whether *phezulu* is higher even than heaven and I stare upwards, imagining what might lie beyond the blue of the sky.

Fact: *A domestic servant earns thirty rand a month (£6) and a farmworker gets eighty rand (£17) plus a ration of mealie and a house to live in.*

Though quieter and less exuberant than Mzamomhle, Eureka can also be entertaining. One day, I noticed a large tent being erected outside a nearby house and women in the yard preparing huge bowls of food. A wedding, surely. The next night, the guests had arrived. The party was going full strength and against the canvas of the tent, which was lit from within by oil lamps, I could see the looming silhouettes of people clapping and dancing. I could stand it no longer. 'Come on,' I said to James. 'Let's party.' As we boogied up to the flap of the tent, an arm reached out and drew me in. Rows of chairs had been set out in opposite lines, all occupied by people swaying and singing. It seemed a jolly sort of carry-on and I was ready to go with it until I looked back and saw James desperately beckoning to me at the entrance to the tent. 'What's the matter?' I asked, swaying my hips. 'Come on in. It's great fun.'

'Come out,' he hissed. 'It's not a party.'

'You could have fooled me.'

'It's not. It's a funeral. An old lady's died.'

And, indeed, the woman of the house had died a few days ago and this was the wake. She was a Xhosa woman, married to a coloured man and was only fifty-five. Next morning, the hearse stopped by the house. I was sorry not to be able to go to the funeral but there was election business to see to. When I got back in the evening, the tent was gone, the chairs had been stacked up and life had reverted to its normal rhythm. I'd already seen the hearse, parked in a shed near the church. Its purchase was part of a rural development programme: cost of hearse, in rand, 15,000; repairs to hearse 5000; wood to make coffins 2000; tools for coffin-making 1000; lowering device 1000.

1 April

The days are changing. The sun is warm but the light is white and cold outside, the shadows of leaves restless on the wall of the church. At an election briefing, we are told that people will be resistant to putting an X on the ballot paper because it signifies a bad mark. In our voter education exercises, we have to make sure people are told to mark only their preferences. The more obvious thing to do is to put a cross against the people you don't want and tick the ones you do. But they mustn't do this. We feel out of it here in the backwater that is Burgersdorp. All the newsworthy events are happening in Cape Town, Johannesburg and Soweto. Stores are looted (affirmative shopping) in

Bophuthatswana, there's a shoot out in Cape Town, more trouble in the Transkei but all is quiet in Burgersdorp. And then word comes through: Mandela is coming to a rally in Aliwal North, a nearby Afrikaner town where some of the white men openly carry guns.

18 April

The rally is due to start at midday but by eight in the morning the roads are thronged with people walking to the town. Some of them started before dawn. I drop off the other observers and go back along the road picking up one carload of walkers after another, ferrying them to the stadium. But then I have to stop because all the observers are needed at the rally. Will everyone still trudging the road get to the stadium in time? I fear not. Of course that's reckoning without African time which is even more elastic than Irish time.

By early afternoon, I'm wilting but the crowd isn't. They're used to waiting and will wait for ever for Madiba. People continue to clap and sing, the majorettes continue to march up and down, the stewards continue to be polite: '*Please*, comrade, don't run under the security barrier.' Eventually, at 3.30, a small aircraft buzzes into our patch of sky and twenty minutes later, the cavalcade arrives. Just inside the gates of the stadium, before the crowd has noticed him, Mandela, wearing a Xhosa headband, stands erect in his open car, a lonely isolated figure, his face blank. And then the car moves forward, the cheering begins and, simultaneously, the famous smile appears on his face. Did he switch it on as the cavalcade crossed the invisible line between private and public? His persona is now so much that of a world statesman that it's easy to forget he is also a canny old ANC politician.

It takes half an hour for the crowd to settle down so that he can address them and, when he does, it becomes clear why they love him. He is their hero, their saviour, their role model but, above all, he is their father. From his platform, he looks down on them with affection, talks soothingly to them, makes little jokes and tells them how to fill in their ballot papers: 'Vote for the handsome one, not the baldy old white fella at the bottom of the ballot paper.' A young minder in his uniform of Umkhonto we Sizwe, the armed wing of the ANC, known as MK and since disbanded, holds an umbrella over him. Another stands ready with a glass of water. A third steps forward to take his spectacles when he's finished reading his speech. He speaks mainly in Xhosa but occasionally the politicians' promise words come through in English, words like electricity, five million unemployed – and flush toilet.

That night, still euphoric, we go to Dukitole (The Lost Cow) – the black township attached to Aliwal North – hoping for some fun but everyone has partied themselves out. In the karaoke-smart nightclub there's no drink on offer and, dismayed, we hang about until hijacked by Maisie, a huge-thighed maiden of strange virtue, who takes us to 'her house' which has a lot of men in it, sitting round drinking. 'You live here?' I ask. 'No, no. It's a shebeen.'

A white man appears, goes through to a back room and an hour later emerges holding the hand of a young black man. Predictably, he takes a dislike to the group of observers: 'When you're finished slumming it here, you'll go back to your comfortable white hotel, I suppose,' he says, raising a hollow laugh among those of us whose cramped quarters mean doubling up two to a room and whose lavatory is outside in the yard and which itself doubles as the dog's kennel. While he continues his tirade, I keep one eye on the murky-screened television, hoping to see a clip of today's rally but all I can see is a snowstorm in Antigua where, at the Antiguan Recreation Ground, an exuberant cricket crowd is celebrating Brian Lara's world-breaking record of 375 runs. I scan the screen for a sight of Russell who, like Deirdre, is now living and working in Antigua but the snowstorm turns into a blizzard and, suddenly reminded of my family, I'm left feeling bereft. Driving back to Burgersdorp at two in the morning, the moon is whitely cold. Autumn is another day nearer.

The *Daily Dispatch* carries a horrible news item: *a man tried to commit suicide by jumping into a cesspit or long-drop lavatory. It contained the takings of ten years. He was pulled out unconscious by local policemen.*

By day, Mzamomhle is pleasing. Some of the houses have a cottagey look to them, cosy as a child's drawing with a door, two windows each side and flower-beds outside. Inside, oilcloths cover the tables and everything is neat, tidy and safe. By night, it is the same except that it all *looks* different. There are no street lights, only tall masts that, carrying the huge township lights, throw a yellow, sickly pall over what now looks like a gulag. The tin roofs are cold and ghostly, as if covered by a fall of snow. Deep shadows draw the eye inwards but to what? A sudden movement, the glow of a cigarette. Young men congregate at corners, black faces invisible against the black of night.

I drive over to Mzamomhle with Charlie who wants to

drop off a book to someone and, as I sit in the car waiting, I notice an indistinct figure across the road. The figure squats down and I keep an eye on it, feeling nervy. But when Charlie emerges, the man comes out of the shadow and crosses the road to talk to him. In fact, to offer to help him with his election rotas. My fears were groundless and I felt angry at the way in which I allowed other people's fears to influence my thoughts. That night, thinking about all this, I felt so angry I couldn't sleep. I even thought of pulling out of the whole operation but, before I could formulate the best way to do this, I'd dropped off.

The design for the new flag has been released and people aren't sure what to make of it. It has no symbols and is described variously as resembling a pair of recumbent Y-fronts, a bureaucratic compromise of an aesthetic concept and a Third-World flag. The international observers have come in for some unflattering attention as well. 'The ballot boxes,' writes someone in a newspaper, 'will be scrutinized by swollen-bellied Western capitalists.' Yep, that's us all right.

Sunday in Eureka

Susie has polished the house and left it sweet-smelling. The sheep's head has been cleaned and is waiting to be put in the pot. I've eaten a bowl of mealie. People are going to church in their white satin and matching high heels. Bob Marley is on the radio. On the lamp post outside our house is a National Party poster with a picture of De Klerk, put there to annoy Charlie. But there's little that annoys Charlie.

How to make mealie:
Add four cups of boiling salted water to two cups of brai pap

or mealie. Form a pyramid and put the lid on. Cook for forty minutes. Stir and replace lid. Leave for ten minutes then pour half a cup of cold water down the sides of the mealie. Stir. Leave for half an hour to steam.

Voter education poster: *Avoid the bullet. Use the ballot.*

There are 7000 candidates for 4000 seats. This includes the regional and national elections both of which are taking place at the same time. The third election is for the president.

9 April

James and I and a few women from Eureka pay a return visit to the nightclub at Dukitole. This time it's open. I hadn't wanted to go because I was tired but it's an outing that's been organized for us so I feel I'd better be sociable. Once there, of course, I have a great time dancing. I acquire two partners that I like and manage to rotate them throughout the night. One, Mithi, is about twenty but who cares? He's civil and respectful of my age and a marvellous dancer. The other, Leonard, is older, a man of the world and an equally good dancer. Both make little encouraging shoo-shoo noises as they move which, under other circumstances, could well urge me to ecstasy.

But at the end of the night, it's James that Leonard really fancies.

12 April

Being part of a group is trying – and I do try but it doesn't come easy. My room-mate is of a nervous disposition and is fearful that, if the window is left open at night, strange men may try to get in. And if not a man, then one of the turkeys, which gobble about outside in the yard, may alight on the window ledge and take it a bit further. I, on the other hand, feel trapped by closed doors and windows. In any case, it gets stuffy at night with no air. I try to reassure her, pointing out that if anything were to come in, man, bird or beast, the intruder would have to deal first with me as my bed is directly below the window. Even James, my soulmate on this adventure, proves more wary than I feel is necessary. Driving back from a rally, we come to Stormberg, the site of a famous battle between the English and the Boers that the latter won, defeating in the process a contingent of the Royal Irish Rifles. The local hill was a focal point in the ambush and, needing some exercise, I suggest we climb it. It was, after all, a grassy slope much lower than anything in Donegal and without the sea mist. James is aghast:

'Up there? In my suit?'

'That's a suit?'

'You have to be equipped for that sort of thing.'

'We are equipped.'

'We're not. We need water.'

'I have a bottle of it here.'

'That's not enough. It's only like a milk bottle. You need two litres of water. At least. Otherwise you'll get renal failure.'

I look longingly at the hill. Such a small one and so historic but, today, not for me.

Fact: *The average size of a class in the primary school in Mzamomhle is forty-seven.*

Fact: *The old age pension is 350 rand per month – about £70. The average monthly loan repayment on a house is 160 rand.*

16 April

We've had a chance to see a sample ballot paper and it looks long and interesting. You vote for the party not the individual and so, with eighteen parties in the running, each has a picture of its leader, a picture of the party symbol and the name of the party. Even if you can't read, there should be no problem picking out who you want. Votes will be distributed according to a system of preferences, excess votes being handed on to the next person on the party list. The ANC has drawn up its list of one hundred candidates. Joe Slovo is number three. Thirty-four million ballot papers have been printed in Britain. The next twelve million will be printed in South Africa. It's estimated that around twenty-six million people will turn out to vote.

When I tried to find one of the outlying polling stations the other day, to check its suitability, I got lost and had to ask the way of a farmer.

'Drive straight on for about ten kilometres and then turn left at the willow tree,' he said.

24 April

We're almost there. Everything is ready and in place. More or less. The Inkatha Freedom Party (IFP), which is supported mainly by Zulu people, has been boycotting the election and its name, therefore, has not appeared on the ballot paper. Now it has decided that, after all, it will run. Everyone is relieved. Without it in, the election could possibly have been declared null and void. However, its name will have to be tacked on at the end of the list, somehow, and this has upset the National Party. The two prime positions on the ballot paper are the top and the bottom. The Pan Africanist Congress has drawn lucky with the top place and the NP had the bottom (slogan: 'Vote for the bottom line') but, now it'll be moved up one and the IFP will get its position (slogan: 'The last shall be first').

25 April, Eve of Poll
I go to bed at 10.30 p.m. ready for an early start and hear on the radio that in New Zealand ex-pat South Africans have already begun voting.

26 April, Polling Day
We leave for our first polling station at 4.30 a.m. and I have to clear the ice from the windscreen before setting out to drive through a surreal landscape. In the western sky is the moon and to the east, the rising sun: twenty-four hours in one. Low mist lies in the valleys and sometimes, as it drifts across the road, I feel as if I'm driving through silky angel hair. Along the way, we stop to pick up two shepherds who are on their way home. It's been a cold night and when they get out of the car they leave behind them the scent of woodsmoke. The flag is flying for the first time over Dordrecht town hall, the cheerful yellow in it picked out by the early morning sun. It looks like a winner.

Voters arrive in a steady stream. One man comes carrying his disabled wife on his back. Another transports his old mother in a wheelbarrow. A couple arrive with their son, a man who is severely brain-damaged in some way. 'Sit,' says the father, pointing and obediently the son sits on the floor and waits while his parents vote. Then it's his turn. It's not an easy process. Identity papers have to be presented and matched against the electoral register. Thumbs have to be marked and checked under an ultraviolet light to ensure against multiple voting. People don't like the idea of something invisible happening to them. If they can't see it, how will they know when it's gone? The opposition has spread a story that the invisible ink is really a poison. When the ballot papers are handed out, the voter is directed to a polling booth. Some can't read. Some can read but stand waiting to be told when to mark their paper. Those that need help must first ask for it. If help is offered too readily there is the suspicion that the voter is being manipulated. All the parties have their observers to watch out for this kind of thing.

Helpers must not indicate in any way how or where the voters should put their mark. Only if they ask for a particular candidate can the helper point out the relevant box. Sometimes, families go into the polling booth in groups, the son, perhaps, to help his parents or a husband to help his wife. And when finally the paper has been marked, it must be folded and put in the box. Some overzealous helpers rush to do this last task for the nervous voter but that practice has to be stopped. Putting the paper in the ballot box is the final step in the liberation struggle and that moment must belong, above all, to the voter.

An old woman, blanket round her shoulders and woolly cap on her head, calls out for help and I go over to her. She's not terribly interested in perusing the list of parties. In fact, she's not even interested in going into the polling booth. She is here, she knows who she wants so what more is there to do?

'You have to find the party you want,' I tell her and cross my fingers behind my back, willing her to find what she's looking for. But she waves the ballot paper away.

'Who do you want to vote for?' I ask her.

'Maun-de-la,' she says in the low, slow local accent and grins wickedly, as if she's just said a deliciously naughty word. I'm not really allowed point to him but I have to make sure he gets his vote.

'ANC,' I hint and wiggle the paper at her. She beams back at me.

'Maun-de-la.'

'Yes,' I say, guiding her towards the polling booth. 'Nelson Mandela. He's there. His picture's there.' She continues to beam. I wiggle the paper some more.

'Can you see his picture?' She peers up and down the list and then she sees him.

'*Maun-de-la!*'

'So that's where you put your mark,' I say and, placing the pencil in her hand, withdraw.

The presidential inauguration was due to be held on 10 May and, with all the election teams gone, I decided to return to Burgersdorp for the celebrations. Moreover, I would stay in Mzamomhle – the first white person, I later learned, to do so.

9 May

I've rented a room for a few days from Zinza, a nurse in the local hospital. Her house has electricity, carpets on the floor, a pink bedroom and lace things round the loo. Yesterday, an old man doing the garden told me Zinza's story. Her parents, who were Xhosa, lived and worked in one of the big towns. Zinza grew up with coloured people who spoke Afrikaans so she did too but when the Group Areas Act was brought in her family was relocated out of the coloured area and sent to a black township in the Xhosa homeland of Transkei. Zinza didn't speak Xhosa and hated it. Now she's settled here in Burgersdorp. Her daughter Priscilla is an insurance sales rep. 'She's beautiful, not like me,' says Zinza who is, of course, as beautiful as her daughter. But she shakes her head in denial: 'No, look,' she says, pointing at a photograph of Priscilla, 'she has an American nose.'

A small delegation has arrived for a welcoming tea party. Mr Solani from next door, a lay preacher, says a prayer and then we have a cup of tea. Last time I was here, he told me he and his wife had no children. She is a teacher, he says, and sees children all day but he would like a child of his own. After the tea party, I leave as I have a meeting with Monica who runs the Mzamomhle Advice Centre. One of the things the new government wants to promote is community radio and Monica thinks it's a great idea. There are eleven official languages in South Africa now but English and Afrikaans predominate. A community radio station would speak to the people in their own language or, rather, the people would speak to the people. There would be music, gospel singing, rock music, reggae, classical and traditional. Health educators and legal people could give advice. Public information could be given out as well as births, deaths and marriages announced. People could ring up with their problems. The more we talked about it, the more excited we became. I would, I promised, find out as much as I could when I went home and pass it all on.

10 May, Inauguration Day

People have started gathering in Zinza's house for the in-auguration and it's not yet 9 a.m. The TV has been placed on the table so that we can all see it. Her neighbour, Raymond, seems to have disguised himself as Basil Brush for the occasion and is resplendent in checked shirt, yellow tie, tweed jacket and country gent's tweedy hat. He's brought a lot of beer with him and, prompted by this, I ask him to go to the rum shop and bring back some pink, sparkly wine which is called champagne. Zinza can't go because, although I've heard bottles clinking in her shopping bag, she's a nurse and it would cause scandal for her to be seen patronizing a rum shop. Everyone is talking, laughing, drinking. A young boy helps me sing 'Sikilel I Africa'. He's Jacob and he's one of Toto Wonga's pupils. Mr Solani puts his arm round his wife but she pushes it away. On television, the ceremony begins and, watching it, my eyes fill with tears. Raymond nudges Zinza and whispers: 'She's crying.' 'No,' says Zinza, 'it's the wine.'

More people arrive, including Violet with her little son. I give him a sweet but as he reaches out a hand to take it, Violet rebukes him sharply. He should extend two hands cupped together when receiving a gift. Mr Solani tries putting his arm round his wife again but is again repulsed. Perhaps she doesn't like him. We've run out of drink so I ask Jacob to go to the rum shop, giving him fifty rand. A bottle of South African champagne costs thirteen rand. He brings back two bottles and gives me ten rand change but who's counting on a day like this? Next time, Zinza sends him and, on his return, she counts her change carefully. Why didn't I do that? Because I'm a lily-livered liberal wet who's afraid of offending a black person, that's why. We need more drink. 'Shall I get some?' asks Jacob but Zinza says: 'Wait. You must consult with Mary first.' I hand over another twenty-five rand. Zinza is talking a lot, announcing plans, fired up with faux-energy brought on by alcohol.

'My daughter must go back to school and get a proper education. I must find the money for it somehow. It's not right.' There's a sudden roar from the TV. The crowd is cheering as someone takes his seat at the ceremony. Zinza glances at the screen: 'Who is this? I don't know him. Is he overseas?'

It's Fidel Castro. 'Cas-tro, Cas-tro, Cas-tro,' the crowd roar and the wine once again floods my eyes with tears. Something's moving on the wall. I'll have to stop drinking this stuff. I stare hard at the wall and see it's an elephant's trunk. Zinza's wall clock comes in the shape of an oriental scene with an elephant in the middle whose trunk tick-tocks back and forth.

Mr Solani leaves without his wife. Raymond dances around the room and into the kitchen. 'Mary,' he calls, 'we have a problem.' We've run out of drink, again. Zinza stares fixedly at the screen. I was sure there was one bottle left in the fridge. 'They drank it,' says Zinza and I hand over another twenty-five rand. I can't believe it: I've spent £50 today on drink. *'Yes, but look at the day that it is,' I say. 'That doesn't matter,' I reply, 'I don't have all that to spare. I'm not a bottomless source of rands, you know.' 'Oh, shut up.'*

And so I do. 'Could you bring me back the change,' I call after Raymond. 'That's if there is any, of course,' I add cravenly. Raymond decides I must become an honorary member of the Xhosa tribe. He gives me my own name – love – and, thrilled, I say a few words in Xhosa: '*Igamma lam ngu Nolunthando*' (My name is Nolunthando). Back in Johannesburg, I recount all this to my lawyer niece who lives there. 'What was the name they gave you?' I tell her and am immediately deflated. 'Oh, they call everyone that.'

25 May, Cape Town: Raadsaal Van Die Parlement, The Parliament Building

'All firearms must be left at the door,' says the notice on the wall and the two men in the queue ahead of us deliver theirs to security. No one is allowed to bring in as much as a biro so I can't make any notes. Instead, I gaze over the balcony and look down on the scene below where the first business sitting of the new parliament is about to take place. On the right, sit National Party members and, behind them, members of the Inkatha Freedom Party. Not that the IFP – supported mainly by Zulus – has a lot in common with the NP, just that they're both in opposition. On the other side and spilling across the political divide into the opposition's territory, sit the ANC members, all 250 of them. *All* of them. Put a frame round the whole thing and you have one of those historic photographs which people pore over, years later, picking out one famous face after another. Or more frivolously, I think, it's not unlike an Oscar ceremony with all the stars present.

For a start, there's Nelson, sitting all on his own, as presidents do. He has a small ornamental desk and is writing at it. Across the floor is De Klerk who, I notice, because he too is writing, is left-handed. Behind him is Chief Mangosuthu Buthelezi, leader of the IFP. The NP members, used to all this, sit back, arms stretched out across the bench seats. Every so often, they raise a finger to one of the attendants who comes forward with a glass of water. After a few minutes, the new boys on the other side get the hang of this and soon they too are signalling for their water. Madam Speaker presides. Ginwala Frene is an Indian lawyer and prominent spokesperson within the ANC on women's affairs. She was proposed for this job by Winnie Mandela. When appointed, Frene had said that, for the official opening of parliament, she would not be wearing the heavy ceremonial outfit of the Speaker which, with its ermine and heavy cloak, was redolent of stuffy colonialism. Instead, she wears, as she usually does, a sari. She sits up at her desk, surveying the other members who have to bow to her before speaking.

The ANC people are still taking their seats – when they can find a free one. Winnie Mandela finds one a few rows behind her husband and sits there alone. No one wants to sit too close to her. She's danger. Eventually, everyone settles down and the proceedings begin. This is the first business meeting of the new parliament but they don't do much business. It's a day for making maiden speeches. All the party leaders get to speak. A few ministers do as well. And beginning as they mean to continue, the NP people address the gathering as colleagues, the ANC as comrades. De Klerk, Nobel Prize winner (with Mandela) gracious in defeat, speaks briefly and urbanely. For the ANC, it's Kader Asmal, stepping in for Thabo Mbeki. Asmal is founder of the Irish

Anti-Apartheid Movement, having spent most of his thirty-years' exile in Dublin. A small, neat man, he bows formally to Madam Speaker as if he's been doing this kind of thing all his life. In measured tones, he makes a speech – in which he quotes Yeats – bows again and sits down. Next up is Mangosuthu Buthelezi. Speaking in Zulu, his speech is long and impassioned. Gradually, however, it changes in tone, evolving into a powerful, foot-stamping Zulu chant that makes Mandela first look up and then stand to receive this tribute from a fellow African and political foe. And as the two men, Zulu and Xhosa, face each other, colonial Europe fades into the margins of history. Their upbringing and their experience of apartheid unite them in a world we know nothing about, a world of tribal loyalties and brotherhood, a world that transcends narrow party politics. An African world. Then, to turn that world upside down, another IFP member rises to make a speech and, though white, addresses the house in Zulu.

The speeches continue. Someone from the National Party goes on a bit too long and Ronnie Kasrils, South African Communist Party member and former adman who ran the MK's information gathering operations, leans back and yawns largely and ostentatiously for the benefit of the friends he has spotted up in the gallery. Kasrils's role is that of bad boy and he plays it well. And then, the best speech of the day from Joe Slovo, his famous red socks bright as traffic lights, semaphoring hope. Joe Slovo, whose wife Ruth First, a glamorous activist and part-time mother, suffered such terrible injuries when blown up by a letter bomb – sent by agents of the apartheid regime – that parts of her body had to be scraped off her office wall. Joe Slovo, the Lithuanian who became Chief of Staff of the MK and General Secretary of the South African Communist Party. Joe Slovo, Minister of Housing in the new government, speaking with passion and conviction, reiterating his promise to build one million houses for the poor and the dispossessed. After that, there was nothing left to say.

CHAPTER SIXTEEN

Ultima Thule: *1996*

Tundra: a vast treeless zone lying between the ice cap and the timber line of North America and Eurasia and having a permanently frozen subsoil. From Lapp tundar*: hill. Related to Finnish* tunturi*: treeless hill.*

Twenty thousand years ago, the ice cap that covered the Arctic was 3000 metres thick. Over the next 10,000 years, as the ice started to melt and the ice cap to shrink, reindeer moved across it and began grazing the land. Four thousand years ago, the people known as the Saami followed the reindeer and began hunting them.

Two hundred kilometres up into the Finnish Arctic, the snow-covered plateau stretched out towards the horizon. A weak sun threw a metallic sheen on the occasional incline that sloped to a barely perceptible rise before drifting away again into an undefined vista of whiteness. In the distance – unmeasurable because of the absence of anything to

measure it against – a herd of reindeer appeared insub-
stantial as a mirage, then faded back into the landscape.
The further we climbed into the freezing tundra, the more
nervous I became. If something happened to Rune, who
would find us in this emptiness? Silence lay everywhere like
a death shroud. Nothing was certain except the horizon and
even that was often indistinct. The tundra remains like this,
day after day, month after month, silent and unchanging,
a wilderness unto itself. Winters last for up to ten long, ice-
bound months. Summers are eight weeks at the most.

The reindeer cows carry their unborn calves all through
the dark, cold winter and only give birth in spring when
the permafrost starts to melt. In summer, the calves are
rounded up and marked. Later, in autumn, the slaugh-
tering begins. The Saami have eight seasons, all related to
the life span and feeding habits of the reindeer. Initially,
the herds provided the Saami communities with meat, milk,
skins and fur but, by the middle of the last millennium,
as the herds diminished in size – all but hunted out of
existence – they took to taming and then farming them.
And because reindeer, like birds, are no respecters of boundaries, the nomadic Saami followed them to grazing grounds
as far apart as Sweden and the distant reaches of eastern
Russia. But then, in the 1700s, the Closed Border Treaties
were signed, the need for these brought about by territo-
rial squabbles between Tsarist Russia, Denmark and
Sweden, of which Finland was a part. The Saami, who
before had been free to follow their herds unimpeded, were
now subject to rules and regulations enforceable under the
Treaties.

As the centuries rolled on, the reindeer people became

more and more marginalized, forbidden to practise their religion, to speak their language, to sing their songs or to make their music. Grazing lands diminished as forests were cleared and land flooded to create reservoirs. Global warming began to shrink the tundra yet again. Reindeer herding is the cultural hallmark of the Saami. Take it from them and you deprive them of their identity, which is a process that is already far advanced. Deforestation has led to a radical change in the environment. The great snowy wastes are no longer protected by trees, which means the snow turns to ice so that, where before the reindeer could snuffle about in the soft snow foraging for lichen, now the ice forms an impenetrable barrier to this lifeline. And climate change is not the only enemy: every year, 4000 reindeer are killed by trains and road traffic. All these factors have had a major, negative effect on the Saami's traditional way of life. In a global population of 70,000, of which 6,500 live in Finland, only 10 per cent are now engaged in reindeer herding. My knowledge of the Saami came from book-learning only but my immediate, practical concern was how I might survive in the desolate landscape in which I now found myself.

Last week, down in Helsinki, the islands beyond the harbour had been spotlit by spring sunshine and the red icebreakers were in dock, their winter work over. Once I begin to travel northwards by train, however, I start to pick up signs of a different world. At Hämeenlinna, the lake is frozen, a cold white sun flickers through the birch trees and people huddle on the platforms with their hoods up. Trundling through forests and small towns, the railway sheds are banked with dirty snow and the brightest things on the

267

tracks are the red stop lights. By afternoon, the pink of the sky is leaking into grey. The forests have become denser, the snow thicker: we've crossed the wolf line. Making my way to the buffet car, I wrestle with the door before noticing that *drag* means pull and *tryck* means push. Pushing it open, I find a spacious buffet car, glowing with light. The polished brass fittings gleam. There's a samovar on the counter and bottles of wine lined up in the cooler. I have a coffee and a hot jam doughnut. I want to stay on this warm comforting train for ever and sod the Arctic.

Finnish trains are not like other trains. There's a small carriage specially for people travelling with pets and children. Occupants: two collies, one other sort of dog, one child, one cat, another fluffy cat in a basket and assorted adults. Walking back along the corridor I find a door wide open, with snow rushing past outside. Is this a Finnish test of some sort, to see if I'll jump or if I'm of stable mind? Or has someone already jumped? Not knowing what to do, I simply walk on. The slender trunks of the silver birch are white. Beyond them, the snow wisps about like a flimsy scarf of low-lying vapour. At 5 p.m. we have a long stop at Oulu. Dogs, children and their respective owners get off for a run-around. The cats, of course, disdain such excessive activity. 6 p.m: we've crossed another boundary, passing into the dark, blue world of night. 8 p.m: we reach Rovaniemi, home of Santa Claus.

Next day, I continue by coach, rocketing on through a blizzard, between banks of snow six feet high and growing. Crawling along behind a snowplough with ten cars behind us, it takes us four and a half hours to do forty kilometres. Last night, the temperature was minus sixteen, this morning minus eight. I decipher the weather page of the local paper and see that what we're having is spring. When the headlights of the coach pick up the sign for Enontekiö, I feel an unaccustomed rush of disaffection for this way of life I've chosen for myself, always arriving at some unknown destination alone, where they speak a strange tongue, uncertain of what lies ahead. I want to stay on the warm, comforting coach for ever. But, of course, I don't.

I'd heard about the Saami long ago, from Ian's friend Robert, an anthropologist who, coming to stay with us in Brill from time to time, would bring with him stories from exotica that, to someone whose highlight of the week was an outing to the pub, were as amazing as Gulliver's travels themselves. But, not only did he bring back stories of the indigenous peoples he was researching, once he even brought one of the indigenous people themselves, in the shape of his Saami wife, Inga.

In one of the display cases in the Pitt-Rivers Museum in Oxford, Inga pointed out to me a small stone – a magic stone – similar to the one she used to use as a child and which, when walking past a rock imbued with some potential for evil, she would hold up between herself and the rock to ward off that evil. Magic, like a set of rosary beads.

There is something that seems to draw me to marginalized peoples which I have never really understood. Perhaps I too feel marginalized and am seeking some understanding of the condition, some way of coping with the habit of a lifetime whereby I always find myself on the edge of a group, never the centre of it. At parties, in customary bridesmaid mode, I make for the gathering of people who seem to be having the most fun only to find myself, two minutes later, standing on my own as they all, inexplicably, drift away to become part of an even more interesting group. Sometimes, in a vain attempt to progress from the edge to the middle, I've thrown into the conversation whatever morsel of gossip I might have acquired, and find that what I'd thought was a secret known only to me is, in fact, common knowledge all over town. If I have a run at a joke, someone else is bound to get to the punchline before me. I have now come to accept that I am neither a team player nor group-oriented, but simply the sort of person who, as a school report once said of Deirdre, performs well in groups of two.

However, none of these theories really explains my interest in the Caribs, the Saami or the Aborigines. I could tell myself, and others, that I am attracted by the fact that they have a close relationship with their ancestral land or that I find their different lifestyles intriguing, their music exciting, their language a challenge. But it was only by jumping in quickly before my auto-censoring device came into play that I could admit that my decision to come to Enontekiö was motivated by sheer, shameless curiosity and that all the other laudable, praiseworthy reasons were nothing more than respectable excuses which travellers have to dredge up from time to time to explain away their self-indulgent inquisitiveness.

But I had to revise my idea of fun when, up in the tundra, I considered what my survival strategy might be if suddenly called to fend for myself in such an alien place for I had entrusted myself to a man about whom I knew little except that he had herded reindeer with the Saami of Enontekiö for ten years. It was Rune himself who had decided I should go into the *tuoddar*, using the Saami word for tundra. And then, that decision taken, that I had a few survival techniques to learn. If I'd thought that the cold weather gear I'd brought was adequate, I was wrong. The ski-trousers were too thin, my gloves laughable and my woolly hat should cover my head, not sit on it. My snow boots were no better than dancing shoes and I'd failed to equip myself with snow goggles. I was dressed, it seemed, for a brisk mid-afternoon walk in Helsinki and nothing more. Instead, Rune instructed, I must clad myself in everything I had and then climb into the snow-proof boiler suit he loaned me which, he said, was just about thick enough to withstand the driving snow and the chill Arctic winds. He himself was wearing the traditional Saami snow boots known as *nutukaat*. These are worn with a lining of soft hay, a sure-fire way of keeping the feet warm and dry.

Then there was our transport to fix up. This consisted of two metal-framed sledges attached to a scarlet snowmobile, one for me to ride in and a smaller one for Karra, Rune's ageing husky. On to my sledge went provisions, a pile of reindeer skins, fur side up, Rune's cross-country skis and his saw. Saami skis are made of wood, with leather straps to tie them to the boot. Mine, sleek, lightweight and bought in Helsinki, were tossed aside. 'Toothpicks,' was Rune's disdainful comment.

The engine revs up and, moving away slowly over the hard-packed snow, we cross the main road. The previous day, I'd ridden pillion, Rune gunning the red snowmobile round icy corners and slaloming through bends banked high with snow so that I had to hang on to him in a way which I hoped did not betray my dismay. Now, however, cocooned in my furs, I sit back and enjoy a more leisurely ride. We skim along the snow, Rune standing, right foot on the running board, left knee resting on the saddle, eyes scanning the horizon, the gallant Karra lolloping along behind us for the first two or three kilometres. Sometimes, we plough through a patch of light snow that sprays over us like sea water. Rune looks back to check I'm OK and smiles.

Just as in the desert, there are no points of reference here to tell us where we are. A few kilometres back, we passed a low wooden sign for Hetta but there are none pointing in the direction we are going. Rune raises a gloved hand towards a small rise to the right and swings the machine towards it. At the base of the hill, we purr to a stop.

'Just want to get some water,' he says. 'There's a stream beneath the snow down here', and without warning, he plunges thigh-deep into the snow, wading through it and out of sight, while I sit, fearful of never seeing him again. Or even if he comes back, what if the snowmobile overturns during one of his spectacular manoeuvres and he's concussed? Or he suffers a simple mishap like a broken arm? Or anything? What would I do? Sit tight and freeze to death or start the machine, assuming I'd be able to, and set off back the way we'd come? But how would I know the way? Would Karra be any help? Probably not. Karra would refuse to leave Rune. I examine the options again: sit tight and freeze to death or set out for home, get lost and freeze to death anyway. I close my eyes in exasperation for I have done something I rarely do, put my trust and my life in the hands of someone else and it's left me feeling vulnerable. There is no hole in the hedge to which I can run.

Rune wades back into sight, waving a can of water over

his head: 'Now we have water for our coffee. Are you all right?' 'Of course. Just admiring the view.'

The tundra is not as empty and devoid of life as it at first seems. Every so often, we pass a small construction of forked willow sticks, interwoven with wire. When a bird strays into it, usually white grouse, it will get enmeshed in the twigs and will be dead by morning. Then the hunter will do the rounds of his traps, collect his bounty and set off for market. Reindeer, too, of course, manage to find life here. Lowering their heads to the snow, they can pick up the scent of lichen or mushrooms three feet below the insulating blanket of snow. Nevertheless, it's still a vista of desolation. Snow in such amounts is daunting to me and when I get out of my seat and immediately plunge knee-deep into it I let out a yelp which makes Rune smile: 'What's the matter? It's only snow.' We drive further up into the tundra. 'Where are we going?' I call out to Rune above the thrumming of the engine. 'To *ultima Thule*,' he shouts and I lie back in the furs, contented.

We hit a small stand of birch and stop. Getting out his saw, Rune cuts down some branches and starts building a fire. He once spent eleven days out here on his own, trapping grouse. 'In those days,' he says, fanning the fire, 'you could get fifty markka for one bird. Now, you're lucky to get twenty. The Russians have moved into the market.' The logs crackle and the flames burn fiercely, startling the surrounding snow with the audacity of their orange brightness. The coffee is strong and hot and I feel it melting my frozen bones. Rune lights up an enormous Honduran cigar and reclines on the furs beside me. We are warm, happy, surrounded by stillness. Across the snow, Karra stands apart from us, motionless, snout raised to the wind. 'He's thinking of the days when he was a young dog,' says Rune. And I think of what Rune's youth, too, must have been like: the adventure, the hunt, the wild nights of drinking and carousing. Until he married and had children and had to stay at home more. Now, unbelievably – for he has a young look to him augmented by a youthful Finnish fringe – he is an expectant grandfather. I pluck up the courage to ask what I should do if I had to fend for myself. 'Stay put. Someone would come to find us.' 'But how would they know where we were? In a place like this, without any landmarks?'

'You're making a common mistake. You think this is a wilderness but there is no such thing as a wilderness. Every kilometre, every hill, every rise of the tundra is known and has a name.'

I think of the townlands of Donegal, each field, road and ruined house with its own name. And think, too, of the Saharawi driver, without any apparent navigational aid, swinging his Land Rover along another line of the compass. There are stars not only in the sand but in the snow as well. Rune nods when I tell him this: 'There's no such thing as a wilderness,' he repeats. Three fat white birds – grouse – scuttle about at the foot of the birch trees and Rune throws another log on the fire. 'Here,' he says, 'we have the thing most people crave and which money can't buy.' 'What's that?' 'Time. We have so much of it we are rich.' And his cigar tip glows bright as the birch logs.

In former days, the Saami stayed put during the snow-bound winter months but, once the first sign of a thaw appeared, they started moving about again, meeting up with other Saami to do business, regularize unions, celebrate winter births, settle scores – and ward off tax collectors. Accustomed to roaming across borders and not therefore always at home when the taxman came calling, reindeer herders were a sitting target during these spring gatherings. Targets not just for one tax collector but for three. Used to living on their wits, however, the Saami devised a neat solution to this seasonal irritation: they would pay off one collector, giving him a little something for himself – danger money in today's parlance – for which reward the favoured taxman from say, Russia, would undertake to keep the other two, from Denmark and Sweden, at bay. There is one such gathering, traditionally they take place around the spring equinox, still held every year at Enontekiö, but since the Christian church colonized the event it has been renamed the Marian Weekend, in honour of the Feast of the Annunciation which falls on 25 March.

It has been a source of sorrow to some Saami that things have developed along such religious lines for, culturally, they are animists who perceive spirits in the forests, rivers and trees of the tundra. Nothing, they maintain, must be done to shatter the balanced ecology of this spiritual world. Their god is Ibmel and their shamans used to beat drums to release their inner spirit, which could then travel through sky and space on their shamanistic business. Determined to rid the people of such pagan practices, however, both Church and State combined to make it unlawful for Saami to sing their songs or for their shamans to beat their drums. Even the drums themselves were to be destroyed. *Joiking*, too, the traditional form of invocatory singing unique to the Saami, was outlawed.

As part of the Enontekiö get-together this year, there were reindeer races, reindeer lasso competitions and drinks available in a bar built entirely of ice blocks. The reindeer were frisky and gave their handlers plenty of grief. But they were de-balled and de-horned and none sported the branch-like antlers I'd been expecting for, although both male and female have antlers, they shed them every year. Close to, these reindeer are relatively small animals and nowhere near as high as a horse. Their fur is smooth and lies along the body though when I sank my fingers into it, I found a good inch of insulation there. Their enemy, apart from urban man, is the wolverine which, when attacking, jumps on top of the reindeer, breaks its neck and then drinks from its jugular vein.

The reindeer races were unnerving, reckless and marvellous to watch. Each animal was put into a cage and then, at a given signal, set free to gallop away dragging behind it a wooden sledge to which clung a prostrate driver. As the race got under way, the driver managed to pull himself upright so that as he ended the one-kilometre race he could hurtle towards the finishing post upright, waving like a triumphant charioteer. Talking to a Saami teacher at the bar, I asked her how large her father's herd was but she shook her head at the impropriety of my question: 'That's something you never ask. The herd is the same as someone's bank balance and you don't ask people how much they've got in the bank, do you?' Later, the prizes were distributed, against the background noise of drinking that filtered through from the bar where, by midnight, men were standing three deep at the counter fearful of their neighbour moving lest they all fall down. As I left, the first row was breaking out.

'You won't believe it,' I said when I called next day to see Rune, 'the chairs were flying by midnight.' Rune was on his hands and knees, hammering reindeer ribs into sizable pieces for the evening meal.

Rune's recipe for reindeer ribs:
Butter your dish well. Break the reindeer ribs into manageable pieces and salt them. Pack them down well in a pot and cover with cold water. Put in an oven for ten minutes at 250 degrees then turn down. Cook slowly for about three hours.

I'd already passed on his reindeer blood sausages that, incidentally, have five times more vitamin C than beef. But I had eaten the delicious golden cloudberries and ligonberries that are harvested in summer when the tundra yields up its fruits. After supper, I wandered out to look up at the starry sky. Kaamos, the polar night, begins in early November when the sun sets, not to rise again until the New Year. When there is a moon during Kaamos, it can be seen hanging in the sky for twenty-four hours at a time.

One night, I went to listen to Wimme Saari and, hearing him, I began to understand something of what *joiking* is all about, for book-learning is a poor medium to explain this rare form of singing. Starting sometimes, though not always, with a rumble deep in the throat, progressing to a resonance echoing from somewhere within the chest, the singer creates the landscape of the tundra and invokes the spirit of nature surrounding him. A *joik* – pronounced yoik – may be a simple chant or a long, complicated epic. '*Joiking* has no beginning and no end. It just stands where it was born, like the open mountains,' writes Nils-Aslak Valkeapää, another well-known singer. Wimme's number was an evocation of a journey through the landscape of his childhood spent here in Enontekiö and, since the form is both historic and contemporary, he conjured up a scene filled with sounds: running water, reindeer bells, the rattle of sledges, the heavy breathing of running reindeer, the revving up of a snowmobile and, as a constant, the powerful, drumming of reindeer hooves, the hot energy of their presence surrounding and finally enveloping the listener.

There was a group of Saami there, too, who had come from Murmansk. This was the first year they had been allowed to cross the Russian border into Finland to join their cousins in Enontekiö. The Murmansk Saami came wearing Russian peasant costumes and, when they tried to dance with the people from Enontekiö, their steps were hesitant and stumbling as if they were trying to remember something long lost to them. Over the years, if they continued to come, they would surely unpeel the layers of culture imposed upon them, cast aside their Russian clothes and become again what they had always been – Saami. But it was not to be. I returned to Enontekiö the following year to find the Murmansk people had been replaced by others from Komi, a reindeer area that lies even deeper into Russia, thousands of miles east of Murmansk. Beyond many borders.

CHAPTER SEVENTEEN

When the Sun Stands Still: 1998

Sweden had always held out on me, keeping back for herself a part of Ian I had never known. Two of his novels are set there and another book, *Seven Beds to Christmas*, is an account of how, finding himself in Stockholm during Christmas week without money, waiting for a cheque to come through, he has to talk his way into – and out of – seven nights' free lodging. To a young foreign writer, some of the beds – fully furnished – came easy. By the time we met he was thirty-three and I was twenty-two – Sweden was part of his past. Sometimes, though, people emerged from that past, arriving in Brill with reminiscences that brought to the surface the subliminal curiosity I always entertained about the country. It was a place, to me, of stereotypes – full of people with flaxen hair, who disapproved of alcohol, lived beside lakes of blue, spent a lot of time in the sauna and had a free and easy attitude to sex. Then I went to Sweden and found the stereotypes were true.

Because he could speak the language, Ian was commissioned from time to time to translate books from Swedish into English or to work on books with a Swedish background. One such book was *The Lions of Longleat*, an account of a project initiated by the Marquess of Bath who was setting up, on his estate at Longleat, one of the first wildlife parks in England. Involved in the project was a Swede called Berggren who had been involved in a similar project near Gothenburg, from where a pride of lions was to be transported to Longleat. Thus, I stood on a railway platform one January to see Ian off to Sweden, turning away from the departing train with misery in my heart, the next two months laid out ahead of me lonely as my first day back at boarding school. And then, in early March, came a letter: I was to gather the children together, pack a bag, drive up to Immingham and take the boat across to Gothenburg where Ian would meet me: the publishers had come good with a bit of extra cash.

No matter that the children then were aged six, five and five months, that I would have a long drive up to the port on my own, a journey made longer by the fact that there would be frequent stops for the baby, Russell, was still being breastfed on demand. None of these things mattered. The long road had been shortened: I was going to see Ian earlier than I'd thought. What did matter, however, was a previous disagreement that had unexpectedly erupted and which I'd thought would resolve itself in time.

As soon as the children had started to arrive, I decided, I would put them on my Irish passport.

'We need a letter from their father,' said the passport office, 'giving his permission.' I was affronted. Was this what our centuries of sacrifice and persecution had been all about? Was this what people had died for during the Easter Rising? I had to get permission from an Englishman, albeit an Irishman *manqué*, to have *my* children on *my* Irish passport? To worsen relations between our two countries even further, Ian refused his permission.

Lancelot Graham Rodger, Ian's father, an ex-public school man like his son, had a distinct aversion to the Irish. 'You people shot us in the back,' he told me once, referring to 1916. We had never been forgiven for that outbreak of foul treachery and nervous of this querulous, unforgiving father-in-law, I failed to point out that many a good Irishman had fought alongside the British during the 1914–18 war and that even James Connolly's Citizen Army had chosen to fight the Kaiser's intruders though not, of course, out of support for the British. And whatever else my father-in-law learned at his public school, it certainly wasn't a knowledge of the geography of the country his forebears had occupied for four hundred years.

'There was a boy from Ireland in my house,' he told me once. 'Fellow's father had a castle in Cork somewhere. You know him by any chance?' The likelihood of my knowing someone who owned a castle anywhere was slim and I replied stiffly: 'No. I'm from Dublin.' 'Well, that's near Cork, isn't it.' When he had to accept the inevitable – that his son was about to marry one of the despised tribe – he took Ian aside and gave him some fatherly advice: 'They breed like rabbits. Be sure to take some sort of precaution. And make sure she doesn't run off with the children.' Someone he knew had married an Irish woman who, when the marriage had broken down, had upped sticks and taken the children back to Ireland. This, then, was the under-lying reason why Ian had refused to have our children put on my passport.

Filtered through the telescope of time, the viewer can choose how to interpret this response: as an appalling lack of trust, as blind prejudice and/or as an attempt by Ian to comply with at least one of his father's wishes. Since the others involved the advisability of joining the Tory Party, shooting Nasser, hanging the traitor Ian Smith and not wasting money on installing baths in council houses where they would only be used to store coal, the passport option was, perhaps, a relatively easy one to run with. To me, blinded by love, it was a simple display of inexplicable pigheadedness, English pigheadedness, of course. And it was a chicken come home to roost when I pointed out – with some relish – that I could not travel to Sweden, or indeed to anywhere, with the children unless they were on my pass-port. Then began a series of frantic phone calls and dashes to the Embassy that characterize the attempt by someone trying to extract a passport in a hurry from a system whose fail-safe design is formatted specially to foil all such attempts. In Stockholm, Ian got Valentine Iremonger – poet, convivialist and, coincidentally, Irish Ambassador to Sweden – to witness his signature and sign the necessary papers. These I sent to the Irish Embassy in London where they promptly disappeared. The system, all by itself, had noted that my passport was due for renewal and had sent it to another department. Finally retrieved, it was set on the appropriate administrative track where it immediately slammed straight into a red light: the date was 17 March, St Patrick's Day when it is never business as usual.

Eventually is the longest word in the dictionary but I did finally drive off the boat at Gothenburg to find myself in a country where no one would stop to tell me the way and where, to my horror, the police wore their firearms openly, for everyone to see. We stayed with the Berggren family and while there I found myself enmeshed in a love triangle – a foursome if you included the elephant – that involved Berggren, his wife Hansi and his female assistant plus assorted wild animals that included not only the lions but also a bull elephant. Berggren had a theory that a zoo should resemble, as far as possible, the Garden of Eden. This meant creating a zoopark in which all the animals – lions and tigers, bears and elephants – roamed freely together. This freedom to roam was a facility that he felt should also be extended to humans and, by the time I arrived, Berggren and his assistant were happily recreating Eden by splashing in the elephant pool with the elephants by day and romping in the straw with each other by night. But that which is a man's Eden may well be a woman's hell. By the time I arrived, Hansi was demoralized, weepy and unable, it seemed, to do anything about her condition. This, then, was Sweden.

Desperate to escape the marital misery, Ian and I decided one evening to go for a drink, unaware that access to alcohol was strictly controlled and that, because we were approaching the Easter weekend, the alcohol outlets were closed and would remain so until the celebrations were over and all danger of overindulgent licentiousness had passed. Our only chance of a drink, we were told, was the local hotel. There, to our relief, we found a horde of secret drinkers – most of them Finns – knocking back as much as they could before the hotel also closed for Easter. This too was Sweden. But another picture of Sweden remained in my mind over the years, a picture of long grasses, meadow flowers and extended sunny days. An image of midsummer, in fact, so that, years later, when I got the opportunity to go there again, I went to Dalarna, where the wooden horses are made and where all things Swedish are to be found.

The axis of my year swings on the twin pivots of midsummer and midwinter. One midsummer in County Cavan, I spent the night outside, warmed by the embers of a bonfire, watching time measured horizontally as fading light from the western sky slowly flowed into two hours of darkness even as the next day's light crept along the horizon towards it from the east. Opinion is divided as to when exactly midsummer is. Diaries note it as 21 June but most fishing and seagoing communities celebrate it on St John's Eve, 23 June. Saint John is associated with seafarers which is why so many coastal places bear his name: St John's in Newfoundland, St John's in Antigua and St John's Point, a narrow isthmus reaching out into Donegal Bay not far from Corkerbeg.

Nineteen ninety-eight was a busy year. I'd seen the New Year in on a flight from Johannesburg to London and in the spring had gone to Australia to spend two months travelling there – and it was still only June. Now, on 20 June, I found myself driving towards the village of Bjursås, in the middle of a Swedish summer that fitted exactly with my preconceptions of it. The scent of recently cut grass rose sweet as toffee to my head, filling it with thoughts of my Ballycorus childhood. Ditches were crowded with wild lupins, cow parsley and buttercups. A couple passed along the road on granny bikes, the handlebars festooned with leafy branches. The timbered houses, each painted with the rusty-coloured ochre extracted from red quartz mined locally, were decorated with greenery and the blue and yellow national flag blew cheerily from flagpoles set into garden lawns. Everything in Sweden, I found, was regulated, neat, tidied up.

Even the dead were kept in order. At the little village of Torsang I stopped to ask the way and, finding none of its two hundred inhabitants around, wandered instead into the ordered, uncrowded graveyard where cropped grass covered each grave and a uniform half moon of earth – no more, no less – was allocated for individual flower displays. For a seemingly secular society, Sweden is well stocked with churches and their congregations play a significant role in village life, which is why, when I finally reached Bjursås, I made straight for the Kyrka knowing something would be happening there. And I was right. With starched aprons covering their striped skirts and white lace bonnets covering their heads, thick-hipped matrons bustled around as only people dressed like that can do. Standing apart in a burlesque attempt at maleness were the menfolk, stern elders of the Lutheran Church – and not all of them elderly – buttoned sedately into black frock coats, wide-brimmed hats on their heads, wearing black knee-breeches and black stockings, each with a frivolous red bobble at the knee.

At the door of the church, a Swedish polka band fiddled energetically but it was the double-bass player who caught my eye. Dressed not in black breeches like all the other men, the trim cheeks of his neat bottom – which he wiggled in time to the music – were encased in the smoothest of cream-coloured moleskin breeches so that it was all I could do to stop myself stroking them. Indeed, when I reread my notes that night I found that I had even made a careful little drawing of this pretty sight. But, like everywhere else, nothing, including Sweden, is what it seems. The rural look achieved by some quaint houses, with their rustic window boxes filled with geraniums, was nothing of the sort. On closer inspection, the wooden boxes proved to be made of plastic with segments of bark stapled on to them. And even Lutheranism had to be called into question. Over the altar of Bjursås Kyrka was not a cross or a statue or even a vase of flowers but a representation of a sunburst. Within the sunburst was a triangle at the heart of which was an eye. It was a cheering discovery, paganism at the core of Christianity, and I looked again at all the churchgoers in their bonnets and breeches and wondered what else might not be what it seemed.

But there was no denying that outward appearances were important. Joining the procession from the church up the hill to the meadow – the horn section of the band led us with great vigour until halfway up it lost its puff, leaving the drums and cymbals to urge us on – I chatted to the woman beside me who explained the dress code. If you were a Bjursås woman, she said, you wore a black bonnet with a white patterned wimple, changing to a plain wimple if you were going to a funeral. Aprons, too, could be social stumbling blocks. Wear the funeral one to a wedding or vice versa and you committed a solecism of gigantic proportions. She herself was wearing the correct Bjursås outfit – black-and-white striped apron over a black worsted dress with red trim on the *inside* of the hem. However, beside her was a woman from another village who was worried that her outfit wasn't wholly correct: the apron was striped when it should have been plain.

'Does it matter?' I asked her. It was, after all, a soft, sunny day and everyone seemed to be enjoying themselves. Did anyone really care about red trims or patterned pinnies?

'Oh, yes, they do. I am from Leksand. Some people from there will notice and frown.'

But these worries were nothing compared to the problems the men had. In the upland meadow, the *majstang* – the maypole – was the largest phallic symbol I'd got close to for a long time: twenty feet, I measured it personally, topped by a crowing cockerel. It had an age-old problem, however, for it lay flat out with no sign of life in it, until, that is, the maypole ceremony began, overseen, I noted uneasily, by the Lutheran pastor.

At a signal from the band, which had now regained its collective breath, a group of men and women approached the pole as it lay supine, supported on trestles, and began to entwine it with garlands, passing the ropes of greenery under and over it in stately, choreographed movements until eventually the whole pole was decked out. Then the women withdrew: the next part, the erection, was men's work. It took twenty minutes to get it up, using a complicated and precarious system of co-ordinated movements involving forked sticks, teamwork and muscle power while the onlookers shouted 'hey-oooo' as more height was gained. Meanwhile, the band played on and on. And on. And I seemed to be the only person who saw anything sexual, and therefore funny, in this exercise. The Swedes did what they had to do, solemnly and determinedly, and I couldn't help wondering if that was what it was like in bed with them as well. But who was I to be judgmental? I was where I wanted to be, it was five o'clock in the afternoon and the sun was still scorchingly hot. By eleven o'clock, it was still there and so were the crowds – dancing, on a platform, as the band played old rock-and-roll numbers and the singer, in cowboy boots, sang songs in an impeccable American accent: 'Aal of me, why don't you take aal of me.' Round and round the dancers went, like bumper cars that never bump, jiving and waltzing in thumping unison while behind them the trunks of the silver birch gleamed white on one side, lit by the near-midnight sun. The sky above was blue and tiny white moths drifted in and out of the pink and purple lupins. I took a walk away from the dancing and the music, up along a lane and back to where the maypole now stood and, looking down at my feet, saw a spread of lily of the valley. For one brief moment, I imagined myself, at some future date, coming to rest in a place like Bjursås, in a small timbered house with a window box full of geraniums, a safe place where even the wild hedges are neat and ordered.

Driving back, just after midnight, none of the few cars I met had their lights on. I pulled over and stopped by a lake. The sky was red, blue clouds drifting across it. Above, among the drooping branches of the birches, leaves stirred in the night wind. And, as I stood there, a shadow seemed to drift across the trees that lined the lake, turning the midnight day into dusk. Then the moment, like a fleeting thought, was gone and it was light again. The midsummer night had happened and I had almost missed it. Later that week, I travelled down to Stockholm and wandered about the city that Ian had once lived in, before he met me. Before he became the person I knew. When he was a different Ian. A moon hung over the city and I remembered the Saami belief that it hangs there in the sky to give light to people as they wander into the darkness of their future. It was 23 June, St John's Eve. On that day, it is said, a person's soul leaves their body and travels to the place where they will die.

Six months later, I lay in bed in the little town of Slane, north of Dublin, listening to the world turning. I could hear its powerful engine humming, its soundless music flowing round me, feel the clanking friction as the great revolving globe moved slowly between the stars, turning its mountains, its rivers and its seas towards the new day's light. Hanging at an angle that took its northern hemisphere furthest away from the sun, bringing us those long, dark winter days. It would remain like that in the sky for three days before beginning its journey back again towards spring. We had reached the winter solstice – the standing still of the sun. I tried to sleep but solar energy had entered my mind and fired it up. Tomorrow, the rising sun would beam in over the capstone at Newgrange and, entering the chamber, hit the floor exactly as it had done for the last five thousand years. And I would be there to see it happen.

The megalithic mound at Newgrange was originally thought to be a passage grave but recent research suggests it was built as a highly precise instrument for measuring time. As the sun enters the inside chamber, at the same time every year, it brings reassurance that the long winter is drawing to a close and, in megalithic times, was a warning to farmers that they should soon think about planting their seeds. Eight years previously, I had written to the Office of

Public Works in Dublin to ask if I could attend this great annual event. The chamber is small and holds no more than a dozen or so people. Since the solstice occurs over a period of three days, the maximum number of people able to witness the sunrise from within Newgrange in any one year is thirty-six. Booking, I'd heard, was vital. I received a letter in reply which said that there was a waiting list and that I was unlikely to be offered a place before the year 2000. In 1992, few people were thinking about the Millennium and this was the first time the year 2000 had really entered my psyche. I filed the letter away as a keepsake but the years passed more swiftly than I'd expected and, in 1998, I wrote to the OPW to enquire again about attending the solstice. This time, the reply said that there was a waiting list and that it was unlikely I would be offered a place for six or seven years. Searching my files, I found the year 2000 letter and dispatched a copy of it to show that I was, in fact, well up the queue. Nothing more was heard until early December 1998 when I was told to present myself at Newgrange at 8.45 a.m. on the morning of the 21st.

I spent the night in nearby Slane and got a taxi out the next morning. A clear starry night had left a covering of frost on the fields around Newgrange. At the gate, I handed my official invitation to a woman from the OPW who pointed out to me the point on the horizon where the sun would rise. The invitees had gathered in the small timbered office and were drinking a warming cup of tea. We were lucky, someone said. This was the first time for four years that the sky had been unclouded and, provided it stayed like that, the sun would be able shine through into the chamber. At half past eight, we crunched across the grass, staining the frost with our footprints, and I broke away from the main group to give myself a moment apart. Although officially the sun had not yet risen, daylight lay across the ground, giving a blue-grey tinge to the frosted surfaces of the fields, and through the sky wheeled three flocks of birds. The mound was surrounded by standing stones, sentinels for this, the year's shortest day. A small crowd had gathered and grouped themselves in twos and threes, waiting quietly. I waited too, until, pulling myself together, I went to join my group. They were nowhere to be seen. 'May I go in?' I asked the woman who had checked my invitation but she shook her head. 'Not yet.' I went back across the field again to rejoin the silent sun-watchers. Among them was a woman with her week-old son in her arms. A Japanese visitor – from the land of the rising sun – had turned up because she'd heard about Newgrange only the previous day. A man was there who had cycled all the way from Dublin. Together, we stood and kept watch. The sun was moments away from coming over the horizon. And then, at four minutes to nine, a golden light radiated upwards and the first segment of the burning ball of fire rose into the sky. And a bird began to sing. But this wasn't right, surely. Weren't we supposed to be inside the chamber for this very moment? I hurried back to the entrance. Over the white quartz mound that housed the chamber hung a pale, watery rainbow.

'I think it's time I was inside,' I said and the woman again barred my way.

'No. No one's allowed in.'

'But I have to be inside. I'm writing about it,' I lied, trying to get past this insurmountable obstacle. Behind me, the sun was another three seconds higher in the sky. More birds had begun to sing.

'No. No one is allowed in.'

'But aren't there people in there already?'

I knew that my colleague, Eileen Battersby, who was covering the event for *The Irish Times*, must surely be in there.

'The only people in there are those who had invitations.'

'But that's me,' I wailed, conscious that another two seconds had ticked past.

'Where is your letter of invitation?'

Five seconds.

'I gave it to you at the gate. Don't you remember, we talked about where the sun would rise and you showed me.' Was my face that unremarkable?

Ten seconds.

Tears of anger and frustration welled up in my eyes. I had waited eight years for this. And though the sun had been hitting the floor of the chamber for the last 5200 years it would never happen again quite like this. Not for me.

Fifteen seconds.

The woman's resolve began to waver.

Twenty seconds.

'You've got to let me in.'

And someone hurried across the frosty field with a message from the office: let her in.

I ducked under the capstone and felt my way down along the dark passage leading to the chamber. A line of thin light spilled along the ground. 'Over to the right,' the guide called out from within the chamber and fearfully I crossed the golden path to the other side of the passage and, as my body interrupted the flow of light, a groan came from the watchers within that was terrible to hear. Then I was in, crouching down out of the way and looking at the fiery blade that cut into the darkness, its edges tinged with yellow and orange, watching as it crept along the floor of the chamber towards the ring of concentric circles. Caught in its power, I put my right hand into the shaft of light, expecting it to be scorched. It came out unscathed for this was a benign fire that brought only good with it. Despite the midwinter frost outside, the chamber was warm and dry, without drip or draught, and it was peaceful to stand there, watching the mysterious laser of light. But how quickly we become accustomed to miracles. People started to talk quietly among themselves, commenting on the way the light was shifting, almost imperceptibly, with the movement of the sun. The presence of a camera crew was irritating and I was puzzled that technology had advanced so little that no way had been found to record, in a less intrusive way, an event that, if not religious, was certainly spiritual. And then, after twenty minutes, the light began to fade, the edges to lose their definition and soon there was nothing. Outside, the sun had disappeared behind a cloud and it had begun to drizzle. The woman who had tried to stop me going into the chamber apologized but I avoided her. I wanted to start the new year without rancour, to carry away with me only positive memories of this glorious, winter solstice.

CHAPTER EIGHTEEN

The Old Gods

As a child, sins and sinning were part of everyday life. 'It's a sin to tell a lie,' sang my mother as she washed the dishes and then would send me to answer the phone to say she wasn't in. In the back seat of the car, sandwiched warmly between two fur coats, I listened to the grown-ups talk. 'You know what that place is?' said Elsie, my mother's friend, as we drove past Appian Way. Momentarily diverted by pictures of chariots whooping along a Dublin thoroughfare – *why* was it called that – I almost failed to pick up one of the many signals that always alerted me to the fact that something interesting was going on above my head. 'It's a home,' continued Elsie but now lowering her voice to a whisper, 'for illegitimate children.' 'Tsk, tsk,' said my mother. Illegitimate. I tried to hold this new word in my head till I could get home and look it up in the dictionary. Anyone who lowered their voice was usually talking about a sin and this sounded to me like a new one. But the dictionary was decidedly unhelpful. Born out of wedlock, said the dictionary. Without knowing what wedlock meant, however, the breadth of my understanding of sinfulness was no further advanced.

To raise your hand against your parents was a truly terrible sin. So awful, a nun told a class of wide-eyed little girls preparing for their First Communion, that she knew of a child, just the same age as we were, who not once but twice hit her mother. When the girl died – naturally, her death followed immediately so as not to keep us waiting in suspense – it was found that the hand she'd struck her mother with would not lie down. Instead, anyone who visited her grave, and here the nun paused for us to shiver at the thought, could see, to this day, the arm sticking up through the mound of clay. I had no intention of hitting my mother. I loved her far too much. Coming home from school in the afternoons and finding her out, I'd run upstairs, open her wardrobe – my father kept his clothes in a smaller wardrobe called, inexplicably, a tall boy – and would bury my face in her fur coat, inhaling the warm, comforting scent of her orange-tinted Elizabeth Arden face powder. Sin, in those days, was fun, something to be explored, an adventure even. When, in the bathroom, Freddy, who, at eight, was the same age as myself, told me he had something to show me I was agog and stared, fascinated, at his little brown mushroom. 'Can I touch it?' I asked but he shook his head. 'No,' he said, 'it's poison', endowing this part of his person with even greater allure.

But when another little boy, Barry – sitting beside me in the Ballycorus woods one Saturday afternoon as we stared intently at one insect mounting another one – told me what was happening, I was bored. Insects were not the same as people and I knew, for sure, that my father would never do that to my mother. Even if she'd let him. Barry, a boy with soft brown eyes and a gentle expression, sighed. 'I won't be able to go to Communion tomorrow now,' he said. 'Why?' 'Because it's a sin to talk about that.'

Next morning, on my way across the fields for the milk, I climbed over a stile and on the other side came upon a group of boys holding Barry spread-eagled on the grass. 'Did he talk to you yesterday about you-know-what?' one of them asked.

Barry looked up at me, his face tear-stained, his frightened eyes beseeching me to save him. But I too was scared of these local boys whose hair was cut short about the ears and who went to the national school, barefoot. 'Yes,' I answered and ran, the milkcan clinking against my bare legs, taking with me the knowledge which I have carried with me ever since, that this was probably Barry's first betrayal by a woman. Both these incidents brought sex into the same arena as sin and with it came other sinister elements such as guilt, sadism and voyeurism. All three stirred together to make that religious porridge, sometimes creamy sometimes lumpy, called Catholicism.

At nine, I went to boarding school in Athlone and there, a child who had a reputation for being bold was found to have transgressed once again. The nun in charge was on the warpath. 'Where is she,' she called out, striding into the dormitory, her long black gown swishing past the curtained cubicles like a cat-o'-nine-tails. 'Where is that child? Let her prepare to meet her doom.' 'She's asleep,' someone told the nun and everyone joined the rush round the far side of the dormitory to see what would happen next. There, face down on her bed, the child lay sleeping in her cotton pyjamas. Whipping the blankets back, the nun's hand sliced through the air and then struck the child's bottom with a stinging slap. I've often tried to imagine what it was like to have been that child, far from the reassurances of home, resting in sleep and then to be awakened by searing, physical pain. I have no further memory of this incident for we were all ordered back to our own cubicles. And we went, each taking with us our own mix of feelings: relief that we were not the culprit, glee that this child had got her comeuppance for she was indeed a naughty child and, more difficult to understand, a certain dark excitement engendered by the sight of someone else suffering. The age of innocence was fading fast.

Later, as the hormones came on line, I fell miserably in love with the only available male, the school chaplain, thus managing neatly to create my own doomed version of the Garden of Eden in which I played Eve and he was the apple. 'Bless me, Father, for I have sinned,' I would whisper to him in the delicious darkness of the confession box, never, of course, confessing that my real sin, my best one, was my desire for the forbidden fruit that I knew he would never give. Had he, I would have been horrified because, if the truth be told, I really knew nothing about sex. At fifteen, I was just in love with being in love.

Ironically, it was the pagan side of Catholicism that attracted me. I liked the way in which the liturgy reflected nature: the black vestments worn by the priest during November, the month of the dead, when the shiny laurel leaves in the school drive, dripping with rain, eventually turned mildewed brown at the edges and we made pious visits to the small nuns' cemetery where each grave had a white, uniform cross. Leading up to Easter, the vestments were purple until Good Friday and the ceremony of Tenebrae, when the tabernacle stood empty, its door open, filling the church with a sense of desolation and loss. And then there was Easter itself, exploding in candles, flowers, vestments of white and gold. I devoured the symbolism of the three steps up to the altar representing the climb up the hill of Calvary, the business with the wine and water, the washing of hands. Enjoyed the discipline of the plain chant. And best of all, I luxuriated in the sensuous cannibalistic climax of the Mass, the *sacrifice* of the Mass, in which the priest ate the flesh and drank the blood of his dead leader while the congregation bowed their heads before this sight too terrible to witness. Latin was everyday language. 'Cor Jesu, Cor Jesu, infinite, amans. Cor Jesu, Cor Jesu, amans et amandum,' we sang as the peonies down by the tennis courts bloomed red as the heart-blood of he who was loving and had to be loved. If I ever had a child, I knew, I would call her Amanda. And wondered why no one had dared to choose the sonorous name Lucifer, the light-bearer, for their offspring.

Later, though I had ceased to practise my inherited religion, I still wondered about the power it might have and, when terminating a wanted pregnancy – illegal then in England – I pinned my Child of Mary medal on my night-gown before being taken into the operating theatre. Just in case it still carried some potential for goodness, just in case it could ensure for me a safe passage through whatever lay ahead. When my mother died, I sat beside my father during the funeral Mass, unable to bring myself to take Communion, grieving that I might be causing him pain with this self-centred show of pig headedness at such an inappropriate time. And envied one of my sisters who took her place in the queue to receive the host but then peeled off early to rejoin my father on the other side, the deed apparently done. Rigid and unbending, I sat unmoving, unable to participate in a duplicity that let everyone off the hook and that harmed no one. Perhaps I'd been living out of Ireland for too long.

Superstition and belief, faith and fingers crossed travelled with me wherever I went, met me wherever I washed up. In Georgia – the land where Jason sought and found the Golden Fleece – Christianity had replaced the old animist religion in which the ram was worshipped, the ceremony presided over by Hera, the oak goddess. Polyphonic choirs now fill the magnificent Georgian Orthodox churches with song and sound, though outside images of bulls still decorate the church walls.

Christianity was the rallying point for Georgians under communism, kept alive somehow during Stalin's dark, oppressive years. But, up in the high snow-clad mountains of Svaneti, there was another sort of darkness, a secret one in which the old religion survived, forgotten and despised by the sophisticates of Tbilisi. In medieval villages linked by mud tracks no car could negotiate, Christian churches remained unlocked and unvisited. Managing to get into one, I found the priest's vestments abandoned on a chair. When I touched them, they crumbled to nothing between my fingers.

In Svaneti, women still went up the mountainside to

collect the herbs Medea had used in her medicinal work. She was a healer, not a sorceress, the Georgians said, speaking as if she had lived only yesterday. I liked this awareness of another, pre-Christian time and knew that if I looked closely enough, I would find evidence of the other religion. And I did. Discovering a church in the mountain village of Latali that *was* locked, I peered through a crack in the old wooden door and saw something that made me go in search of the key. Pushing open the creaking door, I let myself in. There, set into the floor was a tall wooden cross but nailed to the top of this Christian icon was a much older, more powerful one: the unmistakable symbol of fertility – a pair of ram's horns. I had reached journey's end.

Mountains, of course, have always been strongholds of spirituality at whose summits people deposit something of themselves before returning to the anticlimax of life below. The ascent itself is an offering to the gods, a trade-off for a healthy life, for a happy marriage, for the birth of a child, for success in an exam. For good luck. For anything that's on offer. When I climbed Ireland's most sacred mountain, Croagh Patrick, however, any mention of mountain mysticism would have been met with raucous laughter by my fellow climbers. The day was Reek Sunday, the last in July, which is the traditional day for climbing Croagh Patrick. Ger, a tour guide who usually spent her summers taking coach loads of German visitors to see the sights – her look left, look right job, she called it – had a weekend off and had rung me to see if I'd like to do the climb. Like wasn't quite the right word but, yes, I said, I would.

And so, at nine o'clock that Sunday morning we set off to join the straggle of people wending their way up the long sloping track to the first saddle. And although we'd thought of ourselves as early birds, we met quite a few people on their way back down again.

The 2500 foot Croagh Patrick figures large in anecdotal mountain stories. Accounts rooted in the distant past tell of thirty pilgrims perishing on it in 1113 and of a robber who, in 1225, had a hand and a foot amputated as punishment for attacking pilgrims. I'd heard that it was both a doddle and a brute of a climb. That someone, every year, breaks a leg. That the best time to start climbing is five in the morning, or, better still, at midnight. The timing, to me, wasn't important but what did worry me was the possibility I might find myself having to puff through a decade of the rosary at some designated mid-mountain halt, or forced to pray at a statue of the virgin wedged into the rock face. Or that I might be swept up and along by a group of devout pilgrims who had discarded their boots, which is the traditional way of climbing the Reek. The only concession I made to the fact that this was a populist pilgrimage was the purchase of a good strong pilgrim's stick sold to me by a small, freckled-faced entrepreneur who shouted his wares from a ditch: 'Good sticks for sale,' he bawled. 'Good Irish sticks.' I bought one for £1 and asked him where he lived. 'In Castlebar,' he said, 'in a house', this last piece of information revealing that he was a settled traveller.

Equipped with my stick, I dissociated myself from all the other paraphernalia of the pilgrimage, wanting only to climb this ancient mountain as people had been doing long before Catholicism, before Christianity itself had muscled in on it. It came, therefore, as something of a surprise to find myself, halfway through the climb, my boots round my neck, slugging it barefoot along the path of mud and stones that wound itself up towards the summit. We had encountered a few people climbing in their bare feet and when Ger decided to give it a go – her parents had always done it like that – I engaged in an inner battle with myself. She had her own reasons for doing it but for me to do it barefoot would be, I felt, a little over the top, a trifle ostentatious. What on earth would people back in Dublin think? And then, knowing I was merely putting obstacles in the way of doing something that was indeed ostentatious and a trifle over the top, I unlaced my boots, hung them round my neck and paddled off after Ger. Heavy rain had fallen all the previous evening but, by morning, the sun had come out and with blue water glittering among the islands of Clew Bay it seemed as if Tír na nÓg was laid out below us. Once or twice, as we pushed our way upwards, I noticed people taking pictures of the few barefooted climbers among us and decided the photographers were intrusive. This was after all, a pilgrimage and, as such, a private exercise. Of course, my real objections were in no way related to these pious thoughts. What I didn't like was, simply, being photographed by someone I didn't know while looking as I did.

At that moment, I saw a young man squat down to get a picture of Ger, who, with long tanned legs emerging from her shorts and her ponytail bobbing out the back of her red baseball cap, was looking good. Judging from the angle the camera was being held, I, on the other hand, would appear as a puffing, smudgy figure in the background, not half as interesting as Ger. The man, his picture in the can, turned away and, fired up with anger, I stumbled along as quickly as I could to catch up with him. Gasping for breath and unable to close the distance between us, I reached forward with my stick and gave him a whack across his shoulders which made him turn in surprise. 'What do you mean by taking pictures like that?' I shouted angrily. The man looked at me apologetically. A few interested walkers stopped to take a rest and have a bit of entertainment at the same time.

'This is a pilgrimage,' I continued. 'You're intruding into something that's private, you hear?' The man shook his head. He'd been taking a picture of the bay, he said, not of the people.

But I'd often used that lie myself when trying, surreptitiously, to get a good picture to go with a story and I wasn't prepared to believe him. However, since the man had turned out to be German, whose limited command of English compared favourably with my nonexistent German, it was clearly no use continuing my tirade. I flounced on and upwards, digging my stick viciously into the mud. When I looked back, I saw Ger and him deep in convivial conversation, leaving me to contemplate the picture of a middle-aged woman, struggling to get close enough to beat a fellow pilgrim about the shoulders with her pilgrim's stick.

The worst part of the climb was traversing the last 1000 feet or so of shale that lies just below the cone of the summit. Here, jagged chunks of stone angle out of the rock face and the only way to negotiate them is to use legs, arms and whatever else comes in handy. It was at that point that I encountered the annual calamity: a woman being stretchered off the mountain having broken a leg crossing the shale. After nearly three hours and with the weather closing in, we reached the summit and sat on a rock to eat our wet sandwiches. Somewhere near, a priest was saying Mass, his voice coming to us via a PA system. Beside me, a man listened to the proceedings, drawing on his cigarette from time to time. The top of Croagh Patrick, on a soggy morning, was no place for reverential musings on spirituality.

In April 1998, I found myself in Alice Springs. A tourist guide had taken a group of us out to a well-known rock – the Corroboree rock – which used to be a meeting place for Aboriginal people. There he showed us the Red River gums, some of which had been cut down for railway sleepers when the great Ghan railway came to Alice. He showed us the tiny green mannyani plant that, when squeezed, gave out a white juice and that Aboriginal people used as an antiseptic. Crushed, it was also good to smoke. He showed us, too, the tall, white ghost gums, the largest of the gum trees in the MacDonnell Ranges, with whose bark Aboriginal people used to whiten their faces. And then, he showed us some Aboriginal people. 'John,' he shouted and, on cue, a short man in tattered trousers walked out of the bush carrying a bunch of boomerangs. One by one, he tutored us in throwing them, shrugging with disinterest when, giggling, we made a mess of the whole thing. When the boomerang show was over, we were brought to see a group of dancers, middle-aged men and women with sagging skin and tired faces who shuffled one way and then the other while we sat in silence, watching. Finally, we were taken to see some people doing dot paintings. Dot, dot, dot went the brush of a woman whose thin breasts sagged to her waist and whose nose ran with mucus. No one bought anything and, when the bus came to collect us, no one said goodbye. We left the performers sitting on the sand, waiting for the next busload of staring tourists to be delivered to them. At five their own bus would come to take them back to Alice Springs.

To the Aborigines, dying is the most important act of life, more important than a marriage or a birthday. The Corroboree Rock was a sacred site because it had associations with many rituals, including death. In fact the whole of Australia was a sacred site from any small, insignificant pau-pau tree to a huge monolithic red rock such as Uluru. And one day, seeing Uluru, I decided to climb it. The previous week a Japanese tour guide, on Uluru, trying to retrieve the camera of one of his group that had fallen and rolled away from her, had run after it and over the side, to his death. 'We ask people to tie their hats on tightly,' continued the guide. 'If a hat blows off, someone might instinctively run to get it for you and be killed.' There were a lot of plaques set into the base of the rock commemorating people who had lost their lives on Uluru. 'Have you done the climb yourself?' I asked the guide. 'Once or twice. But I don't do it any more. It *is* a sacred mountain and the traditional owners, the Anangu, really would prefer no one to go near it.'

Uluru is a monolithic red rock 1100 feet high. Totally bare of soil or grass, it rises from nothing out of the desert landscape, reducing climbers to ants. The circumference of its base is nearly ten kilometres. The first ten minutes of the ascent takes climbers to a rocky outcrop which doubles as a resting place. From here, the summit is invisible.

Another few minutes' climb takes you to a series of stakes hammered into the rock from which hang chains that the climber can cling on to. As I paused to let people pass, I considered what I was going to do. Most climbers were going up in groups of twos or threes. There were family groups and tour groups, all encouraging each other on. A strong wind blew and nearly everyone was wearing hats tied firmly under the chin, as was mine. I looked up at the chain fence. To get even that far required climbing up a rapidly rising bare rock face, leaning into it at an angle that seemed all wrong. Halfway up, there was a dip in the rock into which the climbers disappeared from view.

'What's it like at the top?' I asked a climber on his way down. 'Blowing hard. We just turned round and came down again.' I sat there for a full twenty minutes, pretending I was getting up courage to start climbing. I would insinuate myself into the next tour group, I told myself. Or tag alongside a friendly family. Or fall in with another lone climber. But all the time, I knew I was going to sit there and finally climb down again. The weight of Aboriginal disapproval was too great to bear, I told myself. But really, it was simply that I was afraid. Afraid that some ghostly presence might edge my foot sideways, might send my body spinning towards the abyss that had claimed the lives of so many people. And it would not, I knew, be an accident but my punishment for tempting fate.

CHAPTER NINETEEN

Bedouin Hospitality: 2000

The baby was three months old and lay, watching us, unsmiling, in her father's arms. Around the pale green formica-topped table were gathered all the usual people. They sat there every evening on metal chairs, shouting, laughing, drinking tea and puffing cigarette smoke at each other. Sometimes, they moved to the room at the end of the wide, echoing corridor to watch football on TV. They were men mostly, though with them this evening was a woman wearing trousers and a pale blue satin pyjama top with a mandarin collar, her hair pulled back tightly in a bun, her eyes made up in a Chinese sort of way. She was smoking a narghile. Could she be the mother of the infant? 'No. The baby mother gone away. She run with Yasser Arafat.' This from Selim, chain-smoking joker of about fifty and, since he called out for tea to be brought to me, the hotel manager. Possibly, even, the owner. It was all difficult to figure out. Were these people hotel guests, like myself?

Or did they live here, as friends of the manager, members of his family even? Or maybe they were hotel employees: one to mop the stairs and the corridor and one to clean the rooms, one to make tea, one to see to guests, one to answer the phone, one to sit in reception and one to sit in reception with him to keep him company – except that there was no reception, just the formica table in the corridor.

'Anyway, *ianni*, you like her?' asked Selim, waving his cigarette ash in the direction of the infant. I looked at the baby who peered back at me blearily. With a tiny gold ring in each ear, the kohl round her eyes smudged, her fiercely black hair plastered to her thin little cheeks, she looked like an exhausted streetwalker.

'She's lovely,' I said. 'Very pretty. *Hilwa.*'

The father nodded and jiggled the child in his arms.

'You like Raqqa?' asked Selim, rolling the first 'r' so that it became a syllable all in its own right.

'Of course.' And everyone nodded. How could I not?

'*Ianni*, where are you from?'

'Ireland.'

'North or south?'

To be from the north was bad. Everyone from there was bad. They knew this from their television.

'I'm from the Republic.'

Selim sat back, relieved. 'Big war there,' he continued, firing shots into the air with the butt of his cigarette.

'*La*,' I said firmly, shaking my head. 'No war now. We have peace.'

He looked surprised: '*Salaam?*'

'Yes, peace. Both sides sat down and talked. Then there was a vote and we got peace.'

How easy it was to be both simplistic and cynical at the same time.

Selim looked at me sadly: 'South Africa, peace. Ireland, peace.'

I nodded.

'So now only Palestine,' he said and pity filled my heart. Selim was not a Palestinian but their war was his war. Syria was their home. *Beyti baytak* – my home is your home – is an old Arab saying. The Palestinians are our brothers, Syrians had said to me, over and over again. I decided to change the subject: 'How far is it to Deir ez Zour?' Selim consulted the audience. I drew audiences round me here in Syria that would make an actor weep. 'Fifty kilometres.' Deir ez Zour was next on my itinerary. It had taken me a week to exhaust the possibilities of Raqqa and I was ready to move on.

Far over on the eastern side of Syria – six hours in a rackety bus from Damascus – Raqqa was a rough and ready desert town full of Bedouins and Kurds. People came here to sell their produce and to buy farm equipment. Village women crowded the pavements in dresses of red and purple, blue and yellow, crimson and black, their long hair tied up with matching scarves fringed with fake coins that gleamed against their dark skin. Some wore dresses that glittered with gold or silver sequins so that they shimmered as they walked along the street. The men wore keffiyehs – red and white or black and white – and strode tall and lean in dusty black, fur-lined cloaks with long, decorative sleeves hanging carelessly free. Red sand lay everywhere for there is nowhere in Syria more than a camel's stride away from the desert. When I called in to the museum, I found the dismembered statues, the broken pillars, the chipped urns all with a veneer of red. Even the Director, when he stood to welcome me with a glass of tea, dislodged tiny puffs of red dust around his chair.

This journey to Syria began in the 1980s when, after travelling to Sudan and later to the West Bank, I knew I needed to learn some Arabic and so started to go to night classes in Oxford. My teacher was a Damascene, Abdel Nabi es Staif (chosen follower of the Prophet). He was working on his D.Phil. and his decision to teach us lowly creatures in the College of Further Education was prompted by a wish to deal with the cultural gap that existed – and still exists – between Arabs and the rest of the world. Language, he had decided, would be the bridge we would use to cross from ignorance to knowledge, from prejudice to tolerance. From darkness to light. And so it proved to be, *el hamdhu lilah*. We learned that the common greeting, *Ahlan wa sahlan*, means, in its extended form, 'unsaddle your camel and stay a while with the people of this valley' – or 'hello' in shorthand. We learned that the numerals we use are Arabic. That it was they who invented the number zero, writing it as a circle and calling it *zuffer*, or cipher as it has become in English. We learned that Salahadin, hate figure in school books on the Crusades, was not, in fact, an Arab but a Kurd and that he died, by choice, in humble poverty. And that, were it not for the Arabs, we would know little about classical culture and early medical practice for it was they who channelled these things through to Europe, via their conquest of Spain.

While trying to decipher an Arabic place name, letter by letter – H-a-l-e-b – I learned that, in English, it became

Aleppo, once the capital of Syria, and one-time home of the hapless merchant who died at Othello's hand. And, of course, there was Damascus itself which till then had meant little to me other than roses and starched tablecloths, and a book by Douglas Hyde about his conversion to communism. But it was a struggle: the unfamiliar alphabet whose vital dots and commas were often omitted, the seeming absence of vowels, the guttural pronunciations that apparently required me to either choke on my words or breathe heavy as a sex maniac on the telephone, the incomprehensible agreement and disagreement of numbers (five houses but fifteen house, seven windows but seventeen window, three doors but thirteen door) and the sudden rush to say what had to be said without prefacing it with windy, European prevarications, such as excuse me, do you mind if, would you be good enough to, and so forth. And as these things started to fall into place something else happened: I developed a growing affection for a people so often and so readily misunderstood, even as their language settled on my shoulders like stardust.

Abdel Nabi gained his doctorate and returned to Syria while I went to Russia, South Africa, America even. We kept in touch. He married, had children, took an academic post in Yemen, then Riyadh. Returned again to Damascus to take up a professorship. He came to Oxford once in a while, to do research for whatever book he was working on. Then, one summer, he came as a visiting fellow and brought his wife, Rima, and their children – and rekindled my interest in Syria. It took a long time to get a visa. Syria was wary then of writers and journalists, knowing that some were recruited to spy for the West. Eventually, however, with a new, younger president who was ready to loosen the knots that had held the country secure for so long, and with help from the Arab League, I was granted my visa, free to travel wherever I wanted. My next destination, Deir ez Zour, was a day's cycling away from Raqqa.

The track descended into a dip filled with rubble and rocks half submerged in muddy, red water. I had left the main road an hour ago, hoping to link up somewhere with the bridge that, according to my map, crossed the Euphrates a few miles further on. But with the sun starting to set, the air was growing chill and I had no idea how far on the bridge was and whether there was a village near it. For the last couple of hours, I had been cycling through an empty landscape. I had no tent but I did have a sleeping bag and knew that, if the worst came to the worst, I would have to find shelter in one of the empty buildings. A truck rattled up behind me and I flagged it down to ask about the bridge. 'Not far,' said the driver, offering to put my bike in the back and take me there but I didn't want that. On the bike, I was a thing apart, surrounded by an invisible wall. I was veiled, could go where I wanted, look at what I wanted, under obligation to nobody. The bike was my magic carpet that no one else could get on. Suddenly, in the fading light of the silent afternoon, I felt desolate, lonely. What was I doing here, in this godforsaken place, in the fag end of a desert, without food or a tent? Why had I not accepted the perfectly sensible offer of a lift along a track that was terrifyingly potholed, from someone who knew where he was going?

I cycled on, getting off to push the bike down into the rocky dip, through the water and up the other side. As I did so, I heard shouts and cries and found myself surrounded by an excited bunch of barefoot children dressed in long ragged dresses, sweaters with the elbows out of the sleeves, anoraks too big for them, djellabiyas too small for them. And found, also, that I had stumbled into a settlement of mud-block houses with hens clucking in the yards, a few bony cows standing motionless under a wooden frame covered in sacking and a group of people standing in the middle of the road, watching me. *El hamdhu lilah!* I was saved . . .

The old woman, Helala al Nasr, sitting cross-legged on the mat that had been spread out for me on the red earth of the farmyard, poured water into a bowl for me to wash my hands. Then, signalling me to take off my sandals, she poured the cool water over my bare feet. Her own feet were encased in small black shoes, the nuns' shoes of my childhood: old, wrinkled, laced up. Age is relative and more to do with cultural practices than wrinkles. Helala al Nasr might have been sixty or eighty. If she gave birth first at fourteen and was now sixty-five, her own daughter could be fifty. The young woman, Mariam, who had invited me into the yard might have been her daughter or her granddaughter for relationships, too, were relative. 'This is my daughter,' said a tall sinewy man with a face as lined as Helala al Nasr's. But daughters leave the parental home when they marry and Mariam seemed mistress – after Helala al Nasr – of this household. I decided, therefore, that she was the daughter-in-law and, having married into the family, had simply become a daughter.

Helala al Nasr, her poor back bent rigid at the hips, held court from her position on the mat. Her face and hands were marked with indigo – faded now since they were first done for her marriage ceremony – and two silvery plaits hung down each side of her face, half concealed by the array of black scarves she wore on her head. Her thick black skirt was dusty from the farmyard and green with age. She was, I could see, the unchallenged matriarch of the family. She was also, I worked out, a widow but having married the eldest of three brothers continued to live in his home. Her son, Suleiman, had married Mariam and brought her into the family. He, in partnership with his dead father's two brothers – both bony, lithe old men – worked the cotton farm, the women sowing and picking, the men packing and loading.

Cotton growing was a break with tradition for the Bedouin. Traditionally, they have followed their herds and grown corn wherever it would sprout in the desert, relying solely on the meagre rainfall, despising those who watered their crops and who, by so doing, were forced to choose a more settled existence. Then, in the 1950s, with the Korean War resulting in a shortage of cotton, the crop was introduced along the banks of the Euphrates and a new way of life had begun. In fact, the traditional way of life had already started to change. Military roads built across the desert made access to distant pastures easier. No longer was it necessary for the Bedouin to set out early in spring driving camel and goat herds across the desert to reach grazing lands ahead of everyone else: the animals could now be trucked there in half the time. Even as I drank my tea, a lorry backed into the farmyard, coming to collect the four huge sacks of cotton that had been stored in a corner and against which I had leaned my bike.

One of Helala's brothers-in-law – a straight-backed, skinny old man who every so often raised not only his voice but his shovel as well to chase away neighbouring children come to stare – slapped the side of the sacks proudly: 'Each one has four hundred kilograms of cotton,' he told me, 'and tomorrow, they will go to Deir ez Zour.' Then he started to heft the sacks up on to the tailgate, the men already on the back of the lorry heaving and pulling, stabbing the sacks with huge Long John Silver hooks to haul them the rest of the way up. When the four sacks were loaded, the lorry left to collect another load from the next family. I'd seen these lorries, the sacks – piled six-high – protruding out into the road on either side, the whole impressive edifice rocking so precariously that I never dared pass one but trailed behind, being waved to and shouted at by the two or three boys that usually rode on top.

Once I'd accepted Mariam's invitation to stay the night, a different tempo settled over the farmyard. Curious neighbouring children were chased away. The men went back to work, Mariam withdrew to the outside kitchen and Helala al Nasr hurried from outhouse to kitchen with pots of water, handfuls of vegetables, bags of flour, supervising the children, the cooking and the farm animals while her senior daughter, Aysha, sat cross-legged beside me kneading dough for the evening meal. Aysha had strange, blue-black skin I mistook at first for a veneer of woodsmoke but which I later realized was due simply to weathering. Two thick plaits hung each side of her face. Like her mother, she had indigo markings on her chin and a bracelet of them on her wrists but, unlike her mother, she had five gold teeth that winked and gleamed whenever she smiled. I liked Aysha. She had a determined mouth and, leaning over the big bowl, worked her strong, countrywoman's arms, rolling and thumping, pulling and slapping, pausing from her work only to straighten up from time to time to ease her back.

It was pleasant watching someone else work and her movements were so mesmeric that I didn't at first notice the commotion across the yard until I looked and saw a headless chicken flapping its wings violently as it staggered among the children's nimble, dancing feet. When it finally sank to the ground in a flurry of heaving feathers, Mariam picked it up and let the blood from its neck drain on to the earth. Then she took a second chicken and laying it on the ground, knelt on its outspread wing to anchor it while she drew the blade across its throat before stabbing the knife back into the earth. The children ran through the yard squealing with excitement, tossing the two heads back and forth. Later, slinking over to where the knife was still stuck in the ground, a farm dog licked up the spilled blood. '*Ana ma fini akull lahem, abdan, abdan, abdan*,' I'd said to Mariam when she'd invited me to eat. It was a phrase I'd rehearsed – and used – over and over again: 'I can't eat meat, ever, ever, ever.' 'Be sure to say *abdan* three times,' a Syrian friend in England had told me, 'then everyone will understand you really mean it. Telling them you're a vegetarian won't mean anything. Only Indians are vegetarian.' Now, however, my rudimentary Arabic had let me down. Chicken was going to be on the menu tonight and I would have no alternative but to eat it. I was a guest of a Bedouin family, after all, and, if I refused their hospitality, Anthony Quinn would surely come galloping in from the desert with his rifle trained on the heart of this ungrateful foreigner.

(I'd made a point of watching *Lawrence of Arabia* again before setting off for Syria.)

When Aysha was satisfied the dough was sufficiently kneaded, she called a child to carry it in a huge aluminium basin across the yard to the kitchen from where it re-appeared in the shape of twenty small soft white rounds, ready for baking.

Down in one corner of the yard, a fire had already been kindled with sticks and over it had been placed a large domed piece of metal, like an inverted wok that, I could see, was now dangerously hot.

While Aysha put more sticks on the fire to keep the flames burning, Mariam picked up a round of dough and started to slap it swiftly from palm to palm so that it stretched and spread until it was a creature in flight, flapping from hand to hand, elastic and unstoppable. Then, when she had it just the right size, she smacked it down on to the metal where it instantly changed colour, browning and blistering in seconds.

Mariam and Aysha smiled at my wonder but it truly was a miracle for the round of dough, no more than five inches in diameter, by the simple act of flying from palm to palm, had been transformed into a round four times its own size.

Then it was Aysha's turn. As the senior woman, she clearly considered she could do better than Mariam and set about whipping the dough back and forth even faster and more rhythmically, her body moving in time to the whole oper-ation, her eyes glancing up at me from time to time to make sure I realized I was now watching a professional. Mariam gave way with grace and took her turn stoking the fire while Aysha worked to get the dough so thin I could

317

clearly see the outline of her hand through it but yet not so thin that it tore.

I wondered about the relationship between these two; what it is was like for Aysha to see a younger woman from an outside family move into her former home and become her mother's lieutenant. In her long black gown, a brown leather belt with a brass buckle at her slim waist, a black and red scarf wound loosely round her long dark hair, Mariam was very beautiful but she was also very clever and clearly knew how to play her role. About twenty-five, she had a quiet air of authority to her and, although she could neither read nor write, she was good on concepts, adept at guessing what word or idea I was reaching for with my basic Arabic. In fact, I even wondered what use the tool of literacy might have been to her. Mistress of her house, gracious in her giving, agile of mind and physically fertile, all her skills had been learned by observation and she had no need of books.

That night, as I'd feared, a large tray of steaming chicken pieces in gravy, tomatoes and rice was carried into the main room and set on the floor. Helala al Nasr sat down cross-legged and invited me to join her. I took a deep breath, suppressed my sense of taste, sent my mind to another part of the desert and scooped up a piece of chicken with the freshly baked bread. It was the first real meal I had had for about four days. I scooped and ate and tried to avoid the larger pieces of chicken while the old woman ate ravenously, chewing the bits assiduously before tossing the bones to the side of the tray. Only when I had finished eating did Mariam and her husband start to eat. Later, we sprawled on the floor, resting our elbows on cushions while the conversation roamed from Ireland – north and south – to whether or not I was married and how old I was. I had been learning fast and, not for the first time, I resurrected Ian, telling my hosts that my husband was an archaeologist working in Damascus. (I had just learned the word for archaeologist.) The lie partly explained why I was travelling alone and deflected the pity and embarrassment that usually greeted the news that my husband was dead and that I was travelling solo. 'Why does your husband not come with you?' asked Suleiman. 'Does he not ride a bike?' 'No. He always falls off.' And Suleiman nodded understandingly. It was reason enough. People came and went, mainly Suleiman's sisters and their husbands, arriving in relays. One woman lowered herself to the ground beside me, a weighty sack on her back. Only as she struggled to her feet to leave – she was heavily pregnant – did I notice a small foot protruding from the sack. 'One in front and one behind,' explained Suleiman, using his hands to demonstrate.

A tin bowl of water was passed round and I remembered I had a bag of nuts in my saddlebag to add to the party. We got to talking about religion. Isa was the Christian prophet, wasn't he, someone asked.

'Yes, in English he's called Jesus.'

'And in Ireland, he is your prophet?'

'Yes, although long ago we had different gods.'

I was thinking of Bridget, the Celtic god – three gods in one, in fact – who was colonized by the Christian church, reinvented as St Brigid and relegated to an inferior position as St Patrick's handmaid. The idea of the Trinity, however, was a concept too difficult for me to convey.

'You have a different name for your god, but you have

only one god?' asked Suleiman, worried. Perhaps they were harbouring a pagan in their midst.

'Yes,' I said reassuringly, 'only one god.' It seemed easier to leave it like that.

The children tired and, one by one, crawled across the floor to settle on Helala's lap where she bundled them into her voluminous skirt, holding them firmly against her breast until they dropped off to sleep and Mariam could take them and settle them on a mattress.

Outside, the night air had a bite to it and the umbrella of the sky was brilliant with stars. Stillness hung over everything thick as the silence that cloaks the countryside after a fall of snow. There were no lights on in any of the nearby houses. Time for everyone to sleep. Mariam waited as, a plastic jug of water in my hand, I stumbled across the rutted earth to where the cattle were. The animals shifted slightly as I squatted for a pee and then washed my hands and teeth. Over the roof of the byre, the rags of sacking stirred softly in the night breeze. Some Bedouins have moved into towns like Raqqa. Others have found a halfway house like this where the night sky is still visible and the earth rough against the feet. Where bedding is a mattress folded up into a corner by day and where food is eaten sitting on the floor. Where the business of living takes precedence over the business of leisure. I stood for a moment longer than was necessary to let the darkness touch my mind and the wind my skin. These were the moments that counted on any journey: the confluence of nature and solitude. The confirmation of the rightness of the solitary state.

Helala al Nasr had gone to sleep with all her clothes on, including her scarf, and I did too but during the night I

320

woke, weighed down by the heavy blanket that had been put over my mattress. I glanced across the floor at Helala who was sharing her mattress with one of Mariam's daughters. Her arthritic old arm was thrown up above her head, the fingers of her work-hardened hand curled with age. Yet she slept soundly until, just before dawn with the stars still in the sky, she rose to wash and pray while I turned over and tried to sleep.

When I next woke, the farmyard was noisy with activity even though it was not yet six o'clock. The cocks were crowing, an ass braying, the dogs barking, a tractor engine revving up, a child crying. Out on the road, a herd of goats passed, their bells ringing urgently as their hooves clipped the dry surface of the track. I paid Sulieman for my night's stay and went in search of Helala. Already, she was busy about the farmyard, shooing the dogs away, throwing scraps to the hens and admonishing noisy children. When she saw me coming, she stopped and taking my right hand, raised it first to her lips and then to her forehead in a farewell gesture of respect though I knew, in my heart, it was she and not I to whom that respect was due.

CHAPTER TWENTY

Once Upon a Time: 2000

The heavy military steam engine, towing its load of ammunition, lumbered through the flat plain of the desert, grey smoke washing into the blue of the sky. From the footplate, a Turkish soldier leaned out, poised to hurl himself on to his quarry – a young man on a motorbike, the collar of his British army greatcoat turned up to protect him from the grains of sand that stung his face, sharp as hailstones. The motorcyclist was a dispatch rider and, every so often, he looked back and saw, through his goggles, that the train was fast gaining on him. Desperately, he opened the throttle right up: the military papers in his dispatch case had to be delivered by nightfall. The steam engine clanked level with the motorbike and as it did so the Turkish soldier flung himself from the footplate on to the dispatch rider, sending man and bike skidding across the hot, red sand. The two men wrestled, the dispatch rider fighting to get the upper hand, but it was the Turkish soldier who managed to scramble to his feet and stand astride his victim, his scimitar – silhouetted against the clear sky – raised for the final, downward stroke . . .

It was an old story this, of how the young soldier had fought against the Turks under the banner of the Royal Dublin Fusiliers. I used to wriggle my toes in anticipation each time I heard it when, as a child on Saturday mornings, I was allowed to climb into bed with the dispatch rider while my mother laboured downstairs in the steamy kitchen, boiling up the silverside cut of beef for dinner. The blade of the scimitar – its curve catching the gleam of the desert sun – hung over my childhood and, like a halo, illuminated this daring young man who, by some inexplicable metamorphosis, turned out to be my father. When I was good, he would show me the two scars – one in his side and the other in his back – that marked the spot where the scimitar had penetrated him and when I was bad, he would berate me mildly with the words: 'You little Turk.' What a Turk was, I never really knew. As I grew older and learned something of that particular war, I began to ask him about it for he himself never spoke of his days in the British Army. Had he seen T. E. Lawrence, for instance? 'I suppose I must have done,' was all he would say.

The idea of the desert railway, the Hejaz Railway, was conceived by the Turks way back in the 1800s. It would run from Damascus, then part of the Ottoman Empire, down through Syria, on into what is now Jordan, swinging eastwards to the Hejaz, the area in what is now Saudi Arabia and in which lie the two great places of Islamic pilgrimage: Mecca and Medina. Anyone who wanted to deviate to make a pilgrimage to Jerusalem could take the branch line to Palestine.

Great majestic buildings – the legacy of colonial powers – were erected at a time when it was inconceivable that things would ever change. These towering constructions, whether law courts, churches or academic meeting places, consolidated the status quo. In Algiers, the French left a palatial Post Office building behind them. In Dublin, the English left the Customs House and, in Damascus, the Ottomans left the Hejaz Railway Terminal. It stands at the top of Saad al Jaberee Street, a stately Turkish façade with keyhole-shaped windows and four pillars supporting an impressive balcony. Nowadays, small makeshift shops selling tea and coffee, cigarettes and cartons of chips push and shove against it like peasants seeking favours from a powerful overlord. Six converging streets conduct swirling traffic round the great open space in front of it while pedestrians dodge the cars to get to that most important component of Arab hospitality, the drinking fountain, beside which an opportunist vendor has spread out his wares: underpants and shampoo.

Up the steps and to one side of the entrance is an old steam engine that age and rust has solidified on to its display block. *Arnold Jung*, reads the brass plate, *locomotif fabrik Nummer 1205. 1908.* Built in Switzerland although it was the Germans who, in the end, got the contract to construct the railway. In the main booking hall a dusty chandelier hangs from the high, painted wooden ceiling. Polished timber and brass barriers surround the ticket windows and the floor is a sequence of the tessellated tiles so beloved of the Ottomans. On the platform, an engine and carriage are set in concrete. The latter, with its plush red seating and tulip-shaped brass lamps, is used now as a tea and coffee bar. Its exterior wall, however, carries the magic words: Damascus, Aleppo, Istanbul, Sofia, Budapest, Vienna, Lyons and Paris for, from here, it was possible to travel northwards to Aleppo and there pick up the Orient Express. Just as Damascus had once been a thriving trading centre for caravans plying the Silk Route so, by the 1900s, it had become the hub of the iron highway.

Standing in the great, empty booking hall, I closed my eyes and heard the din of people shouting out their wares – nuts and oranges, honey cakes and flat bread – the rattle of tin cups against the Turkish coffee pots strapped to the vendor's back. Heard panic-stricken women crying out for lost children and heard the wails, too, of those children not yet found. Men called greetings to each other and the muezzin summoned the pilgrim-travellers to prayer. When I opened my eyes, I could see these ghosts from a hundred years ago: a man in a red tarboosh and black baggy breeches, his friend in a striped djellabia, women veiled and cloaked, imams in mulberry-coloured turbans and white gowns, Turkish soldiers in uniform, beggars in tattered rags.

It was Sultan ul-Hamid II who got the Hejaz project going, announcing it would form a great new link between Damascus and Mecca and adding that it would be financed by the many pilgrims expected to use it. Cynics suspected, however, that there was an ulterior motive and they were right: the Hejaz Railway would also serve as a tool of control, enabling Ottoman troops and munitions to be transported quickly to those outposts of the empire that might consider rebelling. The *haj* is a major part of Islamic practice, however, and donations did indeed come in, from Turkey, Egypt and Iran, as well as from individual pilgrims – some of whom discovered depths of generosity within themselves hitherto unknown when it was learned that a donation could buy them the right to use the title Pasha or Bey.

Work on the railway began in 1900, Turkish troops were drafted in to work on it and within eight years it was finished, at a cost of £8 million. There were two groups of people, however, who viewed the enterprise with alarm: the pilgrim tour operators and the desert tribes. Pilgrimages were big business. The route had to be mapped out, the wells along it checked in advance and guaranteed secure. Camels and camel drivers had to be found. First class travel was by camel and second class by donkey. The rest walked. With anything up to 5000 people in a pilgrim caravan, food had to be provided not only for the pilgrims but also for their pack animals. Guides were essential as were armed guards who accompanied the caravan through hostile terri-tory for the desert was controlled by Arab tribes who gained an informal but regular income from the time-honoured method of collecting danger money from anyone passing through their land. All these, as well as the baggage handlers, tent erectors, servants, itinerant traders and general hangers-on, stood to lose out to the newfangled railway which enabled pilgrims to cover the distance in four days rather than the two months it took by camel train.

The tribesmen hit back by attacking the train whenever they could and when these same tribesmen rebelled against the Turks in 1916 – the Arab Revolt – the British military strategist, T. E. Lawrence, was able to exploit their know-ledge of the rail route and use it to break the Turkish line of communication for, as first suspected, the Hejaz Railway was indeed being used to transport troops and ammunition across the desert, although the net now had widened to include not only the restless Arabs but the British and French as well. Dynamited many times by Lawrence and his desert tribesmen, the Hejaz Railway was put out of action and then eventually left to fall into disrepair. Now, one hundred years after its inception, it makes only one run southwards a week between Syria and Jordan, but the journey takes so long that few people use it.

The Hejaz Railway, however, was part of my childhood – before I ever knew its name. As a young man, my father had joined the Royal Dublin Fusiliers and had been sent to the Middle East where he was employed as a dispatch rider. With a few weeks to go before leaving for Syria, I travelled to the Public Records Office near Kew Gardens, to look up his war records. There, however, the trail stopped: there were none available. The records of all those soldiers whose names began with the letter R had been pulled out of circulation in order that they might be transferred to microfiche. I should come back in six months' time, I was told.

Nevertheless, when I got to Damascus, I discovered there was a small branch line of the Hejaz that Damascenes loved to take and one Friday morning in late November, I bought a ticket to Zabadani, taking my place on a slatted wooden seat as the engine, pulling its four carriages, rattled through the streets of Damascus before branching westwards to begin the long slow climb up into the mountains that divide Syria from Lebanon. This was my second attempt to travel on the rickety little train. The previous Sunday, when I'd arrived at the station, I'd been offered a cup of tea instead of a ticket. The train only ran if there were twenty passengers, the clerk explained. The three would-be travellers looked forlornly at each other. We had failed to add up.

Today, however, was different. Next week, it would be Ramadan when there would be no eating, drinking, smoking or fornicating during the hours of daylight. No railway jaunts either. It was today or never. An air of excitement sparked throughout the train. In the next carriage, a group of students had already started to sing, two of them beating out a complicated and answering rhythm on their drums.

The train rattled through the streets like a tram, unencumbered by fencing or level crossing barriers, its shrill whistle shrieking like an overexcited child. People came to their doors to watch, holding their babies up to see us. At a busy intersection, we cut right through the queue of waiting cars and buses – trains had right of way – and even the traffic policeman stopped blowing his whistle to smile and wave. Children ran along beside us, the more daring ones grabbing a door handle and leaping up to hitch a lift for a few minutes before dropping down on to the street again. In a garden, a bent old woman, sitting in the sun, took her cigarette out of her mouth for a moment as she studied our forty-kilometre-an-hour progress along the narrow-gauge track. We were a carnival on wheels, a mobile fairground. A happy holiday on the move and no one could look at us without smiling.

Leaving Damascus behind, we disappeared into tunnels, cut through gullies and passed between walls of rock, the space between them so narrow I could reach out and touch the jagged surfaces. Sunlight glinted through the trembling leaves of peppercorn trees and lit up the water of the Barada river flowing down to Damascus. And, the higher we climbed, the more excited was the singing and drumming in the next carriage. 'Ya! Ya! Hizbullah!' sang the students exuberantly and suddenly I had a fleeting vision of bloodied death shrouds. The previous evening, I had sat watching TV with some friends. Hizbullah, the Party of God – an Islamic resistance guerrilla group formed after the 1982 Israeli invasion of Lebanon – has its own television station. We watched a series of clips showing black-clad Hizbullah guerrillas abseiling down walls, leaping across buildings, marching along a street. 'Look, look,' said Amir, one of my friends. 'See the flag?' 'What flag? Where?' 'There, on the ground.' And indeed, on the ground was the Israeli flag spread out so that the Hizbullah soldiers could trample it into the mud. And then a small boy of maybe ten or eleven appeared on the screen. 'Now watch this,' cried Amir excitedly. 'Watch how he throws a stone at the soldier.' On cue, an Israeli soldier appeared in the frame. The boy took to his heels but realizing the soldier was not catching up with him, paused, picked up a stone and aimed it at his pursuer.

'See,' cried Amir, 'only a little boy but brave. And now watch the soldier.' He knew the sequence off by heart. We heard the clang of the stone as it struck the soldier's helmet, saw it stop him momentarily in his tracks. The boy too stopped and waited. The soldier, stung by the child's act, again started to run towards him, then paused, turned and ran the other way. Amir was gleeful: 'See, the Israeli soldier is running away from a small child.' It was a bitter little scene. The film had been skilfully edited to gain maximum propaganda from the incident and, despite myself, I felt a certain anxiety for the soldier. How was he to know that the stone-throwing child was not a decoy, placed there to lure him into a death trap? Disliking his uniform and the government that paid him to wear it, I nevertheless felt relieved the soldier had chosen the better part of valour.

I checked my map to try to work out how far up the Barada Valley we had got. The climb was steep and whenever the train stopped, a group of cheery lads – who had been amusing themselves by swinging out across the huge hooks that connected one carriage to the next – would run to the back of the carriage, straddle the interconnecting bit and quickly turn a wheel to apply the brakes and put a halt to the train's backward slide. Then, when the engine had been oiled and got its breath back, the wheel would be turned the other way and we would puff off again. The young men, I finally realized, were train guards.

It was a sunny day, well suited to our slow progress. Ahead, the engine puffed out black smoke, the tender white steam. Leaves fell continuously, like rain. The Barada, its waters low now after the dry summer, flowed through a world of overhanging branches and mossy banks, frothing across rocks and stepping stones. Through the trees, I glimpsed homesteads shaded by vines, men cutting logs, children playing. It was a world far removed from the noise and car fumes of Damascus. We stopped at Ain El Fijeh – the spring of the eye – where the waters of the Barada gather to feed the thirsty Damascenes. And then laboured on and up, the air getting chillier as we climbed higher up into the mountains. Eventually, we lurched into a village called

Maysaloon. I already knew Maysaloon: one of the main streets in Damascus is named after it.

Finding my way round the city had, initially, caused me much grief for, devoid of any sense of direction, I seemed unable to get myself from A to B without going via C and getting lost en route. One day, rotating my street map 180 degrees to try to locate my position, I asked a woman for directions to Maysaloon Street. She pondered, discussed it with a friend, conferred with another passerby, tried to read my English language map before finally working out a route that when I followed it, brought me to a different street altogether. As luck would have it, the hapless woman passed as I was again consulting my map. 'You told me this was the street,' I said, more accusingly than I intended. 'It is,' she said then frowned in puzzlement as she looked at the street sign which clearly read: Asil al Nasr Street. It took me some time to work out that, following independence, streets and squares had been renamed and given patriotic titles which local people either didn't know or couldn't quite place. Maysaloon was one of them. Like pounds, shillings and pence, Morris Minor cars and bus conductors the old Ottoman street names had a nostalgia attached to them that bureaucratic nationalism had failed to erase. People waved dismissively at the street names on my map: 'They're just government names,' they said. 'No one uses them.'

Maysaloon, I later learned, was where perfidy and hope had fought a last battle, the former emerging a temporary victor. For a time, Damascus had been not only at the hub of the railway system but also at the centre of intrigue and betrayal – those two players who, hand in hand, walk the stage in all theatres of war. When T. E. Lawrence set out to break the hold the Ottomans had on the Middle East, a term, incidentally, heartily disliked by people who actually live there, he sought the help of Faisal, second son of the king of Saudia Arabia (Alec Guinness in the film). The deal was that Faisal would appeal to the desert tribes to unite in order to drive out their Ottoman oppressors. In return for this, the land – what is now Jordan, Iraq, Syria, Palestine and Lebanon – would become an entity, with Damascus as its capital, the whole lot, at the end of the war, to be handed over into the control of the Arabs with Faisal as their king. Against all the odds – for the tribes had been warring since before the time of Muhammad – unity was achieved, the Arab Revolt was a success, the Turks were defeated and driven back first from Jerusalem and, a few weeks later, from Damascus. On 1 October 1918, Faisal galloped into Damascus and prepared to take over his new kingdom. But political deals, like promises, are made to be broken and T. E. Lawrence had been presented with a different agenda by his military masters: he was simply to *pretend* to Faisal that this deal would go through when the war had ended. And, loyal to the piper that paid him, this is exactly what he did. Thus, Betrayal stood a shadowy figure at Lawrence's shoulder, even as he promised Faisal that Damascus would one day be his.

The carve-up followed swiftly. Britain got Palestine and France Lebanon, which included the present-day Syria, while Faisal was packed off to Baghdad then under British protection, or control, depending on how you looked at it. To the Damascenes who had just been liberated from four hundred years of Ottoman rule the betrayal was a bitter blow and one that some of their fighters could not accept.

With the war barely ended, a raggle-taggle force of de-mobbed Damascene soldiers put up an ineffectual resist-ance to the advancing French Army and fought their last fight in the mountain village of Maysaloon. They were defeated and, in July 1920, the French took possession of Damascus.

Leaving the village of Maysaloon behind, the train trun-dled on as far as Zabadani, 2000 feet up in the mountains. There, I bought some lunch in a little huckster shop, from an old woman who had given birth to ten sons and four daughters. She spread a mat on the shop floor for me to dine on and brought a pot of tea to go with the dry biscuits and processed cheese. There was barely time to finish this feast, however, for the train had already been shunted into position for the downward journey. Then, as we set off again, I huddled into a corner, wrapping a keffieyeh round me to keep warm for the train windows were without glass and the mountain air was bitterly cold.

The children fell silent and eventually slept. The singing became muted. The last of the sun shone over the rim of the mountain, casting a golden light on golden leaves. Below us lay Damascus, the green lights on all the minarets lit up to welcome us home.

History was everywhere in Syria, its destiny constantly linked with that of Europe's. I thought of my father, a young man from Kerry, joining the British Army and washing up, alongside Australians, New Zealanders, Punjabis and Gujuratis, in this strange country of hot suns and burning sands. And thought again of his bravery in fighting off the Turkish soldier. In adulthood, I had often imagined the two men, one with terror in his eyes the other with hate. Maybe the Turkish soldier wasn't Turkish at all but a Syrian, a man from Damascus perhaps, forced to join the army by his oppressors. And my father, of course wasn't English, even though he wore the uniform of the British Army.

For years, this image of the futility of war stayed with me, freeze-framed in my mind until one day, sitting with one of my sisters in a pub in Dublin, we started talking about our father and I became aware that she was looking at me with incredulity as I recounted his desert heroics.

'What!' she said, 'you're not telling me you believed all that?'

'All what?' Something was in the air and I needed to play for time.

'All that about the desert.'

'But he *was* in the desert.'

'Well, yes. But the rest of it?'

A strip of Elastoplast was being peeled back from a wound that had yet to appear and I was determined not to cry out in pain. I was, after all, a grown woman, mother of three, for heaven's sake, with my own overdraft.

'The story of the Turkish soldier attacking him. You don't still believe that, do you?'

I looked through the plate glass windows of the pub, out on to the quays and O'Connell Bridge, the buses passing as usual, people jostling each other in the early evening rush hour. It all seemed normal and I wanted it to stay like that, my childhood memory intact.

'The marks in his side . . .' I started, hearing myself pleading not to be told the truth.

She laughed: 'Sure they were from the TB he had when he was young. He had to have the bone scraped.' And concealing my sense of betrayal I smiled, laughed even, before drinking the poisoned chalice she had passed to me.

My father's image moved forward a few frames and he went through another incarnation, this time as a teller of tall tales, a spinner of yarns. By then, however, I could look at him and smile as he sat in his fawn knitted cardigan, his limbs bony with age, never talking about his desert days. And I smiled even when he died in the old soldiers' hospital in Dublin, a Union Jack draped over his coffin for the Requiem Mass, and saw two old comrades in their wheelchairs salute his coffin as it was carried out of the church. For, as the hearse moved off through the streets of Dublin, was that not the engine of a motorbike I heard, roaring against the distant sound of train wheels fast catching up with us?

CHAPTER TWENTY-ONE

To Be Continued: 2000

Damascus came back with me to Dublin: the scent of trailing jasmine, the aroma of apple smoke from the narghiles, the warm, crusty smell of baking bread, the low doorways always open but curtained off – beckoning and at the same time warning of secrets and intrigue.

I blocked out the unwanted memories: the din of the rules-free traffic, the horn-happy drivers, the sharp whiff of the *toilettes orientales*, the tiresome men who constantly accosted me in the street wanting only to say hello; inconveniences all and as much a part of Syria as the veiled women, the call to prayer and the souks. But there was something I couldn't block out: a feeling that there was another, unknown presence in the room with me, a shadow that wasn't mine. The memory of a place not yet visited. Then a letter came from an Indian friend recently posted to his embassy in Baghdad and I sat at the kitchen table to read it: 'Please come and visit us. People here are warm and, despite the bombings, they conduct themselves very gracefully. We are only six hundred kilometres from Damascus.'

All the road signs out of Damascus had pointed to Baghdad. When I'd crossed the desert and arrived in Albu Kamal, a small border town on the extreme south-east corner of the country, Iraq was only eleven kilometres away. But I'd had to turn back: the border was closed and, in any case, my business was with Syria. But now? Without ever having visited it, I knew all about Baghdad for had it not displaced Damascus as the first city of the caliphate many years ago? About 1350 years ago, to be more or less precise – AD 750. Damascenes remember the date, the year when their great Umayyad dynasty had been destroyed by their rivals, the Abbasids, who moved the capital to Baghdad thus stealing from Damascus its title of Pearl of the Desert.

I'd gone to a concert of North African-Arab music one evening in one of the old caravanserais – the elegant staging posts where merchants came to stable their camels, drink coffee and, almost as an afterthought, do a bit of business. It was a large airy hall, circular in shape, topped by a series of eight domes, its long arched galleries supported by lime and basalt pillars. Here, the traders stored their goods – silk, aloes and camphor, Tibetan musk and indigo, pearls, sandalwood and ivory – all carried to Damascus by large, slow camels, their huge fringed feet padding across the desert sands from India, China – and Baghdad. Now, as night clouds darkened the glass domes and music infiltrated the building, the wavering, melancholy notes of the flute floated among the pillars like a dirge, a lament for all that had been lost. And yet, not everything had been lost for, despite the Abbasid's ferocious and sustained campaign, one member of the Umayyad clan had managed to escape. Abd al Rahman, twenty-year-old grandson of the caliph, hid out in the desert with a Bedouin tribe that had settled along the Euphrates. There, he lived in comparative safety until word reached him, one day, that Abbasids had been sighted, their approaching banners blowing in the warm wind of the desert. Calling out for his thirteen-year-old brother to join him, he leapt into the river to try to swim to the other side. When they got into difficulty midstream, the watching Abbasids called on them to return, promising them an amnesty. The younger boy struggled back to the river bank where he was promptly killed. Abdal Rahman reached the other side and from there set out on a five-year trek through Palestine and beyond, moving incognito from tribe to tribe until eventually he reached southern Spain. Then, as a tall young man with red hair and a reputation for being something of an adventurer, he set about creating another Umayyad caliphate in what the Arabs called al Andalus – the land of the Vandals.

It is through the gates of Andalusia that Arab culture entered Europe. The Berber warrior Tariq had a mountain named after him, Jebel Tariq, that translates into Gibraltar and the Al Hamra was originally Qalaat al Hambra, the Red Castle. Even as I write these words, the shadowy memory of that warm, rose-scented night in the Damascene caravanserai enters my winter kitchen, drifting in on the music of Francisco Tarrega for it is the strings of the lute and the guitar that mediate between east and west, making familiar that which seems strange and unintelligible. Outside, a continuous fall of January snow has turned white the pavements of Dublin. Inside, the kitchen is warm, lit by the glow of the fire. People ask – where will you go to next? Perhaps I'll go nowhere, stay here. Safe, warm. And then, listening to *Recuerdos de la Alhambra* I think, well, maybe Andalusia, in order to close the chapter on Damascus. But, even as I say it, my hand strays towards the letter still lying on the kitchen table. Baghdad too is part of that story.